UNDERSTANDING COPYRIGHT

BETHANY KLEIN • GILES MOSS • LEE EDWARDS

UNDERSTANDING COPYRIGHT

INTELLECTUAL PROPERTY IN THE DIGITAL AGE

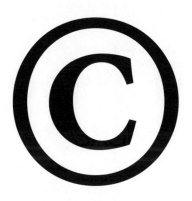

Los Angeles | London | New Delhi
Singapore | Washington DC | Boston

Los Angeles | London | New Delhi
Singapore | Washington DC

SAGE Publications Ltd
1 Oliver's Yard
55 City Road
London EC1Y 1SP

SAGE Publications Inc.
2455 Teller Road
Thousand Oaks, California 91320

SAGE Publications India Pvt Ltd
B 1/I 1 Mohan Cooperative Industrial Area
Mathura Road
New Delhi 110 044

SAGE Publications Asia-Pacific Pte Ltd
3 Church Street
#10-04 Samsung Hub
Singapore 049483

Editor: Mila Steele
Assistant editor: James Piper
Production editor: Imogen Roome
Copyeditor: Bryan Campbell
Indexer: Martin Hargreaves
Marketing manager: Michael Ainsley
Cover design: Jen Crisp
Typeset by: C&M Digitals (P) Ltd, Chennai, India
Printed in Great Britain by Henry Ling Limited
at The Dorset Press, Dorchester, DT1 1HD

Library of Congress Control Number: 2014951148

British Library Cataloguing in Publication data

A catalogue record for this book is available from
the British Library

MIX
Paper from
responsible sources
FSC
www.fsc.org   FSC™ C013985

ISBN 978-1-4462-8583-1
ISBN 978-1-4462-8584-8 (pbk)

At SAGE we take sustainability seriously. Most of our products are printed in the UK using FSC papers and
boards. When we print overseas we ensure sustainable papers are used as measured by the Egmont grading
system. We undertake an annual audit to monitor our sustainability.

CONTENTS

ABOUT THE AUTHORS

Bethany Klein is Head of the School of Media and Communication, University of Leeds. She is the author of *As Heard on TV: Popular Music in Advertising* (Ashgate, 2009).

Giles Moss is Lecturer in Media Policy in the School of Media and Communication, University of Leeds. He is co-editor of *Can the Media Serve Democracy? Essays in Honour of Jay G. Blumer* (Palgrave, 2015).

Lee Edwards is Associate Professor in Communication Studies and PR in the School of Media and Communication, University of Leeds. She is the author of *Power, Diversity and Public Relations* (Routledge, 2014), and co-editor of *Public Relations, Society and Culture: Theoretical and Empirical Explorations* (Routledge, 2011).

ACKNOWLEDGEMENTS

This book grew out of the Economic and Social Research Council-funded project *Communicating Copyright: An Exploration of Copyright Discourses in the Digital Age*; we thank Fiona Philip and David Lee for their contributions to that project and, accordingly, to the foundational ideas that we have drawn on in this book. Thanks to Kate Oakley for providing useful feedback on the manuscript. Other colleagues in the School of Media and Communication at the University of Leeds have supported our work in indirect ways, not least by providing a rich intellectual and research environment: the book has benefited from their interest in and engagement with our work.

Interactions with scholars working in related areas — through invited talks, workshops and conferences — have been enormously valuable in developing and challenging our ideas against the large body of work on intellectual property and copyright which has emerged within legal studies, sociology, media studies and beyond. We especially benefited from the following events, which helped us hone the scope, objectives, and arguments of the book: the 2013 symposium in Durham that brought together contributors to the *SAGE Handbook on Intellectual Property*; the 2013 CREATe conference on empirical methodology; invited talks in the School of Music at the University of Edinburgh and the Media Centre at the University of Sunderland; and the International Communication Association panels on which we presented aspects of this work.

We thank SAGE and Taylor & Francis for allowing us to use some material from articles published in *Convergence*, *New Media and Society*, and the *International Journal of Cultural Policy* in this book. We are grateful for SAGE Senior Commissioning Editor Mila Steele's enthusiasm for critical media issues and commitment to classic American diner breakfasts, the intersection of which resulted in a pivotal chat during the International Communication Association conference in Phoenix in 2012. Thanks also to the rest of the SAGE team for their support, and to the reviewers of the proposal and manuscript for their positive feedback and suggestions, especially Matthew David who provided helpful comments at both the beginning and end stages.

1

INTRODUCTION: UNDERSTANDING COPYRIGHT IN THE DIGITAL AGE

INTRODUCTION

Few aspects of our professional and personal lives have gone untouched by the digital shift. Digital technology is the current that runs through the way we communicate with one another and engage with the world around us. It has changed the manner in which news and entertainment media is produced, distributed and consumed, and it has collapsed the boundaries and roles related to such activities. As a consequence, laws that worked in an analogue world have struggled to keep pace with new digital developments. One area that has been especially stretched to breaking point by digital technologies and activities is intellectual property (IP), and copyright in particular.

How do we know when a law is no longer working as it intended? We might notice that many people do not realize if and when they are breaking the law and we may find that behaviour considered normal or ordinary crosses the line into illegality. We might also recognize that regulatory or enforcement responses to illegal activities seem to many people heavy-handed or inappropriate. Surveys suggest that the line between legal and illegal activity around copyright is, for many, a blurred one (Ofcom, 2012; A. Hill, 2013), and the increasing number of sites and technologies through which we access media has only added to the confusion, with streaming, downloading and sharing legitimated through above-board platforms and subscription-based or adver-tising-supported services. Furthermore, the distinction between sharing analogue and digital versions of media, while significant to media companies and creators, isn't always recognized by users, who may view digital sharing as a simple extension of an activity which has long taken place between friends and family members (Cenite et al., 2009; Caraway, 2012; Edwards et al., 2013b). Finally, the overzealous approach to enforcement by some corporations in the cultural industries, especially in the early days of peer-to-peer (P2P), resulted in lawsuits that were sometimes filed against sym-pathetic defendants, from young children and digitally illiterate grandparents to victims of mistaken identity (see Brainz, n.d.). As these examples suggest, the digital context has widened and revealed a gulf between copyright law and everyday practices.

While the presence of copyright in the lives of ordinary people may have raised the profile of the law, disagreement about copyright protection and enforcement is hardly new. Copyright has been the subject of longstanding debates since its earliest inception. Questions of copyright's objectives, scope and beneficiaries have driven adaptations to the law and have formed the basis of key legal cases which have sought to define and test boundaries around such concepts as parody and plagiarism, fair use and fair dealing, limitations and exceptions. The digital context reignited and modified old copyright debates and introduced new ones. In other words, digitization did not disrupt the functioning of a well-oiled machine: it poured a bucket of water onto a rusted machine. Lots of people disagreed about how to fix it, and that is what brings us to the current situation and to this book, which seeks to understand the copyright debate and propose a strategy for moving the debate forward.

In this chapter, we describe our approach to understanding copyright through a focus on the various parties involved in copyright debates and activities. We seek to understand copyright by focusing not just on the law itself, but through the discourses used to justify particular positions in the copyright debate. We then explain the organization of the book, highlighting the focus of subsequent chapters.

OUR APPROACH TO UNDERSTANDING COPYRIGHT

Copyright is a form of intellectual property (IP) which, in legal terms, describes intangible ideas and creations that come from the mind. (See Box 1.1 for definitions of key terms used throughout this book.) Because IP is not physical property, determining ownership, identifying theft and enforcing protection are not straightforward. Agreements between creators, users and beneficiaries of IP are shaped by the law and formalized in contracts, but vary across geography, industry and circumstance. Copyright is an automatic right which applies when a creative work is 'fixed' through being written down or recorded. Creative works may be musical, literary, theatrical or artistic and can range from a relatively uncomplicated case of a song written and recorded by a single singer-songwriter to a complex production such as a feature film involving the input of hundreds of creators. While anything any of us produces may be protected by copyright as a form of IP, copyright plays a particularly significant financial role in the cultural industries. The rise in the twentieth century of cultural industries based around models of mass distribution and the commercialization of culture set the stage for a more significant role for copyright as a business tool. At the same time, the emergence of new 'information economies' since the 1980s, built on digital technology, provided a political boost for the cultural industries as sectors where commercialized creativity forms the foundation for re-energized economies and communities at the local, regional and national levels (O'Connor, 2000; Bakhshi et al., 2013). As the political and economic importance of cultural industries increased, so too did their involvement in policymaking: protection for rights holders in the digital age has become central to discussions between government and cultural industry representatives, and has played an important role in shaping copyright policy and law.

The advent of digital technologies has been both blessing and burden for the cultural industries. On the one hand, the digital world holds immense possibilities: new forms of cultural texts have emerged; new, and often cheaper, ways of producing and distributing texts have become possible; audiences can be reached in innovative ways — on the move, in their home, and on personal devices with tailored advertising and promotional material. They can consume cultural texts anywhere, and at any time, which means there is no longer any geographical or temporal limit to who can be reached by the cultural industries, and the return on 'big hits' can be in the billions. However, digital technology has also led to new possibilities for creators and users of cultural texts that challenge industry control over production, price and distribution. Digital technology gives creators more freedom to connect directly or through online platforms with their audiences (SoundCloud and Bandcamp are two popular examples for musicians), rather than having to adhere to the processes of production and distribution on which the cultural industries depend. For users, one of the great advantages of digital technology is the fact that it can be used to make copies of texts that are as good as the original. Digital formats can be distributed easily and widely: the architecture of the internet means that users can send copies instantaneously to multiple contacts and download copies from the internet to their personal devices (Lessig, 2006). Users can also engage with cultural texts in ways not intended by the cultural industries, creating parodies, mashups and spoofs, activities that challenge both control over meaning and the limits of copyright.

In sum, digitization has made unauthorized access and distribution of copyrighted work easy and ordinary which, in turn, has provided a catalyst to conversations not simply about how to enforce copyright and punish transgression, but whether copyright, as it is currently understood and regulated, is the right way to encourage and reward creative expression. We could seek to understand copyright by studying the laws themselves but, while changes in the laws over time can suggest a context of shifting perspectives, such an approach cannot fully capture all the noise made behind the scenes: the justifications for copyright protection, the challenges, the drive to produce international standards, the themes of ongoing debates.

Contemporary debates about copyright bring together a number of parties and many perspectives: in order to understand copyright in the digital age, it is essential that we understand how copyright is communicated. Communication has played a crucial and yet arguably under-researched role in the evolution of copyright. In this book, we analyse the digital copyright debate through the perspectives of cultural industries, policymakers, creative workers, intermediaries, and media users. The groups are not discrete: intermediaries and creative workers may also be rights holders, for example, and all parties are made up of media users. Furthermore, competing perspectives on copyright vary not simply between these groups but within them. Yet breaking the debate up into groups — even as the messiness of reality poses obstacles to doing so — allows us to understand copyright as a structured disagreement, where different parties are positioned in particular ways, possess varying degrees of power, and coalesce around specific issues, if not always around the same perspectives on the issues. One way to identify and analyse the position of these groups is through the *discourses* they use. By bringing discourse to the forefront of our analysis, we aim to examine how the different parties involved in the copyright debate view and reflect on copyright and related practices and values.

Box 1.1
Definitions of key terms

Intellectual property: The World Intellectual Property Organization (WIPO) defines intellectual property as 'creations of the mind, such as inventions; literary and artistic works; designs; and symbols, names and images used in commerce' (WIPO, 2014a).

Copyright: Copyright is a form of intellectual property and a legal right given to the originator of a creative work, for a limited period of time, to make copies, distribute, licence and otherwise exploit a creative work. It applies to the breadth of artistic and creative work, from literature, music and art to software, motion pictures and other audio-visual forms.

Copyright exception: Copyright exceptions refer to instances, defined in law, where the use of a copyrighted work is in the public interest and the obligation to inform and pay the rights holder for the use of the work is waived. Exceptions vary from country to country (WIPO, 2014b).

Discourse: The use of spoken or written language as a form of social practice. It contributes to the reproduction of social practices and the constitution of social order (Fairclough, 2003). The term is explored in greater detail below.

Cultural industries: The definition of the cultural industries has been contested, but in this book we use Hesmondhalgh's definition of cultural industries as those industries that produce commodities in the form of symbolic texts that 'influence our understanding and knowledge of the world' (Hesmondhalgh, 2013: 4).

Internet intermediaries: Internet intermediaries are organizations that provide services for distributing, hosting or locating internet content for users (Edwards, 2009).

Our understanding of discourse draws on the work of Fairclough (2003), who uses the term 'discourse' in both a general and a more specific way. In its general sense, discourse is used to emphasize the central role that language (as well as other forms of meaning making, such as visual imagery) plays in social life and its importance in analysing and explaining it. Discourse is an important part of what makes up and holds social practices together and operates alongside other elements of social life, such as material resources, social networks and social actors themselves. At the same time, discourse is also used in a more specific sense to refer to particular ways of understanding and representing the social world. The term may be used, for example, to describe the discourse of the 'free market' or of the 'Romantic artist'. It may also be used to refer to the types of talk and language that characterize particular social groups, as in, for example, the discourse of policymakers or the discourse of file sharers.

Discourse is bound up with power and power relations. Fairclough (2003: 9) describes how certain discourses become dominant and play an ideological role in legitimating and reproducing particular social practices and power relations. Discourse therefore contributes to the power some groups have over others, often combining with other sources of power, such as access to material resources or social networks. However, while certain discourses may be dominant and difficult to displace, social groups have the capacity to resist, reflect on and critique discourses (Dryzek, 2000). Groups may challenge discourses externally by drawing on different and competing ways of representing how the world should be: 'alternative', 'marginal' or 'oppositional' discourses (Fairclough, 2003: 206). They may also critique discourses more internally by questioning them in their own terms.

What do we mean by the idea that discourses may be questioned in their own terms? The discourses that are used to legitimate particular social practices and arrangements involve using justificatory principles or claims about what is good, right and just (Boltanski and Chiapello, 2005 [1999]; Boltanski and Thévenot, 2006 [1991]). So copyright, for example, is commonly defended discursively as being just since it is a legitimate recognition and reward for the labour of creative workers. Such justificatory claims provide some scope for opposition and critique, as other groups contest the interpretation of these principles and the evidence used to support them (Edwards et al., 2014). For example, claims that copyright needs to be strengthened in order to reward and recognize creative workers may be challenged by pointing to the low percentage of music sales that actually go to the artist and so how the interests of corporations and creative workers can diverge. In this case, the justificatory principle that creative workers deserve recognition and reward for their work may be accepted, but the interpretation and realization of this principle in practice is challenged.

We argue in this book that the debate about digital copyright and piracy is especially apt for an analysis focused on competing discourses and justifications. Fairclough (2004) argues that discourse becomes strategically important during periods of economic uncertainty and change, when a previously stable set of practices are challenged and economic actors must compete to re-establish their position. The environment for copyright regulation is constantly changing, and so debates about copyright are ongoing, with discourses mobilized over time by different invested groups to argue their case. In addition, the debate about digital copyright has been riven by 'moral panic', especially concerning the activity of so-called 'pirates' (May, 2003; Lindgren, 2013). Duff (2008) has written of a 'normative crisis' surrounding digital media, referring to 'a breakdown of the framework for value judgments specifically with respect to the social principles and policy bases of the information society'. By focusing on the discourses of the different groups affected by copyright policy, and in particular on the types of justificatory claims they employ, we hope to shed light on the moral dimension of the copyright debate and its connection with questions of justice.

At the same time, we are agnostic about the actual outcomes of the digital copyright debate. We do not aim in this book to set out one particular 'model' of how copyright should work. As will become clear, we are more concerned with the process of the copyright debate than its outcomes. Given disparities in power among groups, we think that certain voices — most notably, those of the public — are less often heard and tend to be excluded or included only asymmetrically in the debate. In normative terms, our perspective is driven by the belief that legitimate copyright policy must involve the public in its construction. We defend a particular form of public engagement in policymaking called 'deliberative'. Deliberative engagement is defined by certain ideals (Habermas, 1997; Mansbridge et al., 2010: 65–72). Firstly, the process of policymaking should be inclusive so that all groups affected by the policy can participate. Secondly, the process should involve open discussion where all options are considered and where participants seek to convince others through arguments, rather than through other sources of influence and power. Thirdly, policy decisions should reflect an agreement among all groups about the common good or, if such a 'rationally motivated consensus' is not possible, at least 'a negotiated agreement' that balances competing interests and values in a fair way (Habermas, 1997: 166). Deliberative ideals may not be realized fully in practice: we may need, as Coleman and Blumler suggest, 'to settle for a more *deliberative democracy*' (2009: 38). Nonetheless, deliberative ideals provide a critical yardstick with which we can evaluate the current copyright debate and policymaking process.

HOW THIS BOOK IS ORGANIZED

While the motivations, perspectives and justifications of the various parties involved in debates over copyright remain necessarily intertwined, this book separates the key groups by chapter in order to explore distinctions between the positions and the discourses that underpin them. But first, it is important to understand the circumstances and legal frameworks in and against which groups have located themselves in the debate, and so we begin with some copyright fundamentals and key historical moments. Chapter 2 sets out the basic historical context of copyright, and describes the way in which digitization relates to important copyright debates. Key moments in the history of copyright are considered and connected to significant questions. For instance, early decisions about copyright often hinged on a belief in serving the public interest through ensuring the distribution of creative work, and so it is notable that the public interest rarely enters modern discussions. When it does, as in recent reviews of copyright policy that acknowledge the importance of the 'public interest' and of copyright exceptions, such recognition has not been substantively incorporated into copyright regulation and policy. Similarly, in the US, extensive industry lobbying against the Public Domain Enhancement Act blocked the possibility of further public interest legislation (Lessig, 2004a). The chapter then looks at digitization as throwing a (golden) spanner in the works: it is the basis of global trade flows in IP and for industrial efficiency savings in terms of production and distribution, but because of the ease with which identical copies can be made and shared, it also threatens cultural industries' revenue, at least in theory. Industry claims to this effect over the last decade have been consistently challenged. Digitization has both revived old debates (for example, in terms of extending the term of copyright and determining what is covered by copyright) and produced new ones (such as how to respond to ordinary infringers, as opposed to the more serious, criminally-connected pirates who were previously the main focus of copyright enforcement).

Chapter 3 explores the role of copyright in the modern creative economy and the approach that cultural industries have taken to shore up their existing power and garner the support of policymakers. Through 'modalities of regulation' (Lessig, 2006) the mainstream, traditional cultural industries (for example, major film and record companies) have sought to influence government decisions and user behaviour, and Chapter 3 will explore some of the approaches taken. As well as attempting to influence the law itself (through precedents set by lawsuits and lobbying), industry players have been involved in less direct forms of regulation. Efforts have been made to modify social norms through education or by running advertising campaigns that characterize file sharers negatively; such efforts have varied in terms of success, with some campaigns resulting in unanticipated consumer backlash or parody. The same scepticism cast on the *Home Taping is Killing Music* campaign in the 1980s was applied to the campaign's digital equivalents in the 2000s. Likewise, public relations work by industry players suggesting copyright infringement activity is damaging the health of the cultural industries has been challenged by contradictory facts and figures.

Arguably more successful than the attempts of industry to influence consumer attitudes and behaviour have been the attempts to determine the market (and thus encourage legal media consumption) and code (technical instructions embedded in software and hardware that will simply make it more difficult to resist regulation). In some cases, such changes have gone beyond protecting copyright to extending copyright, as May (2007) argues of Digital Rights Management. Chapter 3 also explores in detail and through specific cases the range of ways in which copyright is exploited in the cultural industries.

Sitting sometimes uncomfortably between the pressure from industry and government and the activities of media users are intermediaries, like internet service providers (ISPs), technology companies and online platforms like Google or The Pirate Bay; they are the focus of Chapter 4. ISPs, for example, have found themselves pushed by industry and governments to police the end use of their services. Some intermediaries have taken a decidedly oppositional role in the debate: TalkTalk's *Don't Disconnect Us* campaign against the UK's Digital Economy Act revealed the ISP as not only a hesitant enforcement officer, but indeed an ally of ordinary media users. File-sharing platforms like The Pirate Bay (now officially blocked in the UK) make no secret of their anti-copyright position. On the other hand, online platforms such as Google have been generally supportive of the government and cultural industries stance on copyright, though it is notable that they have adopted alternative perspectives in relation to some policies and that Google's own use of copyright material (through linking to and digitizing content) has been subject to debate. Chapter 4 will explore the position of internet intermediaries, located on both sides of the debate (and sometimes as double-agents).

Copyright law can be understood as one of a set of laws and norms that defines and delimits what it means to be a creative worker in the cultural industries. Chapter 5 draws on recent work addressing issues related to creative authorship and creative work in order to frame the various creator perspectives that emerge with respect to copyright.

It considers the experiences of creative workers and the relationship between labour and copyright laws.

Creators have at times served as mouthpieces for industries while others have adopted alternative and oppositional perspectives. Critical perspectives on copyright infringement have been expressed by creative workers, sometimes through lawsuits, though these views are not always well-received by a public that considers many creative workers to be wealthy, privileged and already over-compensated for the work they do. On the other hand, some film and television creators have voiced a more nuanced understanding of piracy as, for example, fan behaviour, a promotional tool and a prompt to examine existing business models. Indeed, many musicians have spoken out in favour of illegal downloading as a means of distribution, relying on profits from touring and merchandising to sustain themselves (although major label contracts are beginning to chase these secondary revenue streams); some have become active proponents of alternative models for making (and making a living through) creative work. The open source movement is one example of an alternative to production and distribution that has gained momentum within the software industry and the philosophy has also been adopted by some creators in other cultural industries. Scholars have explored how copyright law can be understood as actually hindering creativity and innovation and privileging particular (Western, capitalistic) models of cultural production. Chapter 5 looks at creator perspectives in relation to key debates around creative labour.

Users — the focus of Chapter 6 — occupy a shadow presence in the debates that take place among industry, government and intermediaries, and over the years have been positioned through discussion in a number of roles, from naïf to criminal, consumer to citizen, user to producer, with the lines between them frequently obscured. Much of the existing research on users has been initiated by industry and policy researchers, who tend to be closely aligned in their desire to ensure the existence of a copyright system that will protect the commercial benefit derived from creative work. Likewise, many academic contributions across and at the intersections of ethics, marketing and criminology take for granted the legal foundation of copyright and, like policy research, set out to explore why users violate copyright and how legal behaviour might be encouraged. Conversely, scholars adopting a more sociological approach to the system of copyright offer a more contextualized understanding of user behaviour, acknowledging online cultures and communities of sharing, rather than focusing on the so-called deviant behaviour of criminalized individuals. Chapter 6 looks at the user positions outlined across these perspectives and also features the voices of users themselves, made audible through user-based research.

The disjuncture between everyday norms and practices of internet users, on the one hand, and norms that are reflected most prominently in copyright policy and regulation, on the other, suggests widespread rejection of the underlying rationales. Chapter 6 maintains that the dominance of industry and government perspectives in the copyright debate must incorporate an engagement with user perspectives on the fundamental concepts and ideologies that underpin regulation, and around which there are multiple, legitimate competing discourses.

The shape of copyright policy and regulation is ultimately determined through political processes. Chapter 7 examines these processes in more depth, focusing on the nature of copyright policymaking at both national and international levels. The process that decides copyright policy would ideally be a democratic and deliberative one, where the interests and values of all the groups considered in this book are represented and reflected upon equally. In practice, though, the process typically falls short of this ideal. Major corporations tend to dominate, using their economic resources and position to have more influence over decision making. Meanwhile, the imbalance of power in the policymaking process at a national level is mirrored at an international level, where certain governments have been able to internationalize and export their own copyright policies through various international agreements. Yet, despite these inequalities, we describe recent examples where the public have been able to mobilize and influence copyright policy. What the ongoing debate around digital copyright suggests more than anything, we argue, is that public involvement needs to become a more integral part of the policymaking process. We advocate our specifically deliberative understanding of public engagement and ideal policymaking, where decisions are based on the consideration of all viewpoints and where the aim is to reach an outcome that reflects the common good or at least represents a fair compromise among the different perspectives and interests of all groups involved.

Chapter 8 highlights the threads that run throughout the book and summarizes the main tensions and disagreements evident through an analysis of discourses, before looking towards the future. It is clear that in its current state, copyright policy satisfies no one and has limited effectiveness. We suggest that one reason for this is the highly contested nature of the core themes in the copyright debate — the competitiveness and economic health of the cultural industries, the creation and circulation of cultural work, and the relative power of different actors in the cultural industries. We reflect on the different positions taken by different actors in relation to these three ideas, and consider how disagreement prompts shifts in those positions, suggesting that the future of copyright in the digital age is more open to change than might initially be apparent. In our view, an inclusive debate about copyright is essential to developing effective policy that satisfies all parties. Most urgently, users need the tools to be able to voice their position and feel they are heard and understood. We consider the opportunities and limitations of a 'literacy' approach to public engagement with media policy and policymaking and again emphasize the need for a more democratic and deliberative copyright policymaking process.

2

A BRIEF HISTORY OF COPYRIGHT: WHERE WE ARE AND HOW WE GOT HERE

WHY LOOK BACK?

How did a law enacted at the start of the eighteenth century become central to the culture and economy of the twenty-first century? In order to understand contemporary debates about copyright, it is useful to consider the historical context as well as key perspectives, distinctions and changes that have marked copyright's path to the present. Other authors have looked in-depth at these topics: for example, Rose (1993) considers how the notion of authorship is linked to and shaped by the emergence of copyright in the eighteenth century; Deazley (2004) looks at the major changes and challenges to copyright law in eighteenth-century Britain; and Vaidhyanathan (2001) traces the development of copyright in the United States from the eighteenth to the twentieth century. Contributions such as these capture the endurance of early myths and decisions and highlight the value of exploring copyright's history in order to understand issues relevant to its present role and continuing debates. In this chapter, we draw on and synthesize historical work on copyright as a way of providing background for and shedding light on the modern debates and disagreements that drive the communication contests around which subsequent chapters are focused.

KEY COPYRIGHT MOMENTS AND DISTINCTIONS

Although copyright is now a legal concept that spans the globe, the law itself began in England. The starting point of copyright's history is generally identified as the shift initiated by the Statute of Anne in 1709, whereby the right of stationers to publish in perpetuity works purchased was displaced by short-term exclusive rights of authors. Despite various legal twists and turns over the past three centuries, copyright legislation has continued to be understood as seeking a balance between rights of creators (or owners) and availability to the wider public, both goals that have been tethered to the 'public interest' in different ways. Strengthening copyright for owners can be seen as driving creative activity and thus promoting learning for the benefit of the public (through the consumption of copyrighted work) while incorporating exceptions to copyright that allow for free use of material offers wider availability of copyrighted material for the public (Davies, 2002: x).

As countries signed on to the basic principle of copyright, legislation has typically been revisited to reflect new questions about terms and extensions raised by particular cases or through lobbyists. If the goal of copyright is generally understood as the advancement of creative work (or 'To promote the Progress of Science and useful Arts', as the Copyright Clause in the US Constitution puts it), then the pathway to that goal remains a key point of debate. Advancement may be spurred by incentive (through reward) or through circulation (through greater access), and these are notions that developed through influential early landmark acts and cases. The four cases described in Box 2.1 played an influential role in the development of copyright — in the United Kingdom, the United States and in other countries that inherited or adopted laws established in the UK and US — by debating and establishing particular foundational principles which continue to be central to modern debates.

Box 2.1
UK: Millar v Taylor (1769)

The decision made in the 1769 Millar v Taylor case represents one of the important moments in a period which became known as the Battle of the Booksellers, during which competing English and Scottish booksellers clashed over the coverage of the Statute of Anne and the right to reprint works after the protection afforded by the Statute of Anne began to expire. Key to this and related cases were questions of whether the Statute supplanted a common law right for authors and whether the nature of literary 'property' should be regarded in the same way as physical property. In this case, an English bookseller (Andrew Millar) who had purchased the publishing rights to *The Seasons* by poet James Thomson objected to a Scottish bookseller (Robert Taylor) reprinting the poem after the expiration of the rights granted by the Statute. The court ruled in favour of Millar, confirming a common law right of property and allowing for exclusive publishing rights in perpetuity. As Deazley explains, the judge in this case justified the decision based on the claim that 'it is *just*, that an Author should reap the pecuniary Profits of his own Ingenuity and Labour' and that the decision relied 'upon Principles *before* and *independent*' of the Statute of Anne (2006: 15). The idea of incentive (profits) is implicitly promoted through this judgment as just, communicating the purpose of copyright protection as ensuring reward. (And, from that perspective, why shouldn't the reward be perpetual?)

The principles drawn on by the judge may seem surprising since the case did not involve the author, who had died years earlier (hence the expiration of the protection). The decision relied on (and entrenched) the belief, promoted by the London booksellers, in a literary property 'founded on the author's labor, one the author could sell to the bookseller. Though immaterial, this property was no less real and permanent, they argued, than any other kind of estate' (Rose, 1993: 6).

UK: Donaldson v Beckett (1774)

The decision in Millar v Taylor was not the final word on the subject. Just a few years later, in 1774, the Battle of the Booksellers came effectively to an end when the decision was overturned by the ruling on Donaldson v Beckett, a case involving the same James Thomson book.

(Continued)

(Continued)

In this case, Scottish bookseller Alexander Donaldson challenged London bookseller Thomas Beckett's exclusive right to republish the work. (See Rose, 1993: 66–91 for a concise and useful account of the Battle of the Booksellers.) The ruling denied the existence of a perpetual common law copyright, with the impact of such a common law described as endangering knowledge: 'Knowledge and science are not things to be bound in such cobweb chains' (Lord Camden, quoted in Deazley, 2006: 19).

Although ideas inherent to common law copyright arguments persist in subsequent cases and discourse, Donaldson v Beckett is a reminder that encouraging circulation for the greatest benefit of the public was ultimately the triumphant perspective in this period. As Lessig writes, 'Before the case of *Donaldson* v. *Beckett*, there was no clear idea of a public domain in England. Before 1774, there was a strong argument that common law copyrights were perpetual. After 1774, the public domain was born' (2004a: 93).

US: Wheaton v Peters (1834)

The US Supreme Court case of Wheaton v Peters in 1834 represents 'the first major American copyright decision' (Vaidhyanathan, 2001: 202) and provides a US counterpart to Donaldson v Beckett. Henry Wheaton was a court reporter who compiled thorough (and expensive) volumes of court reports. Richard Peters was his successor and, in addition to compiling current reports, he produced abridged — and therefore cheaper — versions of Wheaton's volumes. Wheaton sued on the grounds that Peters had infringed his copyrights through statute and common law. After losing a circuit court case, Wheaton appealed to the Supreme Court and 'Justice McLean declared that the United States recognized no common law notion of copyright, and argued that a perpetual monopoly would not be in the interest of the public' (Vaidhyanathan, 2001: 47).

Here again the tension between the rights of the author (or owner) and the benefits to the public emerges, with priority given to ensuring public availability and accessibility. If one author/owner were able to exert exclusive control in perpetuity, the risk of two threats to public benefit would increase: the work may not be made available at all, or the work may be available at a price that excludes all but the most wealthy buyers. Between these UK and US cases, a precedent was set to reduce such possibilities.

US: Baker v Selden (1879)

One concept that emerged in earlier UK cases (including Millar v Taylor and Donaldson v Beckett) and that was explored in detail in the US Supreme Court case of Baker v Selden (1879) is the idea–expression dichotomy. The concept is used in discussions of copyright to illustrate the principle that it is the expression of ideas, not the ideas themselves, that is protected by copyright. In this case, Charles Selden published several editions of a book that described and provided examples of a system of bookkeeping. W.C.M. Baker later published a book presenting a similar system. Where Selden's book was commercially unsuccessful, Baker's found a market and Selden's widow filed a lawsuit alleging copyright infringement. It was ruled that 'there is a clear distinction between the book, as such, and the art which it is intended to illustrate' (Baker v Selden). In other words, while Selden's book (the expression of the idea) was protected by copyright, the system of bookkeeping (the idea itself) was not, which allowed Baker to publish his own book without infringing copyright.

Although the decision in this case sharpened the distinction that had already been used to rule in previous cases, it did not resolve the challenges of applying the dichotomy within copyright law once and for all. Vaidhyanathan warns, 'When very different words and phrases such as "idea theft," "copyright protection," "appropriation," and "plagiarism," are used interchangeably in the public discourse surrounding the commerce of creativity, the idea–expression dichotomy becomes harder to define, harder to identify, and therefore harder to defend' (2001: 34).

What makes these old cases so important is that they played a large role in shaping key copyright concepts, including property, public domain and the scope of protection, that have continued to form the basis of disagreements and legal judgment ever since. As the landmark cases demonstrate, getting the balance between fair reward and adequate access right is not easy and current debates suggest that we are no closer to agreement about what the appropriate terms are or what exceptions should be covered. On the one hand, some modern critics are concerned that authors do not have enough protection against the infringing activities associated with the emergence of digital technology, where 'the public interest has been invoked, not in favour of strengthening the protection afforded to authors and other right owners to protect them against piracy in cyberspace, but in favour of free and unfettered access by the public to copyright works combined with the means of copying them for personal use' (Davies, 2002: 7). On the other hand, what may seem at first a simple injustice perpetrated by an uncaring public against hardworking artists is rich with complexity and scholars have pointed out that some assumptions about author rights and copyrighted material as property are shaky at best. For example, the idea that authors have property rights emerged at the same time as copyright legislation, so copyright legislation can be understood as constituting the notion of authorial property rights as much as or more than reflecting a shared common sense. Originality only took a central role in cultural production at the same time that the notion of the author's property rights became recognized as an important value; prior to the eighteenth century the concept of authorial literary property was unformed (Rose, 1993). Deazley (2004) offers a useful counterpoint to the assumptions underpinning concerns about authorial rights by challenging the myth produced through countless narratives that consider the history and progression of copyright as naturally, organically culminating in the modern proprietary author. Through an examination of copyright legislation in eighteenth-century Britain, he argues that copyright 'was never simply concerned with the bookseller or the author' and that 'copyright, with both the passing of the Statute of Anne and the factual decision of Donaldson, was primarily defined and justified in the interests of society and not the individual' (2004: 226).

Furthermore, the existence of rights holders who are not authors confuses the principle of reward for creative labour. Because ownership of copyright can be assigned and transferred to non-authors, many of the people and companies who benefit financially from copyright are far from the artists we might imagine. Some scholars claim that a key reason why copyright law 'remains unchanged — despite the contradictions between the Romanticist assumptions about authorship and the very real practices of cultural production — is because the law, as it is currently constituted, works to the advantage of wealthy copyright owners' (McLeod, 2001: 25–6).

While recent debates may overshadow earlier iterations, copyright was always a contentious subject and such disagreements can be understood as contributing to the definition of copyright that is at times taken for granted. As a historian of copyright law reflects on the legal and ontological mid-eighteenth-century debates, 'the real legacy of these years of argument and counter-argument, thesis and antithesis, lies in the fact that, through the process of contesting the meaning of the copyright legislations, the concept of copyright itself came to be defined' (Deazley, 2004: 167). A number of key ideas and distinctions have occupied regular or recurrent places in challenges to and defences of aspects of copyright law, which explains why early legal decisions have continued to resonate over the subsequent centuries and within the context of the modern copyright debate. The following section breaks these ideas and distinctions down into categories: foundational principles, types of rights, and coverage of rights.

Foundational principles

Firstly, and as the above discussion of copyright debates indicates, different perspectives on copyright have been based on different foundational principles. Kretschmer and Kawohl (2004) outline three eighteenth-century justificatory arguments that have shaped the way we think about and understand copyright today. Locke's 'labour theory' of property, which conceived the fruits of one's labour as one's own property, underpinned many of the early statutes and legal decisions relating to copyright. This sense of copyright as property right (and as part of intellectual property (IP)) continues to be the foundation of many developments of and arguments about copyright. Another perspective present in early debates is the 'notion of copyright as a regulation for the benefit of the public, incentivizing creative production' (Kretschmer and Kawohl, 2004: 29) and notably in the copyright clause of the US Constitution 'To promote the Progress of Science and useful Arts, by securing for limited Times to Authors and Inventors the exclusive Right to their respective Writings and Discoveries'. Additionally, philosophical treatises on the significance of authorship and the author's link to his or her intellectual creation embedded the view that '*everything* ever done with the work is associated with the author's personality' (Kretschmer and Kawohl, 2004: 33). These underpinning ideas create distinctions between competing arguments about the purpose of and proposed changes to copyright, with particular principles becoming central in different periods and settings. For instance, the role of copyright in incentivizing creative production became a central tenet of the promotion of creative economies in the 1990s, as we discuss in Chapter 3. Likewise, the eighteenth-century Romantic conception of the author and the increasingly collaborative authorship structures that marked the rise of mass media across the twentieth century pose different challenges to recognizing authorship in copyright law, an area we explore in

Chapter 5. Although these foundational principles have waxed and waned in significance, each continues to be activated in the contemporary context.

Types of rights

Different types of creative works, aspects of creative works and uses of creative works call for slightly different associated rights. The printed material at the centre of early copyright law can seem relatively straightforward in terms of what is covered and how it can be used in comparison with the films, broadcasts and sound recordings later protected: mass media of the twentieth century increased the movement of copyrighted material across platforms and multiplied the types of uses for which permission must be sought. The repurposing and distribution of copyrighted material expedited by the internet introduced further scenarios requiring permission. Using music as an example, licensing is required if somebody other than the holder of the copyright wants to perform a copyrighted piece of music, repackage the piece for distribution, play the piece in public, include the piece as a soundtrack, or sample the piece in another piece of music. Box 2.2 outlines some associated rights.

Box 2.2
Associated rights

Reproduction rights: The exclusive right to make copies of a work (in any medium) or to authorize others to make copies of a work. It is the most basic right afforded to rights holders and applies to parts of the work as well as the whole.

Because 'reproduction' of IP is rarely as straightforward as making exact duplicates there are licences to cover lots of different uses. Consider the following rights associated with musical works:

- Mechanical rights: The rights holder must grant permission for reproduction of a work as a physical product, such as CD, or for digital use, such as streaming or downloads.
- Performing rights: The rights holder has a right to payment when their work is performed or played in public space or through media broadcast.
- Publishing rights: Publishing rights, sometimes assigned to a publishing company by an author, represent the composition of the work, rather than the recording. The rights holder can authorize another artist to record a cover of a song.
- Master use or master recording rights: Permission to use an original sound recording (as opposed to recording a new/cover version of a composition) is covered by master use rights.
- Synchronization rights: A synchronization licence is required when music is reproduced as the soundtrack to visual media. Such a licence requires permission to use both the master recording and the composition, as represented through master use and publishing rights.

(Continued)

(Continued)

A copyright licence agreement may involve multiple categories of economic rights and may identify particular criteria regarding markets and territories, frequency and length of term, and exclusivity.

Government organizations, like the US Copyright Office (www.copyright.gov/) and the Intellectual Property Office in the UK (www.ipo.gov.uk/), provide detailed explanations of rights associated with copyright and how copyright owners can exploit their copyrighted material.

The holder of the copyright stands to benefit economically from each type of use and this economic aspect of copyright can be bought, sold and transferred. In addition to the economic dimension, many copyrighted works also include a moral dimension of copyright, which is concerned not with economic reward but with protecting the reputation of authors. Moral rights, if asserted and not waived, enjoy at a minimum the same term as economic rights and in some countries are assigned indefinitely, but cannot be transferred. In this way, moral rights can be an important protection for creators, though they can be used in practice to stymie creativity, like their economic counterparts, by blocking parodies and adaptations.

Coverage of rights

Finally, as well as different types of rights, the extent of copyright protection has varied across time and place in terms of what is covered and the duration of coverage. While engravings were protected under the Engravers' Act of 1735, until the Fine Art Copyright Act of 1862 paintings and drawings were not protected by UK copyright law (Kretschmer et al., 2010: 5). Copyright term extensions have increased the duration of copyright. The Statute of Anne afforded British authors a 14-year term (renewable once), the same duration echoed in the US Copyright Act of 1790; today the term in US and EU law is a far more generous 70 years after the death of the author. The push to increase or decrease the coverage of rights has been driven by competing and sometimes contradictory justifications. Vaidhyanathan uses the phrases 'thin' and 'thick' protection to describe different approaches to copyright protection, with the former favouring minimal coverage and duration and the latter maximum coverage and duration. He argues for the benefits of thin copyright protection: 'just strong enough to encourage and reward aspiring artists, writers, musicians, and entrepreneurs, yet porous enough to allow full and rich democratic speech and the free flow of information' (2001: 5). However, recent decades have seen a thickening of copyright protection, driven largely by powerful corporations, which may result in maximum profits for existing creative work but, as Vaidhyanathan and other scholars have argued, can also be understood as hindering creativity.

International strengthening of copyright has gone hand in hand with increasing international trade opportunities and agreements. The escalating importance of IP to international trade is evident in the World Trade Organization's (WTO) 1996

Agreement on Trade-Related Aspects of Intellectual Property Rights (TRIPS) and the growth of the World Intellectual Property Organization (WIPO) since its establishment in 1967. We discuss the relationship between internationalization and digitization below and explore the global extension of copyright policy in detail in Chapter 7.

THE DIGITAL DISRUPTION

In the late twentieth century, changing technology associated with digitization began to complicate the foundational ideas and distinctions rooted in copyright's history. Digitization describes the translation of information into a digital format and, more broadly, refers to the shift in communication and media technology from analogue to digital. In the 1980s compact discs replaced cassettes and vinyl records, in the 1990s DVDs replaced videocassettes, and in the 2000s high-speed internet access allowed digital distribution and the virtual marketplace to replace much physical retail activity. Digital media formats are marked by quick and efficient production and reproduction, and distribution through increasingly convergent networks. Such changes offered clear opportunities for media producers to respond to the market while minimizing costs and have thus resulted in significant changes to the economics of media (Doyle, 2013). With the advent of the internet, consumers saw numerous benefits in the form of new media services, greater flexibility and better access. The same digital technology that empowered consumers also challenged suppliers' ability to make money from IP, prompting debates about enforcement of copyright in the digital era.

It should be clear by now that long before the digital turn, copyright attracted much debate and disagreement over who should be served under what conditions and to what extent. Although many non-digital cases have challenged the limitations around borrowing and copying copyrighted material, digitization upped the ante by increasing the speed and accuracy with which material can be copied. So what makes digitization so important to debates over copyright? Digitization changed the way that copyrighted material could be accessed, controlled and exploited, necessitating a re-evaluation of the principles and the processes surrounding copyright law. The following section considers some of the key results of digitization on the way copyright is thought about, talked about and regulated.

Opportunities and challenges

Digitization offered potential for the copyright rich, who reap financial benefits from the use and licensing of copyrighted material, and for the copyright poor, who are typically characterized as end users and purchasers of copyrighted material. For the copyright rich, digital technology offered a faster and cheaper way to make, copy and distribute media. But alongside the tantalizing prospect of wider margins loomed the reality that digital technology was also available to ordinary consumers, who may choose to copy and distribute media through alternative networks. Digitization made copying easier and cheaper *for everyone* and, unlike the analogue copies of earlier eras, the quality of digital reproduction is near flawless, which makes the circulation of unauthorized copies more appealing and more difficult to control (see Chapter 3 for a discussion of how important it is for rights holders to control distribution channels). In other words, the very technology that offered potential to rights owners presented challenges when in the hands (and computer networks) of ordinary media consumers.

The collapse of boundaries

Many of the boundaries which defined the way we originally understood copyright and implemented copyright law have been challenged by changes related to digitization. Vaidhyanathan (2001: 152–3) explains how the 'digital moment', when the process of digitization combined with the rise of networks, 'collapsed some important distinctions' of the copyright system, including the distinctions between idea and expression (is a digital code an idea or an expression?); between accessing and copying (simply accessing a website involves a form of code 'copying'); between producers and consumers; between local and global regulation; and between different types of IP.

Frith and Marshall, editors of the collection *Music and Copyright*, first published in 1993, offered two explanations for growing academic and professional interest in copyright law: 'first, new technologies for the storage and retrieval of knowledge, sounds and images were posing complex problems for legal definitions of work, authorship and use; second, the related globalization of culture was impelling multinational leisure corporations to seek the "harmonization" of copyright regulations across national boundaries' (2004: 1). These reasons, magnified by digital technology, continue to attract interest from scholars, industry players and government bodies: proof that many of the issues remain unresolved.

Laws extended and reinterpreted

Perhaps the most notable consequence of digitization can be found in the actual amendments made to copyright laws, both nationally and internationally. Individual countries amended their copyright laws to take into account the activities that resulted from digitization. Key examples included the 1998 Digital Millennium Copyright Act in the US and the 2010 Digital Economy Act in the UK, which extended media policies to address the technologies and activities associated with digital media, including copyright infringement, enforcement and accountability.

At the same time that individual countries responded with new copyright policy and legislation, international copyright agreements, which had been a source of negotiation since the 1886 Berne Convention for the Protection of Literary and Artistic Works, were cast in a new light. (See Chapter 7 for more on the Berne Convention's role in the internationalization of copyright law.) The nexus of digitization and globalization impelled countries and media companies towards further agreements in an attempt to manage a situation where national law is unable to enforce the (unauthorized) global use of content. Because a small number of countries make the most money from copyrighted material (and arguably stand to lose the most), international agreements can appear to favour the perspectives and preferences of the few over the many. WIPO is a frequent recipient of such criticism. As Fairchild puts it, 'When things got tough, [the music and entertainment industries] flexed their legislative, economic, and communicative muscles in order to enshrine their economic oligopoly, insert draconian restrictions on intellectual property permanently into the law of dozens of countries, and repeatedly insist that their dominance was natural and just' (2008: 4). Because Berne member countries have to be compliant, there isn't a lot of space for flexibility or for an individualized approach that could take country-specific circumstances of production, distribution and consumption into account. Terms of copyright can vary beyond the minimum enshrined by the agreement. Exemptions, too, can vary: unlike the US, many countries include a provision of non-transferable moral rights, as noted above, allowing authors some control over work they've created, even if they no longer control the copyright, and the fair use element of US copyright law is broader than international variations. But ultimately, the foundation and key elements of copyright law are shared through membership in international organizations and ratification of international treaties like TRIPS, which have responded to digitization with updates and extensions to the protection afforded.

Even copyright laws that have stayed the same have been affected by digitization through their interpretation by judges. Litman identifies the shift in copyright law brought about by digitization as one where a system that allowed authors to make a living became 'a tool for copyright owners to use to extract all the potential commercial value from works of authorship, even if that means that uses that have long been deemed legal are now brought within the copyright owner's control' (2000: 3). As she describes, the metaphors and models used to explain copyright have changed over time, resulting in a different interpretation of the law. Where copyright was once viewed as a simple exchange or a bargain that compensated an author, it later was viewed as a system of incentives and, most recently, a system of control. Viewing copyright as a system of control lends itself to an interpretation of the law which grants authors and owners maximum protection.

Fresh discussions

As the previous points suggest, digitization led to a lot of changes for copyright in terms of opportunities and challenges, the relevance of boundaries, and changes to and interpretations of the law. Because digitization introduced new dimensions to conversations about and debates over copyright, scholars were inspired to revisit copyright's history, a context which had been largely neglected during much of the twentieth century.

As Kretschmer et al. (2010) note in 'The History of Copyright History: Notes from an Emerging Discipline', the twentieth century was a period where there was no urgent inquiry or coherent study of copyright history despite previous periods during which copyright history was of high interest to scholars and represented its own academic sub-discipline. While the end of the century saw renewed interest, particularly around the relationship between authors and texts, and galvanized by a number of key publications (Foucault's 'What is an Author?', Woodmansee's 'The Genius and the Copyright' and Rose's 'The Author as Proprietor'), they note that digitization has led copyright lawyers to look to history in order to understand copyright's objectives, functions and promises while an interest in IP as central to a modern economy engaged the interests of a 'new generation of (copyright) scholars' (Kretschmer et al., 2010: 15).

Revisiting copyright's history allows us to go back to some of the early ideas that guided the trajectory of copyright law and to question whether the foundational principles are still relevant or useful today. By considering the development of ideas around authorship and creative works, Kretschmer and Pratt challenge the assumption 'that copyright law regulates pre-existing objects', suggesting instead that 'copyright law constitutes the objects it governs' (2009: 168), what they refer to as 'reverse determinism' (2009: 171) and 'legal determinism' (2009: 172). Despite claims that the musical work or the modern author preceded copyright, they argue that copyright law had a major role in constructing and entrenching these ideas. As a result, when new technology, like the internet, is introduced, the tendency is to extend the laws based on these notions.

In addition to increasing interest from scholars across a range of disciplines, the sum of these changes ignited fresh discussions — sometimes heated — about copyright, among the many groups affected, from rights holders and policymakers to artists and consumers. Perhaps counterintuitively, the renewal of conversations among industry and government players made little use of academic scholarship on the subject, operating in an almost entirely separate universe or drawing only on work from a market perspective that affirmed corporate ideologies underpinning the recommendations of government reports. Alongside renewed discussions among industry and government representatives came the emergence of groups which drew attention to the limits of traditional copyright law in the digital context (Herman, 2013); these included both discourses of liberation and impeding creativity as expressed by advocacy groups like the Electronic Frontier Foundation and the Free Software movement (Vaidhyanathan, 2001: 154–6). The discussions prompted in part by the shifts presented by digitization remain unresolved: they form the basis of ongoing contemporary debates that revolve around power balances and imbalances.

CONTEMPORARY DEBATES IN THE WAKE OF THE DIGITAL MOMENT

If there is one single issue around which modern debates revolve, it is the balance of power that copyright law and regulation reflects. Is the balance of power fair or unfair? How has it changed? Who has the most power and why? What would an alternative balance of power look like? The balance of power between rights holders, artists, licensees and ordinary users varies. But while some scholars suggest that digital technology has increased the power of ordinary users in terms of unauthorized access to copyrighted material, many others have noted the tendency of big, multinational corporations to strengthen their hold on and ability to profit from copyrighted material through campaigning, lobbying, lawsuits and the investment in technological infrastructures that decrease unauthorized access and distribution. Box 2.3 describes three sites through which power over copyrighted material is negotiated.

Box 2.3
New promotions

Although the increasing rate of piracy has been at the centre of debates about regulation of copyrighted material, not all rights holders and creators share the same perspective on whether and how all illegal user access and distribution should be addressed. In fact, in some cases, unauthorized use has been viewed as free publicity that offers to increase profits more than it threatens to eat into them. The television series *Game of Thrones*, available legally in the US through a subscription to HBO, was one of the most pirated shows of 2012, but those closest to its creation were not worried. Jeff Bewkes, CEO of Time Warner, the media conglomerate that owns HBO, described the illegal access and distribution of the programme as 'a tremendous word-of-mouth thing' and noted that the company's experience with illegal sharing of HBO was that it 'leads to more paying subs'. The widespread piracy of the series was also viewed as an accolade: Bewkes said, 'That's better than an Emmy' (Thielman, 2013). His optimistic take on *Game of Thrones* was shared by the show's director David Petrarca, who said, 'It really helps the show's cultural buzz, and it does not impact the bottom line because HBO has more than enough money to keep making the show' (NPR, 2013).

Piracy of music, film and television is often characterized as a cat and mouse game where powerful companies are seeking to control access to copyrighted material through a range of initiatives, policies and technologies: if illegal access is a minor exercise of power on the part of users, it's one that media companies have their sights set on restricting. What this example suggests is that, in some cases, users are able to exercise power through technically illegal but culturally sanctioned activities. Rather than seeking to subjugate non-subscribing fans, HBO celebrates this aspect of fandom as driving the popularity and buzz of the show. We consider in greater detail alternative views that have emerged from corners of the cultural industries in Chapter 3 and among some creators in Chapter 5.

Limited exceptions

Of course examples like that of HBO above are drowning in a sea of rules and demands that restrict the activity of users, even when the distributed material is a creative use that could not be mistaken for a straight copy. Consider, for example, material that is distributed via platforms like the video-sharing site YouTube, one of the key sites that enables users to be producers. YouTube offers a web form for copyright owners to request removal of content on the grounds of infringement (known as 'notice and takedown' requests) and while some such requests are straightforward, others reveal grey areas and legal lines that err on the conservative side. Mash-ups combining multiple copyrighted texts, parodies of copyrighted material and home videos with copyrighted material playing in the background have all been subject to infringement claims. A recent meta-example involved material used by leading copyright scholar Lawrence Lessig in a lecture to demonstrate the sort of creative uses of

(Continued)

(Continued)

copyrighted work that he and organizations like the Electronic Frontier Foundation seek to defend (EFF, 2013). The owners of the copyright for the song used in the example amateur clips filed a claim and, following a counter-notice by Lessig claiming fair use, threatened to sue the professor.

It can sometimes be difficult to establish whether a particular use fulfils the criteria of exceptions allowed under copyright law. Ultimately exceptions are few and the threats presented by digitization have produced an environment in which those in control of copyrighted material are hesitant to loosen the restrictions and allow for more exceptions or more lenient criteria. As a result, the limited legal uses allowed account for a small portion of the user activities and user-generated material that are now woven into everyday life. Examples like these are an important reminder of the continuing role of corporate power in the copyright debates: the big media companies that have defined the terms of copyright also wield their strength to prevent any erosion of the wall of protection they helped erect. Chapter 4 will explore the role of intermediaries (or power brokers) like YouTube and Chapter 7 will look more closely at the power struggles in the policy context.

Changing contracts

Contests of power are not taking place solely between owners and users: imbalances between artists and the companies to which they are contracted have also grown through changes related to copyright. The limited power of artists and the restrictive terms of contracts are not new. Especially in the arena of popular music, artists like Prince and George Michael have spoken out about unfair contractual terms, and it's a tendency that has not gone unnoticed by fans. In fact, some fans have defended their illegal access of music through their commitment to pay for concert tickets and merchandise, the revenue streams of which are assumed to benefit artists more than profits from recordings often do. However, recording companies have responded to the (real or imagined) loss of profits due to illegal downloading by extending the terms of contracts to include all associated activities.

Stahl (2011) explores how contracts have changed as a result of digitization and file sharing by, for example, including activities like touring and merchandising (the '360 deal'). This represents a shift from industry pushing for legislative change to increase the control of companies to contractual change to increase the control of companies; in either approach 'concern with the allocation of intellectual property rights' (2011: 670) remains central. Stahl suggests that as 'contractual forms change under digitalization, familiar political dynamics continue to characterize the relationships between recording artists and the companies that depend on their labor and output' (2011: 668). The prevalence of the '360 deal' is also widening the gap that already existed between the few elite artists and the many (especially new) others (Stahl and Meier, 2012). The '360 deal' reveals how the potential avenues through which artists could exert power become folded into contracts offered by companies unwilling to cede control. Chapter 5's consideration of artists' perspectives in the copyright debate revisits such issues of power.

The balance of power that lies at the heart of copyright debates is replicated at a global level in terms of which countries have the most influence over copyright's application and enforcement, and which countries stand to benefit financially from copyright. Hesmondhalgh argues that 'cultural property rights (especially copyright) are a critical factor in the relationship between imperialism and culture' (2008: 102), noting TRIPS as an example. He explains, 'At the policy level, compliance with TRIPS means huge adjustments in countries that have no notion of intellectual property in the sense in which it is enshrined in "Western" copyright law' (2008: 102). Such agreements legitimize particular perspectives on culture (as driven by reward, as created by individual authors) over alternatives, shoring up the power of specific nation states over others, and demonstrating the imperialism behind efforts to 'internationalize' copyright.

The balance of power is heavily tilted in favour of Western countries and companies, even when the work in question has non-Western origins. For example, McLeod considers the case of world music that draws on or samples the music of indigenous people, noting that the profits are not usually returned to 'the community that labored to create the original cultural product' (2001: 46–7). Furthermore, reducing the discussion of power to profits fails to recognize other dimensions, like cultural significance, that may hold importance to creators. As well as 'increasing opportunities for Western-based corporations', the internationalization of copyright agreements results in 'the commodification and privatization in developing countries of aspects of culture, nature and personhood previously conceived of as outside the market' (Hesmondhalgh, 2008: 107). The same tendency becomes a matter of life and death when viewed through the IP sibling of copyright, patents: the contributions of indigenous people to the development of pharmaceuticals goes unrewarded, while the control of pharmaceutical patents by multinational companies (and the attendant obstruction to more affordable generic versions) continues to receive blame for numerous preventable deaths. The stakes may be lower in the context of copyright and media, but the foundation of inequality is the same: McLeod and Dicola make the point when they write that 'digital sampling and drug manufacturing are on two very different planes of social importance, but the legal and bureaucratic pressures of licensing cause analogous problems in both areas' (2011: 13).

The movement towards streamlined international copyright highlights the influence of a small number of countries on the formulation of copyright around the world. The privileging of an Anglo-American model (which, not coincidentally, benefits Anglo-American companies) discourages consideration of alternative models. One critique of alternatives to copyright, like government grants for creative work or private patronage, suggests an awkward fit between alternatives and an international copyright system (Davies, 2002). If international copyright requires systems that are largely similar, it is easy to see how the model with the most money and power behind it can become a template. We return to these critical issues of power throughout the book.

3

COPYRIGHT AND THE CREATIVE ECONOMY: HOW THE CULTURAL INDUSTRIES EXERT INFLUENCE

UNDERSTANDING THE 'CULTURAL INDUSTRIES'

In the previous chapter, we reflected on the history of copyright, its legal manifestations and the debates that have surrounded its implementation over time. Now we shift our focus to modern discourse, and explore how rights holders in the cultural industries, and those who oppose them, construct different ideas about the status and identity of cultural work, and talk about the role of copyright in ensuring that work continues. Why focus on the cultural industries and their interpretation of copyright? The reason is simple: these industries are global, they cover a wide range of cultural and creative work subject to copyright protection, and they have had a significant influence on the way copyright has evolved. The way they talk about and justify copyright is therefore central to our understanding of the field in the twenty-first century.

In this chapter, we consider the specific nature of the cultural industries, in terms of the kinds of products they produce and the markets they pursue. We consider the role that copyright plays in their business activities, and the efforts they have made to promote copyright as an indispensable means of rewarding artists and other industry workers. Finally, we reflect on voices that challenge the cultural industries' copyright 'talk', with alternative views of the world where copyright is more of a hindrance than a help in rewarding cultural work.

We choose to use the term 'cultural industries' to describe those industries responsible for the production and circulation of the creative work central to copyright debates (see Box 3.1 for some background on the contestation over the concept and term). The definition of cultural industries has been widely debated: activities and organizations that we might count as most obviously 'cultural' (such as theatre performance or museums) are less comfortably categorized as an 'industry', while industries that may be creative and subject to copyright (such as the software industry) are not as obviously 'cultural'. While copyright retains roots in concepts related to fine art and literature, such as notions of individual authorship, the commercialization and monetization of creative work aided by copyright lowers in significance the historical distinctions between elite and popular culture that sociologists of culture have explored (see, for example, Bourdieu, 1984, and Gans, 1999). Miège and Garnham (1979) produced the earliest detailed theorization of cultural industries, in which they tried to identify what could be defined as a 'cultural commodity'. Their analysis was based on identifying the mode of production involved; the risk inherent in production because of the unpredictable ways in which the symbolic value of a cultural product translated into exchange value in the marketplace; and the 'limits of reproducibility', or the ease with which a cultural product can circulate widely. Their approach took account not only of cultural work *per se*, but also of the developing industries that produced the hardware (TV stations, video recorders), facilitating the mass circulation of culture. They identified three types of commodity: reproducible products not requiring the involvement of cultural workers (hardware industries); reproducible products with involvement of cultural workers (music, books, film); and semi-reproducible products (craft products, performances) (Miège and Garnham, 1979: 302–3). Already, then, in these early formulations of the cultural commodity, we can see a blurring of the boundaries of cultural industries; it is certainly debatable as to whether video recorders and other, more current forms of hardware (like MP3 players) are cultural in the sense that they have a particular 'aura' (Benjamin, 1968), but they play an important role in the successful commodification of culture and facilitate both legal and illegal copying and circulation of cultural work.

Box 3.1
Creative or cultural industries? The UK context

In the UK during the 1990s, a growing focus on harnessing creativity to help local, regional, and national economic transition from manufacturing to the new world of the information or knowledge economy affected policy approaches to the cultural industries (O'Connor, 2010). The focus on creativity led to an important change in policy terminology. It began with the publication of the *Creative Industries Mapping Document* (DCMS, 1998) by the UK's New Labour government, a document that became a template for other countries trying to develop their creative economies. The term 'creative industries' replaced 'cultural industries' for both political and economic reasons. 'Cultural industries' was associated with (undesirable and anachronistic) left-wing political policies from the 1980s, and connoted elite cultural work, while the term 'creative' implied inspiration, growth and openness — more 'appropriate' characteristics in the context of the new 'information society' (Garnham, 2005; Galloway and Dunlop, 2007; Hesmondhalgh, 2013). However, the use of 'creative' to describe a particular sector brought its own problems and its inconsistencies have been widely debated ever since (O'Connor, 2000; Bakhshi et al., 2013). It led to a wide range of industries being grouped together, when not all were clearly cultural or equally commercially viable, and with no natural fit other than that a certain level of creativity was central to their work. Some industries — for example, software production and the video/games industries — seemed

(Continued)

(Continued)

to be included because their creativity could be the basis for profitable intellectual property (IP) rights. They could clearly contribute to the new 'information economy' and support economic growth, both desirable political goals (O'Connor, 2000; Garnham, 2005). Others (music, film, publishing) seemed to be on the list because IP could be applied to their commercially viable cultural products, even though most of what they produced would never be successful. And still others, such as antiques and crafts, were clearly cultural and creative but had limited commercial viability.

More recently, the UK's Coalition government has become concerned with its ability to accurately measure the economic contribution of the creative industries, resulting in a consultation process designed to revisit and revise the original classifications (DCMS, 2013). Whether this results in greater clarity has yet to be seen.

The policy and academic debate around creative or cultural terminology has spread to other Commonwealth countries that have used the UK's approach as a model for their own policymaking, such as Australia and Canada. In countries where the UK model has less influence, the debate is much more limited. In the US, for example, the term creative industries is uncontroversial and widely used. In any case, given the politicized background to the term creative industries, and the problems of definition and specificity associated with its use, in this book we use the term cultural industries to describe the industries that produce and circulate cultural work, and use copyright to maximize the revenue they can generate from it.

Other scholars built on Miège and Garnham's work in their attempts to consider what kinds of work might be regarded as 'cultural commodities' (O'Connor, 2000; Pratt, 2005; Throsby, 2008). While any commodity arguably has a cultural dimension, debates continue about how far one might recognize the cultural nature of instrumental goods and services (such as cars or domestic appliances) without losing the meaning of 'cultural production' (Flew, 2002; Negus, 2006; Mato, 2009). For the purposes of this book, we use the argument that the boundaries between cultural and non-cultural industries are recognizably 'porous, provisional and relative' (Hesmondhalgh and Pratt, 2005: 6), but that cultural industries produce commodities in the form of texts that 'influence our understanding and knowledge of the world' (Hesmondhalgh, 2013: 4), primarily through their symbolic rather than functional character. Hesmondhalgh points out that the distinction between a largely functional product (such as a washing machine) and a largely symbolic product (such as a film or a book) is crucial to maintain. The distinction is important to our argument too, since copyright law has traditionally been exercised in relation to works defined by their symbolic, rather than functional, creativity.

Of course, we enjoy a wide range of cultural commodities, some of which are more 'industrial' in production and distribution than others. Hesmondhalgh makes another useful distinction that highlights the industrial element of cultural production. What matters in an analysis of cultural industries, in his view, is not only the symbolic nature of their product, but also the reach that such industries have. In other words, while theatre or dance are certainly intensely cultural, their ability to reproduce and circulate their product is limited by the live format for most performances. In contrast, Hesmondhalgh's core cultural industries produce commodities that have much greater geographical and temporal influence, reaching audiences across the globe without being bound by a particular time or place (see Box 3.2). Once again, the point is important to our argument because among these are the industries that have most vigorously pursued copyright to protect their interests (Bettig, 1996; Drahos and Braithwaite, 2002).

Box 3.2
The core cultural industries

Hesmondhalgh (2013: 17) defines the following industries as 'core cultural industries':

- Broadcasting: radio and television (analogue, digital, cable and satellite)
- Film industries: including distribution of film in DVD, TV and other formats
- Music industries: recording, publishing and live performance
- Print and electronic publishing: including news media, books, magazines, online databases
- Video and computer games
- Advertising, marketing and public relations
- Web design

Hesmondhalgh is careful to make the point that the core cultural industries differ in important ways, but are also intimately connected with each other, in that they compete for consumers' attention, money and time, and all draw on a pool of 'creative and technical labour' (Hesmondhalgh, 2013: 17). Consequently, he argues that they can be defined as a 'linked production system'. In practical terms, the links become clear when one considers how texts might circulate across the different industries: a piece of music, for example, might be incorporated into a film soundtrack; an iconic line from the film might be incorporated into a PR campaign; the PR campaign might include the development of a website which links back to a YouTube video of the music; the popularity of the website might be featured as a news story in the entertainment section of a Sunday paper; and the film's narrative might be developed further as a computer game. Even though each industry produces different artefacts, the success of each is dependent on the popularity of the others. In this kind of a system, applying copyright is a complex process. The rights associated with a particular work and its various components will vary depending on whether the operations take place under the same company or different ones, on the ways in which rights accrue or disappear in different production contexts, and on the degree to which new uses are faithful to, or diverge from, the original.

The linked production system makes clear that the structures of the cultural industries play a significant role in the way copyright is applied and exercised. Importantly, while we frequently associate the cultural industries with global corporations that dominate the production and distribution of cultural texts, the majority of companies are small, sometimes owner-operated, the majority are small, sometimes owner-operated, companies that build on their network connections to survive and co-locate in particular regions and cities, benefiting from corresponding concentrations of infrastructural, labour and environmental resources (O'Connor, 2000; Bell and Jayne, 2004; Oakley, 2006; Pratt, 2008). Nonetheless, while smaller-sized companies may be especially predisposed to re-thinking copyright in the digital age, the big multinationals have the loudest industry voice in the debate and, consequently, control over discourse. For both large and small organizations, though, the possibility of texts achieving the kind of global distribution that may deliver very rapid returns on their investment is accompanied by challenges in terms of their ability to track and monetize every use. Here, the global corporations that dominate the industries have an advantage through the strategies they are able to adopt to mitigate the risk of infringement and the resources they have to enforce their copyright through the courts. In the remainder of this chapter, we consider in more detail why copyright is so important to the cultural industries, and explore the strategies they adopt to protect their rights.

MANAGING RISK AND RETURN IN THE CULTURAL INDUSTRIES

Cultural texts have a number of different characteristics that present particular challenges for the companies that produce them, many of which are exacerbated in the digital era and make copyright an extremely important tool for ensuring their long-term survival. Texts tend to have a high production cost, requiring significant up-front investment, and a low reproduction cost. In other words, the larger the paying audience, the greater the return on the original investment (Hesmondhalgh, 2013). While this means that success can be handsomely rewarded, the low probability and unpredictability of success means there is a risk that the return on an initial investment remains elusive. It also means that control over distribution and price is essential to ensure as large an audience as possible will be able to access and pay for the relatively small portion of cultural work that attains significant popularity (Tschmuck, 2009).

However, both achieving the 'right' price and the most extensive distribution of cultural work are complex processes. Firstly, cultural texts do not have an identifiable, pre-defined value; the revenue they deliver depends on the demand that can be created and sustained for them in a volatile market, susceptible to trends in taste and consumption (Miège and Garnham, 1979; Garnham, 1990). Secondly, cultural texts constitute semi-public goods: their consumption by one person does not prevent others from consuming exactly the same text, and because culture is still frequently regarded as a public good (Miège, 1987), users are inclined to share freely and adapt their copies of a text. This makes it difficult to set a price based on the scarcity of a product, or the balance between supply and demand. If supply is unlimited, the danger is that the text itself becomes economically worthless, no one will pay for it, and the company recoups none of their initial investment. For these reasons, illegal copying is a target for rights holders, since it removes their ability to monitor and monetize consumption, and to limit the supply of a particular work so that its price can cover their costs.

The problems of risk and return that characterize the cultural industries result in a number of practices, or corporate strategies (Negus, 1999), that help make them profitable (Miège and Garnham, 1979). They create and distribute large repertoires of work on the basis that only a few of these works will deliver a financial return. Low reproduction costs mean that the rare big hits they achieve compensate for the losses made by many less successful texts, while the volume of work ensures there is a constant flow of material available to feed consumer demand (Miège, 1987; Hesmondhalgh, 2013). The industries also adopt various 'formatting' techniques to try to maximize the recognition and appeal of products. Formatting includes the 'star system', where creators (actors, TV stars, authors) that attract the highest audiences are most frequently used in texts, most heavily promoted, and handsomely rewarded (O'Connor, 2010). Other formatting techniques include classifying cultural texts as a particular genre (for example, reality TV talent shows), which allows companies to associate successful characteristics with a range of different texts and thereby increase their appeal; and constructing series of products rather than one-off 'editions', which maximizes the revenue obtained from audience loyalty to a particular text (for instance, the Harry Potter series of films and books, or the various Marvel superhero films, comic books and TV series). All of these techniques maximize the opportunities for companies to claim revenue on the basis of their status as rights holders by increasing the size of the audience and the number of channels through which work can be distributed.

The cultural industries must also try to balance the need to foster creativity and innovation among their creators (unpredictable characteristics, but vital for the success of a text that claims to be in some way 'cultural') with the need to ensure commercial viability at the end of the production process. Creators can often be at the rough end of negotiations, with contracts focused on the allocation of rights rather than actual labour, a disproportionately large proportion of their income dependent on royalties, and contractual agreements that generally favour the company (Caves, 2000; Greenfield and Osborn, 2004; Garnham, 2005; Fairchild, 2008; Tschmuck, 2009; Towse, 2011). For example, in the music industry there is a move to establish '360' arrangements as a new contractual norm (see Chapter 2), adding the allocation of rights for touring and merchandising to existing bundles of rights associated with authorship and sound recording. Signing over multiple rights in this way further reduces the power and autonomy of artists *vis-à-vis* corporate interests (Stahl, 2011; Stahl and Meier, 2012). Moreover, the complexity of cultural production means that creators are not the only people affected by the imbalance of power within the industries: a large number of workers contribute to the production process, most of whom are relatively poorly paid and exist on temporary, rather than permanent, contracts (in film, for example, consider the runner, the focus puller, the dresser, the make-up artist, the costume designer, the promotional staff, the drivers, even the people who clean the set after a hard day's shooting) (Hesmondhalgh and Baker, 2011; Hesmondhalgh, 2013).

Finally, cultural industries use a number of tools to address problems of price and distribution. They try to maximize the value associated with their texts by using promotion (PR, marketing and branding techniques) to foster publicity and communicate their symbolic appeal. They also attempt to construct artificial scarcity in their markets by controlling distribution and access to cultural work. A number of techniques come into play as a means of managing the legal, technological, normative and policy environments in which the cultural industries operate (Lessig, 2006), including vertical integration (buying up companies involved in the different stages of cultural production, from creation and marketing to promotion and distribution), promoting and enforcing copyright, introducing technology that can control user activity, and educating users about the importance of industry survival (see Burkart and McCourt, 2006, for a detailed account of the music industry's strategies).

PROTECTING PROFITS THROUGH REGULATION

How does copyright help the cultural industries as they try to manage risk and return in the digital era? For the cultural industries, as owners of cultural texts, its importance is best understood in the context of the industry structures and challenges discussed above. Copyright involves many associated rights, and protects revenue streams by allowing companies to assert their claim to different aspects of IP embedded in the texts they own, over time and across different geographies (Frith and Marshall, 2004). Copyright thus plays a role in assuring the future of the cultural industries: revenue through copyright underpins both employment in the cultural industries and the continued production of cultural work. And because they enforce copyright claims on behalf of contracted creators, the cultural industries are able to argue that copyright is the means by which they protect and encourage creativity, connecting to the politicized discourse of the 'creative economy' as a key source of competitiveness in the global economy. Clearly, copyright is fundamental to the cultural industries' efforts to manage risk and return (Frith and Marshall, 2004; Galloway and Dunlop, 2007; Towse, 2011).

In the process of attempting to preserve copyright, the cultural industries have made huge efforts to assert and enforce their rights, shut down piracy and encourage legal use. Deploying the law as a means of regulating the production and use of cultural work in the digital world — or a modality of regulation, as Lessig (2006) has termed it — the cultural industries have extended their rights, shut down illegal sources for their works, penalized infringers and those who facilitate infringement, and recouped some lost income. In the music industry, the complex case brought against file-sharing site Napster by the Recording Industry Association of America (RIAA) was the first major case of this kind and led to the site closing in 2001, with its financial backer, Bertelsmann AG, being sued for their support of Napster by the National Music Publishers' Association. The case eventually ended after seven years, with Bertelsmann agreeing to pay $130 million damages (Kravets, 2007). In 2010, the Motion Picture Association of America (MPAA) successfully brought a case in the UK courts to shut down Newzbin, a search site giving users access to pirated content.

Newzbin2 was resurrected by the original Newzbin owners in 2011, but subsequently shut down again after the MPAA used the courts to force internet service providers (ISPs) to block access to the site (Jowitt, 2011; Brewster, 2012). More recently, in 2013 the MPAA succeeded in shutting down the online storage site Hotfile and securing $80 million in damages (Dredge, 2013a). As for individual infringers, rights holders have exploited the lack of knowledge and resources that users have about copyright: threatening court proceedings, even if the basis is thin, can be enough to frighten infringers into sanctioned activities (Moss, 2011). At the same time, the success of lawsuits and threats has had mixed results in practical terms: although rights holders were successful in their 2009 lawsuit against peer-to-peer (P2P) site The Pirate Bay (see Chapters 4 and 6 for more detail), it remains alive through proxy sites and moving servers.

Given that the law is not a failsafe means of protection, the cultural industries have drawn on three other modalities of regulation as well: the market, technology and social norms (Lessig, 2006; Murray, 2010: 62–6). One relatively successful approach has been to manipulate market mechanisms in ways that prompt users to change their habits. It includes changing distribution mechanisms, introducing new modes of access and payment, as well as altering formats to provide different ways to consume cultural work. Examples include the introduction of easy access, user-friendly online stores and streaming services for music, film and TV programmes, such as iTunes, Spotify and Netflix. Adapting product portfolios also follows the introduction of new outlets: for example, individual album tracks can be downloaded as MP3s, rather than requiring a consumer to purchase entire albums. Similarly, marketing initiatives such as bundling formats together are becoming more common as a way of catering to users' desires to access the work they buy in different ways without breaking the law: in the resurgent market for vinyl records, for example (Richter, 2014), LPs frequently include a code for downloading their MP3 versions, while publishers bundle hard-copy books with their e-versions, or make e-versions available retrospectively, as in Amazon's KindleMatch service. Magazines frequently 'push' readers of hard copies towards their websites for more in-depth analyses of stories, competitions or other ways of engaging with content. DVDs of films and television series include exclusive behind-the-scenes footage, deleted scenes and producer-narrated excerpts, as a way of encouraging viewers to part with their money. More radical, but still successful, experiments with the market have included invitations to users to pay what they want for books and music (NME, 2008; Flood, 2012) before work is released through more traditional routes.

Related to market manipulation, but perhaps less successful, has been the use of technology as a modality of regulation. Frequently, such measures have been invoked through laws that grant rights holders the power to use technology to both monitor and limit infringers' access to copyrighted work. For example, the original draft of France's 2009 HADOPI law (Haute Autorité pour la diffusion des œuvres et la protection des droits sur internet, or 'law promoting the distribution and protection of creative works on the internet') allowed rights holders to monitor online activity, track down illegal use and then block internet access for that location. Forcing ISPs to block internet access to illegal sites and give up the names of regular infringers was included in the UK's Digital Economy Act (2010), while the Stop Online Piracy and PROTECT IP Acts (SOPA and PIPA) in the US proposed more draconian access limitations and prison sentences for persistent infringers (Sell, 2013). The US Copyright Alert system, introduced in 2013 (see Chapter 4), involves sending infringers six warning letters, after which their internet access will be limited (BBC, 2013a). Such measures are, predictably, unpopular and hotly contested (Halliday, 2012; Van Der Sar, 2013) both within the industry and among users and activist groups. SOPA and PIPA were eventually halted as a result of the widespread protests against them (Herman, 2013; Sell, 2013) while, in the UK, the implementation of the Digital Economy Act has taken much longer than initially planned. In France, the HADOPI measures have been dropped following significant opposition, in favour of imposing fines on users instead (see Chapter 4 for the role of intermediaries in copyright enforcement and Chapter 7 for more detail on changing policies).

As well as using technology to block users from accessing infringing content, the cultural industries have attempted to limit consumers' use of a cultural work *after* they have purchased it, through digital rights management (DRM) technologies. DRM includes technologies that prevent copying by encrypting the original text, limit the use of a work on different devices, or block format shifting (for example, preventing a consumer from printing an e-book they have purchased). Effectively, it removes users' agency by turning technology into a 'black box' that they can't scrutinize. For members of movements like open source, for whom 'design is tampering, where innovation demands investigation' (Gillespie, 2006: 660), DRM is a direct challenge to their creativity, autonomy and to the future quality of the technology itself. Because it writes out user innovation from the start, it is widely regarded as unreasonable by users and anti-copyright activists (Doctorow, 2012) and work-arounds are readily available (see, for example, Sorrel, 2011; Harris, n.d.). As a consequence, its use across the cultural industries is variable. Some forms of DRM remain, but others have been dropped: Apple, for example, has offered a program for users to run that removes DRM technology from everything sold via its iTunes store.

The fourth mode of regulation utilized by the cultural industries is that of social norms. Beliefs and values associated with the production and use of copyrighted work, or copynorms (Schultz, 2006), are influenced in ways that encourage legal, rather than illegal, behaviour. Normative regulation is particularly important in a context where neither the law, technology nor the market have been fully effective in preventing illegal behaviour. Users draw on a range of rationalities when making decisions about how to use copyrighted work, and the cultural industries deploy a variety of communications and education campaigns in order to influence them. The power of discourse and language comes to the fore as a means of constructing particular perceptions of copyright, infringement and legal behaviour in ways that serve the interests of cultural industries (Deazley, 2004; Herman, 2008; Lentz, 2011). In the next section, we outline some of the discursive strategies employed by the cultural industries to deter users from accessing copyright work illegally.

CAMPAIGNING FOR COPYRIGHT

Rights holders have tried to cast infringement in harsh terms, as criminal activity that denies creators their rights, damages the cultural industries, and links to more substantial crimes such as international terrorism, drug smuggling and human trafficking (see Box 3.3). Such campaigns reflect the need for copyright owners to frame infringement not as simple misdemeanour, but as a source of moral panic and a significant danger to society. Demonizing infringement has the obvious advantage of casting the copyright industries in a positive light, as responsible property owners engaged in efforts to protect society rather than their own interests (Patry, 2009). At the same time, campaign narratives preclude the possibility of recognizing some types of infringement as new social norms or creative acts in themselves. Instead, the focus is on the shame and risks associated with infringement as a criminal act.

Box 3.3
The big stick: threats and shaming

Anti-piracy campaigns have been part of the copyright landscape for decades, and have intensified as cheap, user-friendly copying technologies have become more widespread (Yar, 2007). Of the cultural industries, music and film have been most vociferous about their rights and invested heavily in public campaigns defending copyright. One of the most prominent was the campaign *Home Taping is Killing Music*, launched by the British Phonographic Industry (BPI) in the early 1980s to combat the widespread user practice of compiling and sharing mix cassette tapes. Surrounding an adapted image of the skull and crossbones (the skull replaced by the silhouette of a cassette), the message ('Home taping is killing music. And it's illegal.') was an attempt to scare users into compliance, although its call seemed to fall on deaf ears. The campaign prompted resistance rather than compliance, with no discernible fall in home taping and many parodies being produced by bands as well as users, mocking the campaign and challenging its central claim that the music industry would die if home taping continued (Yar, 2007). (See Chapter 6 for more on how users respond creatively to copyrighted work regardless of industry claims about the damage they are doing.)

The threatening tone nonetheless continued in new campaigns responding to challenges presented by the digital era. In the MPAA's 2004 *Piracy. It's a Crime* campaign, for example, piracy is equated with stealing private possessions: 'You wouldn't steal a car. You wouldn't steal a handbag. You wouldn't steal a mobile phone. You wouldn't steal a movie. Piracy is stealing. Stealing is against the law. Piracy. It's a crime.' In the campaign video, grainy images of each criminal act are interspersed with the relevant phrase, with the overall effect that piracy is presented as any other kind of theft, and all 'pirates' framed as criminals, regardless of the scale or purpose of their infringement. Important distinguishing factors are ignored, such as the fact that piracy relates to semi-public, not private, goods, is often enabled by technologies that the

(Continued)

(Continued)

cultural industries promote, and might in some cases extend the audience for some cultural texts. The same approach characterized an online campaign the following year, when the MPAA combined raids on sites streaming movies illegally with replacement screens informing visitors to the (now closed) sites that 'You Can Click, But You Can't Hide' (BBC, 2005).

The film industry in the UK has been no less active, with the Industry Trust launching the 2004 *Piracy is a Crime* campaign, in which commercial piracy was made synonymous with human rights abuses such as people trafficking and illegal employment practices. The blunt messages of the posters made explicit reference to organized criminals, including terrorists and traffickers, with the consumer of pirated goods implicated as a funder of criminal networks. A visual metaphor of a man removing a mask (featuring the face of an uncertain consumer) to reveal the criminal element behind it emphasizes piracy practices as masking darker activities (see Figure 3.1). In 2007, their tone softened slightly with the *Knock off Nigel* campaign. This time, piracy was linked with petty criminality in order to shame users who bought pirated DVDs or illegally downloaded movies. TV and cinema adverts showed Nigel, the guilty party, pictured in his office and out socializing, mocked by his peers because of his behaviour. The song that goes with the film compares Nigel's copyright infringement with other socially unacceptable habits (doing things 'on the cheap', stealing from 'whip-rounds', scrounging drinks, and stealing from his grandmother). The verdict is that he is a 'real creep', 'a grubby little man', and (implicitly) someone whom few people would want to know. The campaign suggests that people like Nigel are justifiably ostracized by friends and colleagues, and once again conveniently ignores the distinction between public and private goods, as well as the fact that illegal downloading can be a social act of sharing rather than being done in isolation (Edwards et al., 2013a).

Figure 3.1

Despite attempts to shame and criminalize users, however, resistance has continued. The campaigns have been parodied extensively online, and in popular culture; the MPAA's *Piracy. It's a Crime* campaign, for example, was parodied in the British hit comedy series *The IT Crowd*. It's no surprise that oppositional views fill the comments sections of new stories about anti-piracy initiatives, as well as the comments sections of YouTube parodies, pointing out the unrealistic links made between piracy and other crime, and mocking the idea that illegal downloading is a shameful activity (see, for example, Bull, 2010; Dredge, 2014). Comments frequently point out the self-interest that drives the cultural industries' efforts to protect their work, and allude to the inequitable structures of the cultural industries as a way of challenging the impression given in the ads that users, not industries, are acting immorally. Resistance to such messages has even extended to the courts; in a recent case, the MPAA was denied the right to use the terms 'piracy', 'theft' and 'stealing' in their lawsuit against Hotfile, a file-hosting site, because they were derogatory terms that might unreasonably influence the jury (techdirt.com, 2013).

Perhaps because the 'big stick' approach to enforcing copyright has had limited effect, the tone of more recent campaigns has softened (Rohrer, 2009; Edwards et al., 2014), with harsher infringement messages communicated only by enforcement arms of the cultural industries such as the Federation Against Copyright Theft (www.fact-uk.org.uk). Instead, marketing and PR initiatives emphasize the idea of a partnership between consumers and producers of cultural texts, and users are made responsible for the survival of the cultural industries. This 'responsibilization' emerges in a number of ways, many of which respond to critiques of previous campaigns (see Box 3.4). One major emphasis has been to withdraw the assumption that all illegal behaviour is intentionally criminal, and instead recognize the difficulties that users encounter in trying to understand copyright legislation and what counts as legal or illegal. The result is campaigns that educate users about the best ways to find and legally obtain copyrighted work. For example, the Motion Picture Distributors Association (India) has collaborated with the Film and Television Producers Guild of India to introduce 'Indian Movie Cop', an educational mobile app that 'facilitates the seamless flow of information on piracy issues' (MPDA, 2013a).

'Creative worker-witnessing' is a second tactic used in less aggressive campaigns, this time responding to the accusation that cultural industry profits derived from copyright tend to rise to the top, feeding the 'star system', but leaving those at the bottom unrewarded. In 'witnessing' campaigns, users are reminded of the hard work that goes into making cultural texts, and creators' entitlement to a reward for that work. Some campaigns leverage fans' commitment to particular stars by arguing that they need rewarding for their effort. Others remind users that illegal behaviour is not a 'victimless' crime (depriving already wealthy stars and executives of extra income), but endangers the livelihoods of creative workers at all levels — technicians, dressers, make-up artists and runners, for example. The Indian arm of the MPA, for example, argues that only a 'robust regulatory environment' will enable 'our young creative generation [to have] their valuable work protected and achieve their full potential' (MPDA, 2013b). Presenting creative workers in this way humanizes the cultural industries and prevents illegal behaviour from being claimed as a protest against an immoral system. Instead, it is transformed into an immoral and personal act that damages innocent individuals who, in the end, are just like the users themselves.

A third tactic has been to appeal to users' self-interest, with campaigns again suggesting that illegal behaviour threatens industry survival, but this time framing the consequences from the perspective of the user: the result of illegal downloading is the loss of cultural texts that they value and desire. Another version of this tactic in the new generation of campaigns emphasizes the active part that legal behaviour plays in the survival of the cultural industries. By legally consuming copyrighted work, users can be incorporated into the production process: buying a ticket, for example, is transformed from an economic transaction into an investment in the work itself. Users are addressed directly as 'makers' of cultural texts, and their loyalty (evidenced by their financial commitment first and foremost) transforms them into active stakeholders in the quality and continuity of the product they love.

Box 3.4
The juicy carrot: partnership and self-interest

A good example of the new generation of campaigns encouraging legal use of copyrighted products is *Music Matters*, a global initiative launched by the BPI and partners in 2010 'to highlight the value and significance of music while educating consumers on where to find and enjoy digital music legally' (BPI, 2014). The introductory campaign video takes the viewer through a set of hand-written statements and drawn images set against a gentle soundtrack, adopting a personal, rather than corporate, tone. The aim is to 'start a conversation' with audience members, appealing to their commonly-held belief in the value of music to suggest that legal use is an 'ethical choice', while illegal use means music is in danger of 'becoming less precious'. The desire to educate users about legal consumption is evident not only in the language used, but also in the introduction of the Music Matters 'trustmark' that consumers can look for in shops and online to guide their music 'choices'. As the campaign blurb explains, 'It means that those who were involved in making music are getting paid. After all, when creators can earn a return on their work, they have the means to continue making the music that matters to all of us.'

In the *Music Matters* narrative, fandom is respected and acknowledged as an important and valued rationale for consuming music, while illegal consumption is put down to simple ignorance of how to access music legally. The communication strategy protects the integrity of the audience and avoids accusations that the industry is coming down too hard on those who contribute to its survival. It also allows a change in industry identity: instead of being the aggressive enforcer, the BPI and its partners offer assistance and information to users in a pedagogic role. Fair remuneration is assumed to take place through existing industry structures, and the campaign neatly sidesteps questions about the legitimacy of current reward systems.

The film industry has adopted a similar tack with its *Moments Worth Paying For* series of film trailers, created through the Industry Trust for IP Awareness, 'the UK film, TV and video industry's consumer education body, promoting the value of copyright and creativity' (Industry Trust, 2014). Launched in 2009, the original series of trailers captured the emotions that play out on viewers' faces, showing their *Shock, Laughter, Tears,* and *Joy*. At the end of each one, users were directed to Findanyfilm.com, a website to help consumers locate legal digital content. A second series, *You Make the Movies,* comprised a range of spoof shorts parodying famous film scenes, such as *Jerry Maguire*'s 'Show me the money' scene. At the end of each, a voiceover reminds viewers, 'You make the Movies. Every time you buy a cinema ticket, Blu-ray disc, DVD or download, your support helps us make the films you love: thank you' (Industry Trust, 2014). The campaign has been revived recently, with short trailers from hits including *The Hunger Games, Muppets Most Wanted* and *Iron Man 3*. '[E]ach unique trailer shone a light on why film is worth paying for in its own way', according to the publicity, while the 'discovery tool, findanyfilm.com' is not only 'inspiring audiences to play fair, but ensuring they're just one click away from being able to do so — whether they're viewing the campaign from their desktop, a tablet or mobile' (Industry Trust, 2013). Once again, the emphasis is on enabling consumers to make the 'right' decision, and appealing to their love and appreciation of film itself as a motivational force to prompt legal behaviour.

In addition to consumer campaigns, the cultural industries have attempted to influence copynorms through educational campaigns in schools and colleges that help students understand the importance of IP and acting legally. For example, in 'Be a Creator: The Value of Copyright', the Center for Copyright Information (an educational charity based in the US and funded by a number of different cultural industry associations) provides videos, guides, and activities for teachers, students and parents, to educate primary school age children about copyright (CCI, 2014). Such campaigns have been criticized for demonizing creative and productive copying by users; ignoring its long history in the cultural industries (Yar, 2008); and imposing a Western, neoliberal approach to cultural work and property (Hesmondhalgh, 2013). In response, organizations campaigning for a more open copyright system provide their own resources for teachers to use in the classroom, providing a less commercially-driven interpretation of copyright law. For example, the Electronic Frontier Foundation provides a free mini-curriculum, *Teaching Copyright*, available online (EFF, 2014), while the Creative Commons website provides a list of open access resources for teachers wishing to educate students without the intervention of the cultural industries (Park, 2013).

Despite all these efforts, industry anti-piracy campaigns seem to have changed little about users' practices: rates of illegal file sharing have not reduced significantly, and users have proved themselves perceptive, rational and cynical 'readers' of industry messages, very aware of the self-interest that underpins them (see Chapter 6). Consequently, the cultural industries have also turned to lobbying to try to influence policy agendas that they hope will influence user behaviour.

LOBBYING FOR PROTECTION DESPITE UNCONVINCING EVIDENCE

To look ahead to a theme we explore in Chapter 7, not all groups have an equal influence over the policymaking process and the cultural industries are able to use their economic clout to make their voices heard among policymakers at the highest levels of government and at national and international levels. Despite the lack of clear estimates of the economic impact of either the creative sector or copyright infringement (Gayer and Shy, 2006; Towse, 2006; Potts and Cunningham, 2008), the size and scope of the cultural industries gives them the resources to employ lobbying experts, to conduct research that supports their perspective on copyright, and to set up industry associations that will act on their behalf. They engage in what Frith (2000: 76) has called a 'politics of rights' and their power behind the scenes is enhanced by the 'revolving door' that links government to corporations, and allows government officials to move easily into lobbying roles supporting industry interests. As Sell (2013: 73–4) points out, these close links underpin rights holders' ability to keep their interests at the forefront of government policy.

The international circulation of cultural texts in the digital age means the cultural industries cannot rely on national policy alone to protect their rights, and efforts to influence policy have addressed international policymaking bodies. IP rights lie within the remit of the powerful World Trade Organization (WTO), which governs global trade structures and is heavily influenced by US and Western trade interests. They are managed by the World Intellectual Property Organization (WIPO) and enshrined in the 1994 Trade-Related Aspects of Intellectual Property (TRIPS) agreement, which internationalized both the application of Western models of copyright and the obligation to enforce them in a way that ensures the interests of cultural industry multinationals take precedence over national cultural, social or legal norms, given that members of the WTO are obligated to implement its policies (Laing, 2004; Hesmondhalgh, 2013; see also Chapter 7). For example, the TRIPS terms are enshrined in the US Digital Millennium Copyright Act (1998), and in the EU Copyright Directive of 2001, while in China the government's efforts to control piracy began in earnest with its accession to the WTO in 2000, after which it established a country-wide network of anti-piracy coalitions made up of Chinese and foreign companies which would help government enforce IP law (Franda, 2002). Enforcing copyright remains much less rigorous in China than in its Western counterparts, partly due to the size of the country and a politicized legal system, but in principle cultural industries can pursue infringers through the Chinese legal system on very similar terms as those found in the West (Beam, 2009; *The Economist*, 2012).

Developing nations bear the brunt of the cost of the international protectionist approach to IP promoted by the cultural industries, and while they can and do challenge normative arguments about the importance of copyright, the imbalance in resources available to them, and other civil society actors, limits the degree to which their voices are heard (Drahos and Braithwaite, 2002; Hesmondhalgh, 2008; Dixon, 2013). Moreover, their position in relation to IP protection can be complex. While they may require greater openness in relation to digital culture, they may also want to protect indigenous knowledge and work from being exploited as 'public' goods, a constant danger when Western models of rights allocation depend on identifying a single author, producer or owner and traditional knowledge may not be created in that mould (Boateng, 2011). In addition, the difficult economic and social circumstances in developing countries may mean that, for many users, legally accessing music, film and other cultural work is impractical and sometimes impossible (see Box 3.5).

Box 3.5
Copyright in South Africa: apartheid legacies, informal economies and cultural resistance

Like other emerging economies, the copyright regime in South Africa is marked by the country's desire to become a more significant global economy, and the fact that large numbers of its population live in poverty without the resources to consume copyrighted texts legally. South Africa is a signatory to the TRIPS and WIPO agreements, and its domestic copyright law reflects some of the international norms that these agreements impose as part of the process of harmonization. However, South Africa's specific history of repression during apartheid and the current high levels of poverty mean that infringement is rife (Primo and Lloyd, 2011).

During apartheid, restrictions on the movement of black citizens and the extreme poverty in which they lived led to local informal economies emerging to meet the need for access to information and media texts. Post-apartheid South Africa is nominally 'free' and with a much wider range of media and cultural texts available, but a racialized media economy still exists, marked by geographical and economic divisions between whites and blacks, and between different regions. In this context, informal economies continue to thrive, and infringement is a normalized and widespread practice in all areas of copyright (Primo and Lloyd, 2011).

Many criticisms of the South African copyright regime are driven by the country's development needs and an understanding of access to information and cultural texts as a human right, rather than a commercial exchange (Visser, 2006). This is most marked in education, where copying textbooks is an important 'grey' industry and the only way to access knowledge for many students, because the high prices of original copies are out of their reach. In this respect, the South African market reflects the rest of southern Africa, where copying texts is normal practice for the same reasons (Rens et al., 2006). Other critics suggest that South Africa's relatively uncritical adoption of international standards in copyright law is particularly punitive on cultural grounds. It does not challenge the primacy of individual ownership over collective ownership of culture, nor does it do anything to address the racialized systems of media and cultural ownership in the country.

The rejection of policy norms by South African audiences is reflected in continuing infringement, even in the face of stern industry messages equating piracy with theft. In response, South

(Continued)

(Continued)

African enforcement agencies have only limited success whether acting on behalf of international or domestic interests, and the over-stretched legal system tends neither to prioritize infringement cases, nor to penalize infringers particularly severely. Collecting royalties is also fraught with problems, including corruption among collecting societies themselves. As a result, domestic artists who should be benefiting from copyright law have seen very limited returns (Darch, 2014).

As Darch neatly puts it, the complex historical and current context of South Africa means 'The South African IP landscape is ... a cacophonous environment in which different voices strive to be heard above the others, and in which agreement about the social, economic and legal function of the elements of IP is rarely found' (2014: 275–6). As awareness of the importance of IP regimes grows, the debate will only increase.

We have explained how the international IP regime favours the cultural industries, and in particular the big multinationals, over users. Cultural industries establish another layer of support for their position by lobbying at national levels, with a focus on both influencing specific policy decisions and ensuring that IP rights remain on the government's agenda. Copyright has received particular attention with industry bodies promoting a 'common-sense' understanding of the wisdom of the old copyright regime and alignment with international treaties that is clearly reflected in policy statements and documentation (Cloonan, 2007; Armstrong et al., 2010). Extending the scope and terms of copyright has been a major focus, and the cultural industries have been largely successful in getting their way. In India, for example, the Copyright Amendment Bill (2012) makes Indian copyright law compliant with WIPO frameworks even though India itself is not a signatory to the relevant treaties: the Amendment extends copyright terms, protecting works that originate from outside India but where infringement occurs within India, and provides for ISP liability in certain cases (Prakash, 2012). Other examples of term extensions that have resulted from lobbying by the cultural industries include the 1998 Copyright Term Extension Act in the US and the 2013 Copyright and Duration of Rights in Performances Regulations in the EU (see Chapter 7 for more detail on these extensions). That said, the cultural industries don't always win out over national interests: term extensions notwithstanding, Indian copyright law retains an element of protection for the specific needs of the most disadvantaged groups in the country (see Box 3.6).

Box 3.6

India: meeting global obligations, managing national needs

Over the past two decades, India has enjoyed rapid growth in its knowledge industries and entertainment sectors. The country has a vibrant Bollywood movie industry whose scale exceeds that of Hollywood, it has a thriving technology industry, and digital content and platforms are increasingly widely available. However, the country's economic success con-trasts with the fact that well over half the Indian population live in poverty. As a result, and like many other developing countries, Indian governments dealing with copyright must balance pressure to conform to global agreements with the need to cater to the information and access needs of some of the world's most disadvantaged people.

As Thomas (2014) describes, the issue of copyright protection and enforcement in India has become more acute since the 1990s, and successive governments have strengthened insti-tutions and systems for copyright protection in line with the country's obligations as a TRIPS signatory and a WTO member. Moreover, the apparent scale of piracy in the country has led to India being designated a 'Priority Watch' country by the US, vulnerable to pressure via Section 301 trade sanctions. In response, Indian enforcement agencies such as the Copyright Enforcement Advisory Council have cooperated more effectively with the global media indus-tries and copyright enforcement bodies (for instance, the Business Software Alliance (BSA) and the MPAA) to prevent counterfeiting, although with limited effect.

Despite this pressure, India retains a degree of sovereignty over both its copyright law and modes of enforcement. It has not signed WIPO copyright-related treaties, and while the Indian Copyright (Amendment) Act of 2012 reflects many of the measures required by WIPO signatories, it also incorporates measures that address the specificities of the Indian context. Indian governments have explicitly recognized knowledge as a public good and have actively protected this position.

For example, Thomas (2014) notes that the scale of disability among the Indian popula-tion means their rights to access and information are more readily recognized and, in the case of the visually impaired, the 2012 Copyright Amendment Act now enshrines access as a national right (in stark contrast to the situation within WIPO, where the issue of accessible formats remains marginalized). The Traditional Knowledge Digital Project is a collaborative effort between a number of government ministries and research institutions to document and archive traditional forms of Indian knowledge such as Ayurvedic medicine and yoga, in order to protect them from exploitation by overseas interests. Finally, investments in free and open source software have become increasingly important as Indian governments have moved towards systems of e-Governance, where government accountability, transparency and cit-izens' participation in civic life depend on the ability to access and use information systems, regardless of economic status or physical well-being.

In addition to lobbying in traditional terms, the cultural industries take advantage of opportunities to contribute to formal government consultations, where policymakers seek input from interested parties into discussions about the development of IP policy. Here, the cultural industries can present themselves as experts and make full use of research that demonstrates the value and validity of copyright. The result of these different engagements with policymakers is that cultural industries enjoy substantial formal and informal influence on the policymaking process. The reality is that oppos-ing voices do not have the same access as the major rights holders and, as a result, there is a tendency for policymakers to uncritically accept the arguments of industry beneficiaries, and for policy itself to more obviously reflect the interests of big busi-ness rather than users and the public good (Cloonan, 2007; Armstrong et al., 2010; Edwards et al., 2014). This state of affairs is all the more worrying since both scholars and industry players alike have continually expressed doubt about the wisdom and efficacy of such rigid and costly enforcement of copyright, not only because of the limitations it places on creativity, but also because of the effort it requires from the cultural industries to police a never-ending battle with users and artists who insist on retaining some sort of control of their use of cultural work (Frith and Marshall, 2004; Hesmondhalgh, 2013).

Although the rhetoric of the cultural industries has insisted on the devastating economic effect of copyright infringement, what do we know about the actual effects of infringement on the cultural industries? The answer is: we are not sure. Despite the energetic industry defence of copyright, there is no clear evidence that it does in fact promote cultural production, creativity and improve revenue streams (Yar, 2005; Towse, 2011). Industry claims of the damage inflicted by copyright abuse are contested regularly, as is the (often implicit) assumption that the best way to reward creativity is through existing formal and controlled industry structures. As a result, debates about copyright, its value and management, continue.

For the most part, cultural industry representatives engaged in the debate remain loyal to traditional copyright models and perpetuate the idea that illegal file sharing is a form of criminality. In its report *Digital Music Nation* (BPI, 2013), the BPI argues that illegal downloading via BitTorrent sites or P2P file sharing (see Chapter 4) is still damaging the industry despite significant growth in the use of legal digital music services. With BitTorrent downloads in 2012 standing at 345 million tracks, compared to 239 million tracks downloaded via legal services, the BPI states, 'Illegal downloading is holding back the digital growth not just of music, but also of other creative sectors like publishing, sport, TV and film' (BPI, 2013: 26). The association also presents data that shows illegal file sharers spend less on music per annum than those who consume music legally, countering a common anti-copyright argument (BPI, 2013: 18–19). Similarly, NetNames, a British 'Brand Protection' company focused on online brand protection and portfolio management for commercial companies, published *Sizing the Piracy Universe* in 2013. Commissioned by NBCUniversal, the report describes infringement through 'piracy ecosystems' as 'tenacious and persistent' (Price, 2013: 2), attracting ever larger numbers of users and using up bandwidth exponentially. Suggestions of an uncontrollable, undisciplined online audience are evident in claims of a 'voracious online appetite for pirated content', that 'the practice of piracy itself morphs to altered circumstances' (2013: 7), and that 'piracy is rampant across the internet' (2013: 90). The report concludes that the 'piracy universe' in January 2013 equated to 432 million copyright-infringing unique internet users, over half of whom were located in Europe. Policymakers, influenced by the claims of cultural industries, tend to communicate similar messages.

Claims about the damage caused by infringement and the centrality of copyright to industry survival are contested by alternative voices in the copyright debate (Hintz and Milan, 2011; Sell, 2013; Dobusch and Schüßler, 2014). For example, the Media Policy Project at the London School of Economics has published two reports investigating cultural industry claims that file sharing has damaged revenues (Cammaerts and Meng, 2011; Cammaerts et al., 2013). The reports challenge claims that file sharing is to blame for falling sales of music and argue that wider distribution of music has supported significant increases in revenues from live performance, from which the industries have benefited. In the case of film, they argue that file sharing has contributed to the development of digital cinema, and offers new distribution opportunities to independent filmmakers (see, for example VODO (www.vodo.net), an online service that promotes and distributes work by independent creators using an audience-driven payment model). In sum, and drawing on data available for the music, film, publishing and gaming industries, they demonstrate that reports of an overall decline in the cultural industries are vastly exaggerated, and new innovations facilitated by digital technologies are providing plenty of impetus for growth.

Other organizations challenge the general claims that the cultural industries put forward as the basis for a stronger enforcement regime. For example, the global Association for Progressive Communications (APC) compiles and circulates good practice and information guides for internet users around the world, and has published an Internet Rights Charter specifying, among other things, the right to share content in the process of learning and communication. Commercial interests, they argue, are subordinate to these public rights: 'Protection of the interests of creators must occur in a way consistent with open and free participation in scientific and cultural knowledge flows' (APC, 2014). In the UK, campaigning organization Open Rights Group (ORG) contests industry calls for a more robust IP framework, by arguing for greater freedom and flexibility in copyright policy and practice to fuel economic growth: 'The creative economy is driven by the use, reuse and exploitation of information. Our contention is that the evidence demonstrates that copyright needs to create a permissive environment in order to fuel that reuse and exploitation' (ORG, 2011: 6). From ORG's perspective, the cultural industries' reliance on laws with their origins in an analogue world is too rigid for a digital age. Instead, they argue that the explosion in public creativity that characterizes the digital era should be nurtured and recognized as inherently valuable in and of itself. They define 'fair use' not in terms of legal or illegal behaviour, but as a balance of commercial interests with the cultural value derived from the free circulation of texts (ORG, 2014). ORG's arguments challenge the cultural industries by redefining user infringement as creativity, and thereby locating the production of cultural texts outside, rather than only within, the cultural industries themselves. In a slightly different take on the same theme, Pang (2008) illustrates the complex relationship between counterfeits and original commodities, authenticity and nationhood in China. She illustrates how readings of 'creativity' that reify the original commodity in opposition to the copy ignore the fact that counterfeit products are 'an extreme manifestation of commodity obsession' (2008: 134) and are thus inseparable from the originals. Such arguments show that, in arguing the case for a more flexible copyright regime, activists also challenge the cultural industries' apparent power over the production and circulation of culture in the digital era. Chapters 5 and 7 consider some of the organizations that challenge the perspectives of the cultural industries, including those that represent the very creators whose interests the cultural industries purport to represent.

But perhaps the strongest contestation of the cultural industry position on copyright comes from users themselves. Infringement has not disappeared: sharing, creative adaptation of texts, sampling and copying all survive despite the industry's best efforts to enforce their rights using different modalities of regulation. Attempts to designate file sharers as 'pirates' and then tar them with the same brush as those engaged in more socially damaging criminal activity have backfired with piracy attracting kudos among some users that makes it more, rather than less, attractive (David, 2013; Burkart, 2014). Chapter 6 digs deeper into the views of users through examining their practices and their voices.

This chapter has reviewed the nature of the cultural industries, the role that copyright plays in their business models and the various approaches they take to protecting their rights in the face of rapidly changing markets, technologies and user behaviour. While the dominant multinationals tend to set the agenda for copyright policy and law because of the resources and influence they enjoy, their positions are not uncontested. Plenty of scepticism exists about the validity of their claims regarding the importance of existing copyright systems; the damage that illegal uses of copyright work actually inflicts on them and on artists; and the ways in which they define illegality in the context of everyday, reasonable user practices. If copyright policy is to balance industry and user interests, providing adequate protection for creators while facilitating innovation and development, then it seems clear to us that these alternative voices must be given space in the copyright debates at national and international levels.

In the next chapter, we consider how one particularly important group of organizations, the intermediaries who host and distribute cultural texts, lies at the heart of the struggle between the cultural industries, on the one hand, and users and their advocates, on the other, to control the use and distribution of copyrighted work.

TECHNOLOGIES AND CORPORATIONS IN THE MIDDLE: HOW INTERNET INTERMEDIARIES ARE DRAWN INTO THE DEBATE

INTRODUCTION

Before the cultural industries and rights holders can make any money from the texts they produce, they have to find ways to distribute those texts effectively and to the widest audience possible. Internet intermediaries are central to how digital content is distributed and so are an important part of the networks of actors that comprise the context for copyright regulation and enforcement (Wang and Zhu, 2003), occupying a complex and often contested space between rights holders, creative workers and users. Indeed, the World Intellectual Property Organization (WIPO) has called their role the 'main challenge for copyright in the digital environment' (Estavillo, 2012). There is no single way to distribute material: the versatility of the networked digital world has resulted in various mechanisms, both legal and illegal, through which content (treated often simultaneously as a public good and private property) may circulate, and different types of organizations that facilitate this movement. The Organization for Economic Co-operation and Development (OECD) defines internet intermediaries as organizations that 'give access to, host, transmit, and index content, products and services originated by third parties on the internet or provide internet-based services to third parties' (OECD, 2010: 20). This definition is broad enough to cover a wide range of intermediaries with different objectives, both commercial and non-commercial, legal and illegal, and private and public.

For the cultural industries, intermediaries represent an important locus of control for the enforcement of rights. But while all intermediaries host, distribute and/or locate internet content (Edwards, 2009), not all of that content is copyrighted. In addition to copyright, intermediaries can have a significant impact on our human rights online, such as freedom of speech, access to information and knowledge, security and privacy (Klang and Murray, 2005). It is this fact that makes attempts by rights holders to use intermediaries as a means of enforcing copyright a complicated and contested matter. Operating at the intersection of public and private interests online, intermediaries constitute a battleground for regulation that is fought over by anti-copyright activists and rights holders alike. In this chapter, we consider the role of intermediaries in the debate about copyright, and the dilemmas of regulating their activity when they cater to both public and private interests, distribute both public and private goods, and protect and promote fundamental human rights.

WHAT ARE INTERNET INTERMEDIARIES AND WHY ARE THEY IMPORTANT?

Intermediaries are central to what we do online. As Kohl describes, 'our actions and communications are, in the offline world *often* and in the online world *always*, mediated by third parties' (2012: 186). Intermediaries serve different economic, cultural, and political purposes and they are a significant group of organizations in their own right, regardless of their relation to copyright. Yet they are also central to copyright debates since they provide the means by which copyrighted material is circulated legally and illegally. Intermediaries are crucial for corporate rights holders both in finding a market for their products (since intermediaries allows users to locate and sort cultural products, and to access them, view them, listen to them and buy them) and in tackling online copyright infringement for which intermediaries are a (knowing or unknowing) conduit. In other words, intermediaries are an important locus of control for cultural industries to manage both risk and return as they produce and distribute their texts (see Chapter 3).

Following Kohl (2012, 2013), it is useful to distinguish among different types of internet intermediary. Firstly, there are 'connectivity intermediaries' or internet service providers (ISPs) that provide us with access to the internet. These intermediaries are especially significant since they own and control the networks (both fixed and mobile) through which we gain access to the internet in the first place. Secondly, there are various 'navigation intermediaries', such as search engines and aggregation services, which help us to locate relevant content online. Thirdly, there are a number of large social networks and other platforms that host applications and content and a range of other smaller hosts. These different internet intermediaries can have different relations to copyright and to media users, the cultural industries, and creative workers. As we explore below, some intermediaries are viewed as 'legitimate' by corporate rights holders, working with and returning money to the cultural industries. Others are viewed as illegal and illegitimate sites that facilitate and indeed may induce copyright infringement. There are also other intermediaries, from online organizations like the Wikimedia Foundation (which hosts the internet encyclopaedia Wikipedia) to public service broadcasters and other public institutions, which are associated with alternative copyright practices and discourses and the promotion of the public domain and the commons, the content of which can be used freely.

Given their central role, intermediaries appear well placed to regulate internet use and therefore prevent copyright infringement. This is clear in the case of ISPs as connectivity intermediaries. Since everything we do online is mediated by ISPs, they are an obvious means of regulatory control. But other internet intermediaries also have significant regulatory power too, especially those which attract large numbers of users. While the internet has historically been viewed as a decentralized and distributed space, and still is in certain respects, we have seen the emergence of some very large intermediaries — 'mega networked intermediaries', in Pessach's (2013: 833) terms — that tend to dominate online space and much of the attention of users. There is a tendency for the market online to become more concentrated, as is the case for the cultural industries more generally (McChesney, 2013). On the internet, as Freedman notes, 'one thing that has remained constant is the structure of a "winner takes all" market which systematises the need for huge concentrations of online and offline capital' (2012a: 115). As of May 2014, according to the list of top global sites produced by Alexa (2014), Google.com (search engine) is the most visited site on the web around the world. It is followed by Facebook.com (social networking site), Youtube.com (video distribution platform owned by Google), Yahoo.com (internet portal and search engine), and Baudi.com (Chinese language search engine). Wikipedia, the non-commercial internet encyclopaedia that is collaboratively produced, is sixth most popular on the list. However, it is something of an exception as the vast majority of the top sites are commercial.

The regulatory role of intermediaries is framed by the global provisions for copyright law set out by international trade bodies such as the World Intellectual Property Organization (WIPO) and the World Trade Organization (WTO), as well as treaties such as the Agreement on Trade-Related Aspects of Intellectual Property Rights (TRIPS, administered by the WTO). They have a major impact on the flexibility that signatories to such agreements actually have in their own jurisdictions (see Chapters 2, 3 and 7 for further discussion of these global agreements). As a result, the management of copyright across different national legal systems has converged. In most jurisdictions, the general principle applies that intermediaries are not responsible for copyright infringement that happens via their service. However, as we shall see in the next section, the ability of intermediaries to claim this immunity is conditional on a number of qualifiers relating to the degree of knowledge they have about the content transmitted, the amount of control they can exert over the content and its transmission, whether the content infringes copyright law, and whether they stand to gain from distributing the material in question (Edwards, 2009; OECD, 2010).

While overall patterns of managing intermediary liability reflect the WIPO regime, individual countries do have to introduce their own laws and policies. The two main models that have provided templates for many countries are the EU European Copyright Directive (ECD) of 2001 and the US Digital Millennium Copyright Act (DMCA) of 1998. In these acts, intermediaries are permitted immunity if they are 'mere conduits' — transmitting third-party material without engaging with it in any way — or are simply caching third-party material. There is no legal obligation for intermediaries to police all the material they host and they are not automatically liable for copyright infringement. However, rights holders are entitled to seek redress if their rights are being infringed, which puts intermediaries at risk of being prosecuted if they are found to have knowledge of infringement but do nothing about it. Prosecution can be avoided if intermediaries make clear attempts to remove the offending material, once they know it is there, and within a reasonable timeframe (Edwards, 2009) — the so-called 'notice and takedown' approach.

The model of conditional immunity adopted in the ECD and DCMA has been adopted across the globe (Edwards, 2009). Such laws do not go uncontested and debates about the ways in which rights holders extend their power through the control of intermediaries can be vociferous. In Chile, for example, amendments to the IP law passed in 2010 made it the first country in South America to regulate intermediaries, introducing immunity as long as the intermediaries remove infringing content once they receive legal notice of its existence (MacKenzie, 2010). However, the law requires a court order before intermediaries remove infringing content, meaning that the decision is not just left to private companies to make (see Box 4.1).

Box 4.1
Chile: global regulation and social inequality

Even as international agreements lead to increasing standardization of IP regulation around the globe, variation in IP-related activity on the ground persists. Different social and cultural settings produce responses that may not always align with those intended by laws and regulations, and some contexts have prompted a wider debate about the power of internet companies and the rights of users. Millaleo and Cadenas (2014) relate the situation in Chile, for example, where a social structure involving deep inequalities intersects with a number of intellectual property (IP) areas: as a consequence, Berne and TRIPS signatory Chile is 'a country with highly developed institutions, especially in the case of IP rights, but with a high rate of deviation from its norms' (2014: 133). Millaleo and Cadenas explore how this context of 'inequality and exclusion has important consequences for access to the digital world and for IP issues' (2014: 133).

As Chile struggled to meet the obligations of TRIPS and a related Free Trade Agreement with the US, a 'long and intense public debate was generated concerning the limits and purposes of IP rights' (2014: 139), resulting in laws which represent a notable compromise between IP supporters and those opposing the strengthening of IP. In 2010 Chile passed a law requiring a court order for ISPs to take down copyright-infringing material (preventing notice and takedown procedures being held only by private companies) as well as the first net neutrality law limiting the control of internet companies over user access and data (more on the concept of net neutrality below). The passage of both suggests that not all countries are equally comfortable with the role of multinational corporations and the power they wield in the contest over IP.

Millaleo and Cadenas also note the very high rates of piracy in Chile, which are seemingly at odds with the country's development but easily explained by persistent inequality and social exclusion. Piracy can be seen as giving those who are economically disadvantaged a chance to enter the public sphere from which they are otherwise excluded. Critics of the IP regime in Chile draw attention to the socio-structural context of piracy and push for free culture and open access.

Even with the existence of formal policies on intermediary regulation, grey areas remain that national courts have to clarify on a case-by-case basis. In China, for example, the Chinese Regulation on Protection of the Right to Network Dissemination of Information (2006) states that intermediary liability arises if intermediaries know, or 'ought to' know, about infringement. The rather vague wording leaves open in what circumstances knowledge of infringement should exist. In the 2007 case of the *International Federation of Phonographic Industries vs Yahoo.cn*, the Beijing Supreme Court found that Yahoo, having been notified of infringing copies of certain songs, was not only obliged to take them down (which it did), but was also obliged to monitor all other copies of the songs being transmitted or hosted on its network (Wang, 2008). More recently, China's popular search engine Baidu was held liable for search results that pointed to infringing content, on the basis that it should remove all links to the content on an ongoing basis (Tao, 2012). Despite more recent clarification from the Chinese courts about the circumstances in which intermediaries 'should know' about and act upon infringing content, these kinds of decisions — and the fact that Chinese courts are not always consistent in their verdicts (Tao, 2012) — suggest that intermediaries in China are likely to be faced with a heavier burden of responsibility for monitoring content if they want to avoid lawsuits.

In recent years, rights holders and governments have increasingly called upon intermediaries, and in particular ISPs, to help in their efforts to tackle copyright infringement. But in encouraging intermediaries to play a greater regulatory role, policymakers need to weigh up different values. Asking intermediaries to regulate the behaviour of their users and constraining their ability to host and distribute content may help to tackle copyright infringement, but it can also affect the other important roles intermediaries play. Fundamental human rights, such as freedom of speech, access to information and knowledge as well as an individual's right to privacy, could be threatened if intermediaries seek to regulate our online activities too heavily in line with the interests of rights holders. At the same time, intermediaries themselves are not exactly passive observers in this debate and have resisted taking on too strong a regulatory role. As we discuss further below, some are hugely significant corporate actors in their own right. While they may use discourses of users' human rights and freedoms to justify their position publicly, they are also motivated to protect their own economic interests and their relationships with users as consumers.

THE WAR AGAINST PIRACY AND FILE-SHARING SITES

Given that it is difficult to identify and take legal action against large numbers of individuals involved in copyright infringement, intermediaries and their services that help facilitate infringement have been a major focus in the war against piracy waged by rights holders since the early 2000s. However, an ongoing challenge for rights holders and the courts has been to define exactly what 'infringement' is and how intermediaries facilitate it as new technologies emerge and their activity takes different forms. As Yar (2005) argues, it is important to remember that the notion of 'illegality' is socially constructed, a product of the existing legal regime at any one time. He notes that 'the global growth of "piracy" can be attributed in part to a shifting of the legal "goal posts", rather than simply to any dramatic increase in practices of copying' (Yar, 2005: 686). There is no straightforward definition of piracy as a particular form of activity, and the same term is used to refer to both civil infringement that individuals commit, such as format shifting or file sharing with friends and family, and to commercial infringement, which happens on a much larger scale and is clearly profit-oriented. To complicate matters further, intermediaries frequently facilitate both legitimate and illegitimate use of copyrighted material, so that their role in relation to piracy is not clear-cut.

In addition, and as illustrated above, while limited liability has become a norm across many jurisdictions (Sutter, 2005), the limitations are not as straightforward as they sound: difficult questions arise as to what constitutes 'knowledge' of content and whether intermediaries should be responsible for deciding whether or not content infringes copyright. Such debates have become more important as the cultural industries have developed sophisticated techniques for enforcing their rights in recent years and sought to put increased pressure on policymakers and intermediaries to take action. There are a number of key legal cases against intermediaries for copyright infringement that demonstrate the principles around intermediary liability and show the development of file-sharing technologies (see Box 4.2).

Box 4.2
Courtroom battles over file sharing

Murray (2010: 233–54) has reviewed a number of key legal cases in relation to file sharing. The first is *UMG Recordings, Inc. v MP3.com, Inc.* in the United States in 2000. This case centred on an internet service called My.MP3.com, which aimed to provide users with a way to access their music online. My.MP3.com uploaded music to a central server and users were then able to access this music if they could prove they owned a copy (by either purchasing the CD from an allied retailer or placing a copy of the CD in the CD-ROM). A number of rights holders in the music industry took legal action against the site, arguing that the actions of MP3.com constituted copyright infringement. To defend themselves against the action, MP3.com looked for previous legal precedents. Most notably, this included the Sony Betamax (*Sony Corp of America v Universal City Studio, Inc.*) case from 1984, which had considered whether Sony's videocassette recorder was legal given that it might be used for recording programmes and so for copyright infringement. In that case, it was decided that Sony was not liable for copyright infringement: most viewers would only use the videocassette recorder to record programmes to watch later (a process known as 'time shifting'), a practice most rights holders would be unlikely to oppose, and it was not clear that the recorder would have a significant negative economic impact on industry. MP3.com used a similar defence in the case of *UMG Recordings, Inc. v MP3.com, Inc.*, arguing that the service allowed users to 'space shift'. However, the court decided that MP3.com was copying and distributing the material itself (rather than just selling a device that could do this, as was the case with Sony) and so was liable for copyright infringement.

At the same time, 18 Recording Industry Association of America (RIAA) members had initiated legal action against the file-sharing service Napster. *A&M Records, Inc. v Napster, Inc.* is a particularly significant and well-known legal case (see also Chapters 3 and 6). Indeed, according to Murray, 'the Napster case is possibly the most famous information society case to date' (2010: 236). Napster was a popular music site and network that allowed its users to share music files. Unlike My.Mp3.com, Napster used a peer-to-peer (P2P) model where the files are stored on the computers of users and are exchanged by users themselves. Since media users themselves appeared to be committing the infringement, the Napster case seemed on the face of it to be more like Sony Betamax than MP3.com. However, Napster was not fully decentralized: Napster did record information about the users and the files they were sharing and so in theory could stop the sharing from happening. As a result, Napster was accused of 'contributory and vicarious federal copyright infringement' (Murray, 2010: 238). The claim of 'contributory infringement' was based on the charge that Napster knew about the infringement and contributed to it. To test 'vicarious infringement', the court had to decide whether Napster was also technically able to prevent the activity from happening and whether it benefited financially. The court concluded that Napster was able to stop the infringement and that the site had grown so popular as a result of it being used for sharing copyrighted products that it did profit from it. Napster was eventually required to remove content when requested to by rights holders, but this proved too difficult to manage and the site closed in 2001. The service was subsequently reopened as a legal site and now runs as a subscription-based service under the same name.

After Napster, a number of legal cases followed against other intermediaries associated with P2P file sharing (Murray, 2010: 241–50). The technology used by both MP3.com and Napster meant that they had the capacity to monitor and control the content they distributed. But with subsequent P2P systems, such as Grokster and Morpheus, control was more decentralized and users exchanged files anonymously. Legal action was taken by a number of rights holders against Grokster Ltd (the supplier of Grokster) and StreamCast Networks (the supplier of Morpheus) in the United States in 2003 (*MGM Studios, Inc. v Grokster, Ltd.*). Initially, the court decided in favour of Grokster and StreamCast, given that they did not necessarily have knowledge of the infringement and because, unlike MP3.com and Napster, they were unable to prevent it. However, following a legal appeal, the Supreme Court overturned the initial decision in 2005. The Supreme Court applied an 'active inducement' principle, deciding that Grokster and StreamCast had actively encouraged copyright infringement. Both companies offered a service designed to be used for copyright infringement, put in place no technical measures to prevent it, and benefitted financially. As Justice Souter explained, 'the more the software is used, the more ads are sent out and the greater the advertising revenue becomes' (Souter, cited in Murray, 2010: 245–6).

Not all courts have reached the same verdict as the StreamCast and Grokster case. Murray (2010: 247–8) also discusses an important case that took place in the Netherlands in 2001–2002, involving a P2P network called KaZaA (*BUMA & STERMA v KaZaA*). A Dutch court had

(Continued)

(Continued)

initially decided that KaZaA must take measures to prevent the copyright infringement that users were committing through the use of its software. However, this decision was appealed by KaZaA and later overturned: the Dutch Court of Appeal decided that KaZaA was not responsible for the copyright infringement its users committed and that the service is not just used for copyright infringement but for the distribution of products that were in the public domain or where the distribution had been permitted. In contrast with the Grokster and Streamcast case in the United States, KaZaA was therefore not deemed liable for the copyright infringement. However, during the legal proceedings, the software for KaZaA had been sold to companies based in Australia (Sharman Networks), which meant that the legal proceedings moved there. In a legal case in 2005 (*Universal Music Australia Pty Ltd v Sharman License Holdings Ltd)*, the Australian court took the view that KaZaA had infringed copyright. Like the StreamCast and Grokster case, the reasoning was that the company profited financially from the file sharing and encouraged it to happen and that no technical measures were taken to prevent it (Murray, 2010: 249).

The final legal case discussed by Murray (2010: 250–4) involves The Pirate Bay in Sweden (see also Chapter 6). The Pirate Bay is the best-known intermediary service based on the use of BitTorrent software, which allows efficient and quick sharing by splitting files into different parts which are shared among users. Unlike traditional P2P sites, there are in effect multiple uploaders of the copyright material. The process is facilitated by BitTorrent indexes, which track and list Torrent files, such as that offered by The Pirate Bay. From 2006 to 2008, The Pirate Bay was investigated by the Swedish authorities for copyright infringement. Eventually four people involved (Gottfrid Svartholm, Fredrick Neij, Peter Sunde and Carl Lundsröm) were charged with 'promoting other people's infringement of copyright law' (Murray, 2010: 251). The defendants argued that The Pirate Bay was no different from any other navigation intermediary, which help users to locate cultural products, and can be used to access both legal and illegal content. However, following the same 'active inducement' principle raised in the Grokster and StreamCast case, the court decided that The Pirate Bay had incited copyright infringement and had benefitted from it. In 2009, the Swedish court sentenced each of the four people to one year in prison and found them liable for significant damages. The decision was appealed and The Pirate Bay continues its operations, although it is blocked by ISPs in some countries, as discussed below.

The legal cases that have targeted file-sharing services illustrate how the role of internet intermediaries is complex and difficult to regulate. New technologies mean that the roles of intermediaries continually evolve and are not easily interpreted by courts. Technology cannot be prosecuted, and so if intermediaries are to be used as a locus of regulation, governments, corporations and the courts have to find a way to connect the intermediary organizations with the outcomes of their service, even when new technologies increase the distance between those organizations and the activities of users. Intermediary knowledge and financial benefit have been used as a proxy for this, but they remain contested. Moreover, previous legal decisions and precedents cannot always be used as guides for future cases.

While legal cases against intermediaries have been successful (see Bo
sharing has continued on a large scale. Rights holders have therefore adopte
tactics in order to try to address copyright infringement. As discussed in Chapter 6,
as well as targeting users themselves with warnings and occasionally lawsuits, rights
holders have sought to enlist the help of ISPs or 'connectivity intermediaries' (Kohl,
2012). As already noted, 'connectivity intermediaries' are especially significant, since
they are the organizations which own and control the networks through which we
gain access to the internet and upon which other intermediaries and applications rely.
Rights holders have therefore sought to take legal action to mandate them to block
access to sites associated with copyright infringement. One example was the court
decision in the UK in 2011, which required British Telecom — a major ISP — to
block access to Newzbin2, since it had been found guilty of copyright infringement
(BBC, 2011). This case has significant implications. As Kohl explains,

> The upshot of the case for ISPs (and possibly other connectivity intermediar-
> ies) is that once a court finds a third party guilty of copyright infringement, a
> blocking injunction is easily obtained against them. Certainly, this case sets the
> scene for a much more active involvement of ISPs in copyright enforcement in
> the UK (a position that is replicated in many other EU countries) and signals
> the beginning of more effective copyright enforcement on the Internet, or at
> least its more aggressive enforcement. (2012: 194)

Indeed, after the Newzbin2 case, corporate rights holders requested that similar
actions be taken against other sites, including The Pirate Bay, discussed above.

Corporate rights holders have also lobbied for so-called 'graduated-response' policies and legislation, which would require ISPs to take 'technical measures' against users
who ignore initial warnings about copyright infringement. In France, the HADOPI law
(Haute Autorité pour la diffusion des œuvres et la protection des droits sur internet, or
'law promoting the distribution and protection of creative works on the internet') was
passed in 2009 and included provisions for ISPs to monitor, and potentially suspend
the internet accounts of recidivist copyright infringers. The Digital Economy Act was
passed in the UK in 2010 and included similar provisions (Digital Economy Act 2010,
section 10) (Corrigan, 2011). Meanwhile, in 2011–2012, two bills designed to enlist
intermediaries in tackling copyright infringement were considered in the United States:
the Stop Online Piracy and the PROTECT IP Acts (SOPA and PIPA). In 2011 in New
Zealand, the controversial 'Skynet' Law was passed, creating a graduated response
regime where ISP account holders are held responsible for their accounts regardless
of whether they actually committed a detected infringement, where the power to challenge an accusation of infringement is limited, and where overall, the onus is on the
defendant to prove their innocence, rather than on (better-resourced and funded) rights
holders to prove wrongdoing (Keall, 2013; Giblin, 2014).

The effectiveness of 'graduated response' policies is unclear; they have faced significant resistance from users (see Chapter 7), and have also been actively opposed
by intermediaries. For example, in the UK, ISPs were critical of the Digital Economy

Act. The ISP TalkTalk initiated a campaign called *Don't Disconnect Us*, which argued that the legislation threatened the rights and freedoms of its users, and both BT and TalkTalk initiated subsequent legal challenges. Meanwhile, various intermediaries, including Facebook and Google, played a crucial role in resisting SOPA and PIPA in the United States, and in New Zealand, the Telecommunications Carriers Forum, representing the country's largest ISPs, joined the opposition against the first iteration of the Skynet law (Gower, 2009).

Many internet intermediaries, and not just the file-sharing sites considered in this section, are dependent on the 'safe harbour' provision for immunity from prosecution for copyright infringement. ISPs, social networks and other platforms for user-generated content have typically resisted assuming regulatory responsibility for the content they carry. They are keen to emphasize their role as 'mere conduits' or 'platforms': since they distribute content neutrally and without discrimination, they argue that they should not be responsible for it (Gillespie, 2010). To defend their position, intermediaries often draw upon the discourse of user rights and freedom, emphasizing the importance of freedom of speech and information and access to knowledge and culture. However, the position of intermediaries is contested: as we have seen, legal cases necessarily draw intermediaries into debates about what is and isn't illegal, whether they like it or not, and policymakers and rights holders have put more pressure on intermediaries to play a greater regulatory role. At the same time, partly in response to these pressures but also to protect their own commercial interests, legal internet intermediaries have collaborated more with rights holders in recent years, putting in place measures to strengthen copy-right protection and generating revenue that can be returned to the cultural industries. So while intermediaries and rights holders have often been at odds with one another, as described in this section, it is not always the case. Indeed, intermediaries can be rights holders themselves, further blurring the distinction between the two roles.

THE 'TURN TO PRIVATE ORDERING' AND THE PRIVATE INTERESTS OF INTERMEDIARIES

While the law is one way of obliging intermediaries to regulate and prevent unau-thorized sharing of copyrighted content, it is a slow, time-consuming, and expensive solution for rights holders. Consequently, in recent years there has been a shift towards closer cooperation between rights holders and 'legitimate' intermediaries (mainly ISPs and social media platforms) as a more speedy and effective way to achieve rights holders' objectives. The resulting private agreements either return profits to rights holders and/or help in the battle against copyright infringement. Following Bridy, we can describe this as a 'turn to private ordering in copyright enforcement' (2010: 81). For example, the defeat of SOPA and PIPA in 2012 (see above and Chapter 7) prompted US-based media corporations, in agreement with ISPs, to set up the Centre for Copyright Information (see www.copyrightinformation.org) as a system through which infringing material can be identified, the user's computer identified, and a 'copyright alert' sent to the machine by the ISP. In the case of repeated infringements, the ISP may also disrupt internet access (BBC, 2013a).

Technologies available to ISPs which allow 'deep packet inspection' are significant in supporting this development. Deep packet inspection gives ISPs the potential to examine the content that goes through their networks and so control the data streams carried with precision. Tackling copyright infringement is one way in which deep packet inspection can be used, providing a technological solution to the problem of piracy. As Bridy explains, 'Using DPI [deep packet inspection], ISPs have the ability to automate and centralize the previously dispersed processes of monitoring, notice, and termination, which are the essential elements of graduated response' (2010: 105).

The management of traffic by ISPs raises the heated debate about 'net neutrality' (Marsden, 2010). Net neutrality involves a complex set of issues, but at its heart is the question of how internet traffic is managed and whether ISPs should be able to discriminate among the data streams they carry over their networks. ISPs have argued that they should be allowed to manage internet traffic not just for technical reasons, but also for commercial ones. The concern is that they may then choose to privilege the media content and services they own or are affiliated with and limit access to the content and services of competitors (for example, internet telephone services may be blocked by mobile networks, since these services threaten their profitability). As already noted, the interests of rights holders and intermediaries do not always diverge: intermediaries may be rights holders themselves or establish mutually beneficial economic alliances with rights holders.

However, the more ISPs manage traffic and seek to profit from it, the more their discursive claim to be 'mere conduits', which have no knowledge of the content they carry, can be disputed. As such, their immunity from legal responsibility is also put in question. In Bridy's terms, 'As broadband providers have abandoned the end-to-end model of data transit in favor of intrusive traffic management or shaping, their continuing eligibility for the "mere conduit" safe harbor in § 512(a) has become questionable' (2010: 106).

Another example of the 'turn to private ordering' comes from search engines that operate as 'navigation intermediaries' (Kohl, 2012). Google (the most visited site and most popular search engine by a substantial margin) removes URLs so that they do not appear in its search results. Removal requests from rights holders have increased markedly in recent years. At the time of writing in May 2014, Google (2014a) reports that it has received 25,509,549 requests in the past month. It is not clear how many of these requests Google responds to, but the corporation explains that it 'removed 97% of search results specified in requests that we received between July and December 2011' (Google, 2014b). At the same time, Google has also used the removal request data to adapt its algorithm for search results, so that sites associated with copyright infringement appear lower in search results and are less visible to users, while legitimate sites are prioritized. As Google explained in a blog post in 2012, 'Sites with high numbers of removal notices may appear lower in our results. This ranking change should help users find legitimate, quality sources of content more easily — whether it's a song previewed on NPR's music website, a TV show on Hulu or new music streamed from Spotify' (Google, 2012).

Given all the attention rights holders place on the adverse economic impact of online copyright infringement, it is easy to miss the fact that legal digital services, where there is collaboration between rights holders and intermediaries, are both plentiful and increasingly profitable. Intermediaries that provide these services can benefit from their success just as the cultural industries do. Revenues from digital services — be it through online subscriptions, advertising or per-copy payments — are increasing across the cultural industries (Cammaerts et al., 2013). According to the BPI (2012), for example, revenues for recorded music in the UK rose by 2.7 percent in the first quarter of 2012, with digital revenue accounting for the majority (55.5 percent) of this revenue for the first time. As Zittrain suggests, the 'lines for détente on straight-out copying are drawn: there's been uptake of all-you-can-eat subscriptions through services such as Spotify or Netflix, and pay-per-item stores such as the iTunes store' (2012, n.p.). In Box 4.3 we have listed some of the best-known digital services of this kind.

Box 4.3
Legal intermediaries

Some well-known and popular intermediary services for cultural work include:

Spotify, Deezer: Spotify and Deezer are subscription-based music streaming services that work across multiple devices and through which users can access their favourite music, receive suggestions for other music they like, and share their playlists with friends. The success of streaming services such as these made an important contribution to an increase in digital music revenues worldwide in 2013 (IFPI, 2014).

Hulu, Netflix, Amazon Prime: These services provide users with free or subscription-based access to a range of films and television programmes. While Hulu is an advertising-supported service, neither Netflix nor Amazon show advertisements on their services. All the services have negotiated licensing deals with content providers and return a proportion of their revenues to rights holders. The services are enormous businesses: Netflix had 44 million viewers at the end of 2013 (BBC, 2014), Amazon Prime had over 20 million subscribers in December 2013 (Yarow, 2014), while Hulu (currently based only in the US) had 5 million subscribers by the same point and has enjoyed very rapid revenue growth (Solsman, 2013).

iTunes: iTunes, although originally a music-specific service introduced by Apple, now allows users to find, purchase and organize music, movies, TV programmes, podcasts, and books. The service had 575 million accounts as of June 2013 (BBC, 2013b).

In addition to online subscriptions and per-copy payments, intermediaries can also collaborate with rights holders by 'monetizing' infringing content through advertising. Of course, internet intermediaries dealing just with official content may be funded by advertising: online services such as Hulu, for example, provide free access to films and television programmes, but generate funding through advertising and return this money to rights holders. But monetization through advertising has also happened in the case of sites where infringing content may be shared among users.

In the case of Google's YouTube, for example, the rights holder can decide either to take content down or to 'monetize' it through advertising once infringing content is identified, a system which is facilitated through the use of a Content ID system (see Box 4.4 and Figure 4.1).

Box 4.4
YouTube's Content ID system

Google's YouTube uses a Content ID system, which works by checking uploaded files against those provided by corporate rights holders (Google, 2014c). If there is a match, YouTube will do what rights holders have decided should be done with that video. For example, rights holders can opt to block the video or mute it so that the sound does not play. Alternatively, and significantly, they can decide to 'monetize' the video by receiving some of the money which the advertising next to the content generates. In addition, rights holders are able to take different decisions in different countries, deciding, say, to block the video in one country and to monetize it in other countries.

Such initiatives follow a long tradition of rights holders waiving rights because of the promotional return from exposure through a particular outlet. In the nineteenth century, for example, music publishers would pay to have their music played in dance halls and by popular musicians, while more recently product placement in films has been negotiated in a similar way. In a recent study of the Canadian market, Andersen and Frenz (2010) found that different forms of entertainment — music, movies and watching live performances, for example — complement, rather than substitute for each other, suggesting that rights holders may be able to exploit illegal distribution of content if they promote other cultural work when infringing content is being consumed.

Figure 4.1

Internet intermediaries such as Google's YouTube have been keen to present themselves discursively as distinct from existing cultural industries and media: they appear as a democratic platform for users to express themselves, rather than be passive consumers of mass media. And yet, as Gillespie describes, 'from early on, YouTube has aggressively sought strategic partnerships with professional media companies, to include commercial media content alongside its user-generated submissions. Although commercial media are still a minority of YouTube's total content, they dominate the lists of most popular and most viewed, particularly music videos from major label artists' (2010: 353). Indeed, intermediaries like YouTube are arguably in a particularly strong position *vis-à-vis* rights holders, given their hold over distribution. As mentioned above, Pessach (2013) has referred to corporations such as Google and Facebook as 'mega networked intermediaries'. Unlike corporate rights holders, the position of these corporations is based not so much on ownership of rights as their domination of audience attention. The high numbers of users they manage to attract (combined with their knowledge about the users gained through the data they collect) allows them to be powerful platforms for advertising. As Pessach explains, 'Although these intermediaries do not necessarily extract direct revenues from selling copyrighted content, they still occupy functions similar to those of traditional corporate media in terms of their centrality within the distribution layer, control over audience attention and implicitly, cultural production' (2013: 838).

The 'cloud' and the move to more controllable devices have offered additional ways for companies to exercise 'private ordering' over copyright. As Zittrain (2009a) has argued, companies which control software and data in the 'cloud' become particularly important, as we move from the use of open PCs to more closed, controllable, and 'tethered' devices such as games consoles, smart phones and internet-connected televisions. The shift to tethered devices allows companies to exercise more control over copyright, because the content is hosted on a remote server, rather than on our own personal devices, or because the company is able to exercise control over the device remotely. As Zittrain explains, 'Any device that is tethered to the cloud could have its contents changed at the request of a publisher, author or angry subject' (2013). An infamous example occurred in 2009 when Amazon removed copies of George Orwell's *Nineteen Eighty-Four* remotely from Kindle devices. A Kindle version of *Nineteen Eighty-Four* had been made available to purchase by a third party, but the distribution of the book had not been approved by the rights holders. In a classic Big Brother move, Amazon responded by remotely removing the book from the Kindles of those who had purchased the book, which sparked consternation among users. The company later apologized for the action it took, but the incident demonstrated the control that can be exercised through tethered devices. Zittrain quips, 'Orwell would be amused' (2009b).

INTERMEDIARIES AND OTHER IMPORTANT VALUES

As we noted in our introduction, internet intermediaries are not simply a mechanism through which cultural products are exchanged between the cultural industries and their audiences. Intermediaries are central to how we communicate with each other and to our lives as citizens as well as consumers; those who provide internet services to us are at least as important to our engagement in the social world and public life as the telephone, television or the postal service. Placing constraints on the role of intermediaries, for whatever reason, must recognize the potential impact on our right to freedom of speech as well as our access to information, culture and knowledge. Policymakers must therefore balance the public interest in freedom of speech and access to information with the private interests of corporations as rights holders.

Moreover, since intermediaries connect public and private domains, the regulation of intermediaries can also have implications for privacy. Intervention by intermediaries to prevent copyright infringement may be predicated upon access to private information which in turn encroaches on our right to privacy (Edwards, 2009). In most circumstances, the police would need a warrant to come into our homes and prevent us from undertaking any particular activity. In contrast, notices of infringement of the type found in graduated response regimes need only be based on an accusation, rather than proof of wrongdoing, before steps are taken to identify a machine, its location, and the person who holds the ISP account for it. Access to sites can be blocked, effectively imposing sanctions on a user's activity without any requirement to provide evidence of wrongdoing. Such issues take on additional significance when one considers that intermediaries themselves, if rights holders had their way, would frequently be acting as judge and jury in cases of possible infringement, exacting punishment before either illegal behaviour or harm is actually proven (Moss, 2011; De Nardis, 2012). They do not require any check on accuracy of infringement claims, and the costs of policing infringement will ultimately be passed on to users and intermediaries, rather than being carried by rights holders (De Nardis, 2012). Indeed, the current copyright regime has prompted ISPs to 'self-censor', pre-empting rights holder actions by taking down sites that present a possible risk of infringement following rights holder notification, even when the infringement itself is unlikely (Edwards, 2009: 12). Given that the decision-making processes and the technological systems that facilitate these actions both exist beyond public view, they implicate intermediaries in what is ultimately a significant threat to the public interest.

The value of creativity and access to culture and knowledge also have to be recognized by the law, and weighed up against the impact that intermediary control over content would have on the diversity of creative life in any particular society. Copying and reusing material is, and always has been, inherent to cultural development. As Pang (2008) has argued, markets, not users, reify originals. Lessig suggests that a more open copyright regime would provide scope for user creativity and the 'cut and paste' culture of the digital age. He points out that a 'society that defends the ideals of free culture must preserve precisely the opportunity for new creativity to threaten the old' (Lessig, 2004a: 119). It is this balance between openness to novelty and protection of creative work that courts must also consider when reflecting on how intermediary activity should be regulated.

There are already intermediaries that seek to facilitate access to and reuse of content, helping to promote what Murdock calls the 'digital commons' (Murdock, 2004, 2014). Public service broadcasters and other public institutions have sought to develop systems that make material freely available to the public and help to further the public circulation of culture and knowledge. Within Higher Education, 'open access' publishing, where research is made available on an open platform and subject to a Creative Commons licence (see below) rather than via closed, subscription-based journals, has become increasingly popular among academics and funding bodies alike. At the same time, public libraries and museums have recently been digitizing collections and archives with the aim of ensuring they are available for anyone to access in the future as well as the present (Murdock, 2014). Europeana (Europeana.eu), for example, has assembled and made available a huge library of digitized cultural products from across Europe, many of which fall in the public domain. However, the ease with which archiving can happen may vary depending on the medium. In the US, for example, printed materials may be readily archived under the terms of 'fair use', but neither film nor television programmes are always made available. With the exception of 'ephemeral' material that was never copyrighted (see https://archive.org/details/ephemera), they tend to remain under the control of the rights holders, deposited in a private, rather than public, archive, if, in fact, they are preserved at all (Lessig, 2004a).

While the commercialization of the internet is a reality, the importance of the free circulation of knowledge and information was central to its early development (McChesney, 2013). Indeed, the philosophy of shared knowledge is still present in many respects. The internet encyclopaedia Wikipedia is one example. As noted above, Wikipedia is among the most popular sites on the internet, and yet it is based on the volunteer contributions of individual users and the material it produces is freely available for others to use. Proponents of a digital commons argue that these spaces should be protected, and that rights holders' interests should not be privileged over the development of public knowledge and creativity. Traditional approaches to copyright would not allow this and so alternative approaches and licences have emerged (Berry, 2008). Particularly significant is the Free Software Foundation, established by Richard Stallman, and the subsequent emergence of the Open-Source Software movement. There is also the Creative Commons organization and set of licences, a system adopted by hundreds of organizations across the globe as a way of managing copyright in a more autonomous and user-friendly way. The Creative Commons 'develops, supports, and stewards legal and technical infrastructure that maximizes digital creativity, sharing, and innovation' (Creative Commons, 2014). Creative Commons licence holders can permit specific uses (for example, non-profit uses) while limiting others (for example, commercial use), or can also place their work officially in the commons (see Box 4.5). The author, rather than any other rights holder or intermediary, controls the decision about how their work should be used.

Box 4.5
Creative Commons Licences

There are various different Creative Commons Licences available:

Attribution (CC BY): 'This license lets others distribute, remix, tweak, and build upon your work, even commercially, as long as they credit you for the original creation' (Creative Commons, 2014).

Attribution-NoDerivs (CC BY-ND): 'This license allows for redistribution, commercial and non-commercial, as long as it is passed along unchanged and in whole, with credit to you' (Creative Commons, 2014).

Attribution-NonCommercial-ShareAlike (CC BY-NC-SA): 'This license lets others remix, tweak, and build upon your work non-commercially, as long as they credit you and license their new creations under the identical terms' (Creative Commons, 2014).

Attribution-ShareAlike (CC BY-SA): 'This license lets others remix, tweak, and build upon your work even for commercial purposes, as long as they credit you and license their new creations under the identical terms' (Creative Commons, 2014).

Attribution-NonCommercial (CC BY-NC): 'This license lets others remix, tweak, and build upon your work non-commercially, and although their new works must also acknowledge you and be non-commercial, they don't have to license their derivative works on the same terms' (Creative Commons, 2014).

Attribution-NonCommercial-NoDerivs (CC BY-NC-ND): 'This license is the most restrictive of our six main licenses, only allowing others to download your works and share them with others as long as they credit you, but they can't change them in any way or use them commercially' (Creative Commons, 2014).

Copyleft is a key but contentious aspect of free software and some open source and Creative Commons licences. Leaving goods in the public domain may allow others to adapt them and claim rights over them. Copyleft (all rights reversed) prevents this. It requires that all future work based on the original work must also be shared on the same terms by other users, ensuring that the work forms part of a digital commons and so is always freely available to others. In this way, copyleft uses copyright law, but turns it on its head. GNU General Public License (developed by the Free Software Foundation and Stallman) is copyleft, as is the ShareAlike Creative Commons License, but there are Creative Commons and open source licences without copyleft requirements (for example, BSD unix, which just requires attribution). The majority of Wikipedia text and many of its images are made available using a Creative Commons Attribution License (CC-BY-SA) and the GNU Free Documentation License (GFDL) (Wikipedia, 2014). As noted above, an increasing amount of academic work is now released using Creative Commons licences, following the development of Open Access policies.

These examples demonstrate how some intermediaries can contribute to fostering a digital commons by drawing on alternative frameworks and principles for sharing content. At the same time, it is important to recognize how the commons and private enterprise on the net are often linked. Commercial intermediaries have become adept at co-opting and commodifying the collaborative principles of open source, either by identifying the 'work' done by users as a marketing opportunity, or using open-source materials as the basis for developing proprietary work or making profit from it in other ways (Freedman, 2012b). Such an approach is consistent with a familiar pattern of capitalist expansion, where corporations draw on resources in the most cost-effective way possible to maximize their own profits (McChesney, 2013). Indeed, the corporate strategies of the most successful internet companies, such as Google and Facebook, are traditional, competitive rather than collaborative, and driven by commercial interests rather than the public good (Freedman, 2012b).

While intermediaries may position themselves as the defenders of user rights such as freedom of speech and access to knowledge, the values and interests of private intermediaries do not necessarily correspond with the values and interests of users any more than those of rights holders necessarily do. As one example, Murdock (2014) describes how the interests of the public and private corporations may not converge in major digitization projects. He writes,

> The Google Book Project, in which Google has digitalized the collections of a number of major European libraries, including the Bodleian at Oxford University, points up the potential problems. The way in which the process has been organized has prompted unease in the professional library community, particularly with regard to the pre-emptive inclusion of orphan works, together with a growing recognition that Google's first-mover advantage has given it a *de facto* monopoly over the digitalization of major public collections. (Murdock, 2014: 159)

In thinking about digital copyright today, it is important that we acknowledge the extent to which large, private intermediaries are central and powerful players in the debate.

In this chapter, we have discussed the pivotal role that intermediaries play in debates about digital copyright and in particular about when, where and how copyright infringement takes place. By providing the means by which cultural products are circulated, intermediaries are crucial players in the development of copyright regulation. Far from being disinterested 'conduits', they are central to discussions about how public and private interests are balanced in the digital age, and the actions they take have a significant material impact on the ways in which we, as individuals, are able to communicate, play, share and create using copyrighted work. Alongside the cultural industries, internet intermediaries help to determine the production and distribution opportunities available to creators of copyrighted material: while the regulatory activities of big corporations — cultural industries and intermediaries alike — are often described in terms of supporting and protecting creative workers, the position of creators in the debate is less straightforward. In the next chapter, we explore the assumptions attached to creators of copyrighted content and consider the various ways in which creators relate to copyright.

5

CREATIVE WORKERS AND COPYRIGHT: HOW CURRENT AND FUTURE CREATORS BENEFIT FROM CULTURAL LABOUR

WHO ARE THE CREATORS?

Whether we view creative work as necessitating a system of reward in the form of copyright or copyright as constituting the very concept of the original author whose intellectual property (IP) requires protection (see Chapter 2), there is no doubt that creators are the central party around which copyright debates revolve. We use the words author, creator, artist and creative worker interchangeably in this discussion, though it is clear that the use of a particular phrase in a particular setting can shift the meaning and prompt different associations (for example, 'artist' may trade on specific assumptions about originality and authenticity, and 'creative worker' may include those less likely to be labelled artists, such as software designers). This chapter addresses the position and views of those involved in the creation of work typically protected under copyright law. Chapter 3 considered the discourses circulated by the cultural industries with the intent of strengthening and enforcing copyright protection. Industry demands and pleas often rely on examples of those at the heart of cultural production, creators, suffering from unauthorized use of their material or an insufficient system of reward and regulation. It might seem, then, that the perspective of creative workers has already been addressed. So why the focus of this chapter on creative workers themselves?

Creative workers must be investigated separately from the industries to which they are affiliated precisely because copyright embeds such a distinction, usually to the disadvantage of creators. Creators may be at the heart of cultural production, but they are rarely the key beneficiary of copyright revenue. Litman draws attention to the need to separate artists from industries when she explains that most people agree that artists need to get paid, 'But at the moment, the authors and content owners who just want to get paid are at least officially aligned with the content owners who insist they need perfect control. We need to separate them. We need to try to foster an environment in which it is easy to pay and to get paid but real hard to exercise the kind of control that content owners insist they need and are entitled to' (2000: 11).

Of course, creators have varying relationships to the companies they're attached to and the agreements that set the terms of their reward. Firstly, creators vary from amateur to professional with very different sets of expectations and needs assigned to the opposite ends of the spectrum. On the amateur side, we can include creative users of work that may include copyrighted material. These amateur content creators will be explored more fully in the following chapter: for current purposes, they represent a type of creator that probably does not expect to make money from their creations and may not recognize the terms and conditions of using YouTube, for example, as equivalent to a contract that a working artist has with a production or distribution company. Further along the spectrum are amateur or semi-professional creators who may sell their creative works, but do not, and do not intend to, make a living through their creative work, while the other end of the spectrum includes creators who hope to, expect to or indeed do make a living through their creative work. Copyright and its attendant issues may be of greater importance to these professional creators.

On the professional end of the spectrum there are further gradations between working artists and elites, with revenues varying dramatically. For every multi-millionaire musician, for instance, there are thousands struggling to make ends meet. Toynbee considers the flawed copyright norms that divide, reward or do not reward musicians of various types in various ways and demonstrates how copyright privileges a particular type of musical production, disadvantaging those outside a narrow category, favouring 'big corporations over the supposed beneficiaries of the system, music makers' and creating 'inequality between music makers, especially between stars and small-time music makers' (2004: 124). The inequality between creative workers exists across the cultural industries, and is exacerbated by inconsistent distribution of revenue derived through copyright, though the exact details of the uneven distribution of copyright earnings can be difficult to calculate or trace. Towse highlights research on the reality of earnings through copyright and in particular

> the so-called winner-takes-all phenomenon, whereby the top earners, the few superstar singers, bands, authors, film directors and suchlike who dominate the markets in the cultural industries, also earn the highest royalties. The available evidence (and there is very little of it made public) shows that the top few receive highly disproportionate shares of the total revenues, while many members (sometimes 50% or so) earn less than the minimum that is distributed. (Towse, 2006: 578)

Whereas elite artists may be able to negotiate generous contractual terms, most will agree to standard contracts that are not adapted to the particular circumstances of individual creators (Towse, 2006: 575) and, for most working artists, copyright likely contributes a small amount to earnings.

As Chapter 3 demonstrated, the cultural industries are not monolithic in their approach to copyright: some sectors are more open than others to alternative approaches and smaller-sized companies may be especially predisposed to re-thinking copyright in the digital age, but the most powerful of the cultural industries, the big multinationals, have the loudest industry voice in the debate and, consequently, control over discourse. In terms of the experiences of individual creators, working with an independent or self-owned company will offer different benefits and contracts than working with a multinational. Whereas small or independent companies cannot offer the rare riches experienced by elite creators, they can be more adaptive to the needs of individual creators and have fewer parties demanding a slice of the pie. They also tend to have a more nuanced view of copyright, proposed changes to legislation and perceived threats (see Hogan, 2012, for one take on anti-piracy legislation and independent music labels).

Multinationals are less flexible in their position towards copyright and continued efforts to expand protection, yet the representation of increased protection hides the reality for many artists: as Garnham notes, 'the rights of large corporations have been extended on the grounds that only thus can the incentive to invest in new content be protected, as though it were protecting the rights of the original creators when in fact those rights and the returns from them are transferred under very unequal relations of contractual power from the original creator to the employing corporation' (2005: 25). While lobbying organizations may claim to be protecting the rights of authors, it is often not the creators who hold the copyright: use of the ambiguous phrase 'copyright holders', argues Fairchild, is one approach to hiding the reality that the action of lobby groups shows an interest in protecting media corporations (2008: 61).

As this section has indicated, the position of creators with respect to copyright protection and creative reward varies. But the *positioning* of creators in the debate relies on key assumptions. Much of the industry discourse — which is picked up and circulated by other parties, including policymakers and users — assumes that stronger copyright protection leads to greater rewards for creatives and that stronger copyright protection provides incentive for creativity, leading to more creativity and more innovation. This chapter aims to address those assumptions by exploring the meaning of authorship and creative work, and by considering the diverse perspectives of creative workers.

UNDERSTANDING AND REWARDING CREATIVE WORK

Agreement over copyright's terms and scope would require, as a foundation, a shared understanding of what constitutes creative work and how creative work should be rewarded. This is easier said than done. While some forms of creative work are easily delineated and creators easily identified, others prompt questions about the nature of creativity and authorship.

Copyright laws include the proviso that the terms apply to works that meet the criteria laid out 'irrespective of artistic quality' (or a similar phrase) in order to avoid legal decisions wading into such territory. It is not for judges to decide whether a work is art or not, or whether a work is good or bad, but simply whether it meets the criteria against which copyright applies under the law. Yet, if the law has not addressed the more abstract or philosophical questions regarding art, legal decisions and legislation have relied on a number of assumptions which represent particular — and not uncontested — perspectives on authorship and creativity. These assumptions include the notion of the Romantic author, the characterization of authorship as a solitary activity, and the link between financial incentive and innovation. The historical and continuing reliance on these assumptions across various sites of discourse encourages a taken-for-grantedness that is rarely challenged.

The Romantic author

One of the key assumptions underlying copyright tenets and rulings in contested cases revolves around the notion of the Romantic author. By 'Romantic', we do not mean authors proffering roses and chocolates, but a conception of authorship influenced by the characteristics of eighteenth-century Romanticism, which viewed art as the expression of feeling and imagination and which championed originality as the mark of creative genius. Counter to earlier beliefs about artists and art, the Romantic movement emphasized artists as defined not by their ability to follow rules or re-create, but through a special, spiritual quality and production of original work. Here it is worth recalling that copyright, in its initial form, served to protect booksellers (not authors) from the competition of unauthorized reproduction. As other categories of work were added to copyright law and with the influence of Romanticism, an association of authorship with originality and genius was established.

Woodmansee (1984) traces the concept of the author to the eighteenth century, when writers attempted to make a living through the sale of their writings to the public at a time when the decline of traditional patronage had not given way to a fair alternative: honoraria were relatively meagre and publishers enjoying the profits was viewed as an injustice. Of course, publishers didn't have it so good either, as the reprinting of books without publisher permission became more common, and there were limited legal arrangements to allow printers to profit before work could be reprinted by others. Woodmansee looks at the emergence of the concept of the original genius (from the earlier characterization of the craftsman with moments of inspiration) as driving the notion that the product is the property of the writer (1984: 427). This sense of ownership could then be used to justify copyright law.

Copyright did not simply reflect an understanding of authorship but helped constitute it: 'No institutional embodiment of the author–work relation ... is more fundamental than copyright, which not only makes possible the profitable manufacture and distribution of books, films, and other commodities but also, by endowing it with legal reality, helps to produce and affirm the very identity of author as author' (Rose, 1993: 1–2). The relatively modern Romantic notion of authorship, with its emphasis on individual genius and originality, provided a foundation and justification for copyright, but also neglected the more complicated reality of creative works, where the use of conventional forms and re-use of works that came before are commonplace (Rose, 1993: 2).

The role of the Romantic author in shaping the ways in which copyright is understood and legislated has drawn the attention of many scholars critical of the influence of the category and its consequences. Copyright scholars have looked at the emergence and naturalization of the category of the Romantic author (Rose, 1993; Boyle, 1996); considered the negative consequences of the Romantic myth on copyright law in terms of privileging some types of creative work and excluding others (for example, indigenous artists [Jaszi and Woodmansee, 1996]); and argued that 'the Romantic author and copyright are both forms of the same social relations and that they combine to provide a way of managing the commodification of culture in capitalist modernity' (Marshall, 2005: 2). Barron argues that 'Romantic determinism' has resulted from excessive attention on authors rather than the work protected by copyright law and that it is the definitions of 'work' and the root of copyright in the logic of property that presents problems: the property analogy doesn't fit in many cases of creative work (and somehow manages to fit things we might not expect to be covered). Although Barron argues that the problems with copyright law are not related to aesthetics or questions of art or originality, she acknowledges that Romanticism is 'bound up with the concealment of copyright's commercial purposes and functions' (2002: 398). Certainly the idea of the Romantic author underpins particular aspects of copyright law and rulings taken.

The solitary author

Closely related to the myth of the Romantic author is the myth of the solitary author: in other words, not only is creative work the expression of an original genius, but that genius is generally assumed to work alone (as sole author, sole painter, sole composer). Rose explains that the original genius notion that continues to be used in copyright discourse 'obscures the fact that cultural production is always a matter of appropriation and transformation', and ignores others involved in the process (like publishers and producers), as well as the means of production (1993: 135). Modern media products are most obviously the result of collaborative networks, but even pre-digital creative expressions emerged through networks of influence and input. Explorations into the sociology of art have sought to situate artists and artistic activity within broader contexts of production.

In *Art Worlds,* Becker explores the collaborative nature of the production of art, beginning with the (intentionally tautological) definition of an art world as 'the network of people whose cooperative activity, organized by their joint knowledge of conventional means of doing things, produces the kind of art works that the art world is noted for' (1982: x). Becker explores the various activities involved in the production of art in a range of worlds — from classical music to jazz and rock, from dance and theatre to feature film — and while the differences between the worlds are interesting, it is the similarities, the reliance on cooperation and the difficulties of defining absolutely artistic activity, that drive his thesis. Bourdieu's (1993) work on fields of cultural production likewise challenges the myth of the independent creator by examining the wider institutional and power structures relevant to creators. Hesmondhalgh has drawn attention to the ways in which Bourdieu's field theory (which attends primarily to art and literature in its exploration of cultural production) ignores large-scale media production and the 'much more complex divisions of labour characteristic of modern, commercial media production' (2006: 227) though praises the work for highlighting the interconnectedness between fields of cultural production and, importantly, to power. While such collaborative production is often associated with popular media like film and digital media like software, Becker and Bourdieu demonstrate, as Toynbee notes, the complex webs involved even in so-called 'high' arts like classical music: 'Thus, even in the heartland of aesthetic individualism, authorship is social and compositions are more like moments in a continuing cycle of production than unique and original creations' (2004: 131). But it is probably true to say that agreeing a reward structure for a work like a feature film or a proprietary software application, where hundreds of people might contribute to the creative expression, presents particular difficulties, as described in Box 5.1.

Box 5.1
The complex web of creative collaboration

Consider, for example, the many creators involved in making a feature film. Even if we limit our list to the most inarguably 'creative' roles, we can include screenwriters, producers, directors, actors, cinematographers, composers, set designers, costume designers among the many creators. And alongside these many creators are multiple layers and many variations of copyright. The World Intellectual Property Organization's (WIPO) booklet *From Script to Screen: The Importance of Copyright in the Distribution of Films* describes in detail, and from the perspective of a distributor, the steps that a producer and distributor must take, from start to finish, to ensure 'That the creative effort of everyone who has contributed intellectual property to the project has been properly recognized, that all have been compensated for their contributions and that the rights they granted have been properly recorded' (WIPO, 2011: 45). Through this process of rights assignment, which is thoroughly documented, the large number of creative authors allow a single entity to claim ownership of the film. The WIPO booklet outlines the standard processes used in the film industry to manage the complex web of creativity, but standard processes also entrench particular hierarchies and reward structures, such that some creators benefit enormously from blockbuster success, while others earn little or nothing through copyright.

The fact that creative work so often requires the collaboration and involvement of many people whose extent and type of contribution can vary substantially poses challenges to the application of copyright law. It would be impossible for copyright law, for example, to define or determine a standard distribution of reward. Some collaborators may have a more typically creative role, others may have put the most time in, and still others may have been responsible for a technical process without which the creative work could not be made. Who should be considered to have the greatest stake of ownership? In addition, each individual situation will vary in terms of number and types of role contributing to the production of a creative work. One solution is to grant 'primary copyright status to "producers" of film, television and music products' (Laing, 2004: 75), an approach Laing identifies as demonstrating the tendency of US and UK copyright law to favour the interests of corporate owners and distributors of cultural products over the creators. A variation of this solution, which has addressed the challenges posed by collaborative production, is corporate authorship through the recognition of a work as 'work for hire'.

Corporate authorship describes the capacity of a company to claim ownership of (and control over) collectively produced IP. Creative contributions in such cases are designated in contracts as 'works made for hire' or as part of employment, transferring any copyright rights from employee to employer. Scholars have critiqued the impact of corporate authorship on the autonomy and rights of artists working in such areas as the popular music industry (Fairchild, 2008) and the film animation industry (Stahl, 2010). Ultimately, corporate authorship may simplify the application and regulation of copyright, but it muddies the system of reward implied by the assumptions about authorship that continue to inform debates about copyright. Would fans adjust their attitude and behaviour towards copyrighted material if they learned the individuals they understand to be creators in fact transferred their (economic) rights to companies under a 'work for hire' contract? Certainly some fans use their knowledge about contracts and the relatively powerless position of artists as a justification for unauthorized access and distribution (we deal with this trend in greater detail in Chapter 6).

Author motivation

Another assumption about authorship and creativity that underpins copyright law is the idea that economic rewards act as an incentive for creators and thus lead to innovation. As detailed in earlier chapters, this is one of the key justifications for the existence of the copyright system. But of course it simplifies the varied relationships that creators have had historically and continue to have today to the creative process and economic reward.

There are lots of examples — from both before and after the implementation of copyright — of creativity flourishing without any economic reward, and certainly without a guarantee of economic reward. While the notion of 'art for art's sake' represents a similarly reductive extreme in understanding creative work, it is one that is lost in the straightforward economic model. The assumption that creators require economic reward as incentive also assumes that the creator of a copyrighted work necessarily benefits from the economic reward provided by copyright but, as we have seen, there are many instances in which creators do not benefit from copyright, either because the rights are assigned to somebody else or because a lack of success does not translate into noticeable reward. Caves (2000) offers the 'nobody knows' principle to describe the unpredictability of the creative markets and the inability of creators to predict how their work will be received by consumers. If not for guaranteed economic reward, then, how do we explain why creators continue to create? Is it because of the hope that next time, maybe, the economic reward will come? Or could it be that at least some creators are driven by non-financial motivations as well? How do motivations vary over time and space?

The assumption that authors require financial reward — and, in particular, royalties earned through the copyright system — does not speak to the experiences or views of all creators. It is important to recognize that many of our ideas about authors and creative work and assumptions about incentive are bound up with the advent of copyright (and conveniently ignore contradictions or prior history). And the assumptions are used to justify strengthening the copyright regime despite the lack of or conflicting evidence: 'We have to stop simply assuming that stronger copyright means higher earnings for artists and that this therefore leads to greater and better creative output. It is not an easy task to test these relationships — indeed, cultural economists who have worked in this area know how difficult it is to research artists' labour markets — but lack of information on the subject does not strengthen the case for copyright; it weakens it' (Towse, 2006: 580).

ASSUMPTIONS VERSUS REALITY

The above exploration of some basic assumptions underpinning ideas about authorship and creativity that inform copyright opens space to consider the reality of creative work. Recent trends only move us further from the imagined solitary genius for whom financial incentive is a viable motivation. Chief among these trends is the movement towards more casualized and flexible labour across the range of cultural industries, and particularly within the industries that have produced the most vocal and powerful proponents of a strengthened copyright regime.

Commenting on artists at the start of their careers in popular music, Greenfield and Osborn observe, 'the desire to sign any offered contract immediately almost always outweighs any thought of reading the small print' (2004: 100), adding that 'the party in the stronger bargaining position is always more easily able to exact the contractual terms they wish, and that this party is almost always the corporation rather than the individual. This is as true of contracts involving copyright as of any other commercial deal' (2004: 100). Their estimation of entry into a popular music career resonates across a range of creative careers, where the awareness of the rarity of chances to break in has created a severe power imbalance and circumstances in which many new entrants are willing to work under precarious conditions.

As we mentioned in Chapter 3, one of the key features of the cultural industries is reliance on a reservoir of low-paid workers (Hesmondhalgh and Baker, 2011). In many cases, this means an environment of casualized or flexible labour, where creators are on short-term or part-time contracts, always hustling for the next job with no guarantee of a more stable or secure position. In terms of copyright specifically, such an environment translates into an increase in work-for-hire contracts, where a creator transfers copyright and subsequent royalties to the employer, and other contracts that minimize or remove reward for IP (see Stahl and Meier, 2012; Marshall, 2013). As industries work to regain control after the perceived loss threatened by copyright infringement, one of the obvious areas of focus has been contracts and the ways in which IP and royalties are defined for contractual purposes. In this respect, the already poor position of artists has been compounded by legislative changes which can shift the legal definitions of terms; Fairchild notes, for instance, how money received from anti-piracy actions and copyright laws (like the Digital Millennium Copyright Act) did not go back to artists because of how terms are defined and understood (Fairchild,

2008: 63). Furthermore, the increasing availability of amateur content and contributions, through technologies like high-spec cameras on phones and through activities like internet-based creative competitions, will necessarily drive down the value of creative work: why pay the professional well when an amateur can supply work for less or nothing at all?

Changes in this area have not gone uncontested: in 1999 'sound recording' was added to the list of categories of work which can have 'work for hire' status in the US Satellite Home Viewer Improvement Act in 1999 (at the urging of the Recording Industry Association of America (RIAA)). The addition 'appeared to transfer the authorship and ownership of copyrights in sound recordings from recording artists to their record companies' (Stahl, 2011: 680) and, when discovered and publicized, was met with much opposition: the Recording Artists' Coalition was formed in order to counter the lobbying power of the music industry. While opposition was successful in drawing attention to the problems of the addition (and ultimately in repealing it), this is one example of many legal moves that continue to reproduce an imbalance of power between creators and their respective cultural industries. (Plus, as some critics noted, the effectiveness of the opposition was reliant on a coalition of some of the most powerful creators, further evidence that many ordinary artists have no input: see Edlund, 2002.)

The above descriptions of current trends and directions should illustrate how many of the characteristics that have defined creative work in contrast to assumptions underpinning copyright are as true now as they ever were (and sometimes more prominent). Firstly, there is a wide, and widening, gap between most creators and the elite, most successful creators. While a small number of creators are multi-millionaires, most are not making a living through creative work. Perversely, the elite creators also tend to be those who are most likely to benefit from copyright by maintaining a stake in the rights and by achieving the level of sales necessary for significant royalties. Secondly, creative work has always relied on more than a single, solitary author and much of the creative work for which copyright is relevant involves a great number of authors, in one form or another. Software, television and film are among the examples for which authorship (and copyright) can be spread thinly and, from some perspectives, unevenly. Finally, just as art flourished in eras prior to copyright legislation, it continues to flourish in environments free from or less encumbered by copyright, whether amateur communities or non-Western art worlds. If anything, there is a growing mismatch between the assumptions that drive industry and policy narratives and the reality for the majority of creative authors. And the assumptions are not simply unhelpful, but potentially damaging. As Toynbee (2013) notes, the 'specialness' of cultural work — represented by the values of creativity and autonomy that structure the myth of the Romantic, solitary author — is mobilized by industry as a justification for copyright protection, even as the benefit to creators is uneven at best. It also 'provides a kind of mythological backdrop for the performance of cultural work. Artists, authors, actors and musicians tolerate insecurity and impecuniousness which would not be accepted in other sectors in part because the aura of specialness that surrounds them provides a certain compensation. In other words, the attribution of special status helps the cultural industries to dominate and exploit workers in this insecure and unequal corner of the labour market' (Toynbee, 2013: 97). As for the assumption that copyright provides an incentive for creators to innovate, what remains hidden is the actual and unsettled relationship between copyright and innovation. Many scholars have explored how copyright does not clearly lead to innovation and, on the contrary, there is evidence that in some cases it *stifles* innovation. McLeod and Dicola's (2011) consideration of music sampling demonstrates how classic hip-hop albums, credited with invaluable innovations in popular music, would not have been made in the stricter environment that followed their success. In many other cases, the effect on innovation needs to be viewed in terms of what a creative work *could have been* if copyright protection was more relaxed. For example, documentary filmmakers can find copyright clearance a challenge, both because of the financial hurdles but also because copyright owners may be hesitant to grant permission for material linked to controversial subjects or where the material is used in an unintended way: consider, for example, NBC's refusal to licence a clip of George W. Bush for Robert Greenwald's *Uncovered: The Whole Truth about the Iraq War* because it was viewed by the network as 'not very flattering to the president' (Lessig, 2004b).

CREATOR VIEWS AND VOICES

This chapter has so far explored the role of the author in the copyright debate, challenging some of the assumptions that support arguments in favour of strengthening copyright and highlighting the ways in which creators — already less powerful than the companies to which they are contracted — are continuing to lose the benefits implied by the copyright system. In the remainder of the chapter, we explore the varied views and voices of creators to understand how authors themselves have discursively produced positions that at times support and at times challenge the existing legislation and regulation of copyright. We also consider perspectives put forward on behalf of creators and alternatives to the existing system that seek to favour creators over the companies to which they are contracted.

A *New York Times* article called a 2004 survey by the Pew Internet and American Life Project 'the first large-scale snapshot of what the people who actually produce the goods that downloaders seek (and that the industry jealously guards) think about the Internet and file-sharing' (Zeller, 2004). In order to capture the opinions of artists and musicians, rather than the industries that often speak on their behalf, US researchers 'conducted a random and nationally representative telephone survey of 809 American adults who said they are artists' and 'administered a non-random online survey of 2,793 musicians, songwriters and music publishers' (Madden, 2004: ii). The report of the survey results, *Artists, Musicians and the Internet*, offered evidence that artists are hardly in agreement about file-sharing services. Artists were 'evenly divided in their assessment about whether filesharing programs are a net good or a net bad for their colleagues' and musicians were 'more likely to see the positive aspects of file-sharing' (Madden, 2004: vi). Artists and musicians surveyed were similarly split in their judgements of whether sharing with a friend should be considered an infringing activity.

In the decade that followed, there was no sign that creators were nearer to reaching a consensus on the issues of copyright infringement and the costs versus benefits of digital technology (DiCola, 2013, demonstrates the persistent diversity of opinions among musicians).

Pro-copyright and vocal about the need for enforcement

Certainly there have been and continue to be many cases of creators acting as mouthpieces for the key messages of the cultural industries, reciting the justifications employed in industry campaigns and communications, and creators who are insistent about the value of copyright as an incentive for creative work and the threat of infringement to the just reward of creators. The threat is communicated in multiple ways: it may directly affect creators whose incomes are reliant at least in part on copyright-derived royalties. Or it may be indirect through the potential harm caused to their relationship with the corporation under which they are contracted (which itself derives profits through copyright). Individual creators and organized groups have expressed variations of such concerns.

Many individual artists across the range of cultural industries have spoken out against copyright infringement and have promoted measures to strengthen copyright, such as Digital Rights Management (DRM) technology, prosecution of infringers and the extension of copyright terms. Such views have been shared through artists' own public-facing communication (for instance, artists' websites), quotes provided to media outlets and visible efforts as spokespeople for campaigns. For example, in 2005 actors Jackie Chan and Arnold Schwarzenegger (Governor of California at the time) starred in an anti-piracy advertisement which aired on Chinese television, and in 2011 John Hurt narrated a dark anti-piracy spot ('The Last Cinema') commissioned by the UK Film Distributors' Association. Singer Lily Allen started (very briefly) a blog called *It's Not Alright* to encourage musicians to rally together against piracy and Cliff Richard was such a vocal supporter of extending the copyright term for sound recordings that the 2011 EU extension has been called 'Cliff's Law', echoing the naming of the 1998 US Copyright Term Extension Act for Sonny Bono.

At the extreme end, views have been made clear through lawsuits filed. One of the highest-profile lawsuits featured heavy metal band Metallica, who challenged the file-sharing platform Napster (see Box 5.2). This suit received a lot of attention because it dealt with the relatively new trend of peer-to-peer (P2P) file-sharing platforms, and thus would set a precedent, but also because it revolved around an activity in which many ordinary users were implicated. Other creators have threatened legal action over perceived copyright infringement both before and after this case: in terms of just popular music, these include cases of artists suing over sound or video samples that have not been cleared and artists (or their representatives) making 'notice and takedown' requests over material posted on video-sharing sites like YouTube. Music is an obvious example to highlight lawsuits because end consumers are seen as at least partly responsible for the threat, the music industries have been behind long-standing campaigns and creators (as opposed to corporations) are sometimes named, plaintiffs (as opposed to say, lawsuits filed by film industry representatives). But there are also numerous non-music examples, sometimes featuring creators for whom alternative sources of revenue or alternative models of distribution are less easy to imagine: consider, for example, the copyright infringement lawsuit filed in October 2013 by photographers against the National Football League (NFL), Getty Images and the Associated Press. In this case, the plaintiffs claimed that the licensing agents, competing for exclusive licensing bids for the NFL, encouraged the NFL to use photographs without gaining consent from the photographers (Heitner, 2013).

Box 5.2

Metallica's battle with Napster

The first and probably best-known case of an artist filing a lawsuit against a P2P software company occurred in 2000. Heavy metal band Metallica sued Napster for copyright infringement and racketeering by enabling users of the platform to share the band's catalogue of music.
Metallica drummer Lars Ulrich noted in a statement at the time,

> With each project, we go through a grueling creative process to achieve music that we feel is representative of Metallica at that very moment in our lives. We take our craft — whether it be the music, the lyrics, or the photos and artwork — very seriously, as do most artists. It is therefore sickening to know that our art is being traded like a commodity rather than the art that it is. From a business standpoint, this is about piracy — a/k/a taking something that doesn't belong to you; and that is morally and legally wrong. The trading of such information — whether it's music, videos, photos, or whatever — is, in effect, trafficking in stolen goods. (Uhelszki, 2000)

In contrast, CEO of Napster Eileen Richardson described the band's perspective:

> It's a bit crazy. It just shows, though, that they're not that familiar yet with the Internet as a medium. They're unfamiliar with how their fans are using it, and how it could benefit the band in the future. And so that's just an education process. I don't know that it's any different from what happened with radio when it was a new medium. Everyone then was up in arms, 'Oh my God, how are people going to get paid; it's free and it shouldn't be.' We're running into some of those same issues here.

> Another analogy is the movie industry. Today, Blockbuster, and the video marketplace in general, is an $18 billion marketplace; and movies, the box office, is only a $7.4 billion marketplace. When the VCR first came out, everyone said 'Oh my God, nobody's going to see another movie.' But it never ended up happening because there is a market for going to movies and there is also a market for renting them and bringing them home. The effect of that was that the movie industry grew by two and a half times. And we believe the music industry will grow much larger because of us. The Soundscan numbers came out, revealing that record-industry profits rose by 8 percent last year'. (Cave, 2000)

Napster was forced to block users who shared the band's music and was ultimately bank-rupted by this and the RIAA case described in the previous chapter. It relaunched in 2011 as an aboveboard, subscription-based music site and, a year later, the band struck a deal with Spotify and made their catalogue available via the streaming site. Reflecting on the newfound partnership, Napster co-founder and Spotify investor Sean Parker commented, 'The lesson of the story is that, when you have two parties that are set up in opposition to each other, you start to think of the other person's perspective being much more polarized than it actually is' (Lee, 2012), perhaps understating the very different discourses drawn on at the time. Now Parker has entered the legitimate music distribution market and Metallica accept that the online access and distribution of music is here to stay and that opting out prevents artists from reaping potential rewards. (The business deal has even extended into friendship in one case: Ulrich attended Parker's wedding in 2013 (Topel, 2013).)

These examples offer a picture of some creators acting out in support of copyright. Most cultural industries are also home to organized groups of pro-copyright cre-ators, from those with broad coverage, like Artists Against Digital Theft, which represents artists across the range of cultural industries, to more specialized groups like the American country-music focused Save the Music America. The UK's Federation Against Copyright Theft represents some of the most powerful media corporations, including Virgin Media and the Walt Disney Company, while Berlin-based We Are the Creators was organized by a group of artists opposed to the growing German Pirate Party. By joining efforts in organized groups, creators may be granted greater legitimacy and greater power to ensure their position is heard and to lobby for change.

Many other artists have spoken out against the traditional copyright system and the industries perceived to exploit particularly new entrants, positions reflecting the mixed and often minimal benefits of copyright, as well as personal politics and alter-native responses to changing technology. Creator perspectives that eschew the current copyright system are not new: there are historical cases of creators who have dis-missed the value of copyright and who have emphasized the way in which art draws on previous work (calling into question the criterion of originality) and the importance of unfettered circulation of culture. Near the end of his life, author Leo Tolstoy signed a will placing his work in the public domain (as documented in the novel and film *The Last Station*). A century later, in 2010, filmmaker Jean Luc Godard asserted, 'There is no such thing as intellectual property' as he made a donation towards the legal fees facing a French media user accused of copyright infringement.

Like the artists who have joined together to lobby for the strengthening of copyright, so too have creators critical of the copyright system established organizations, ranging from those intent on adapting the system so that creators are the main beneficiaries to those that are opposed to copyright altogether. In the UK, the Featured Artists Coalition campaigns for 'all artists to have more control of their music and a much fairer share of the profits it generates in the digital age' (www.featuredartistscoalition.com/). Creative Commons record labels (creativecommons.org/record-labels) and music communities (creativecommons.org/music-communities) provide opportunities for artists in favour of a more open alternative to traditional copyright. The following section outlines some of the key ideas promoted by creators seeking reform and alternatives.

Not anti-copyright but against the current implementation

Some creators are looking at how the current system can be adapted or complemented to make up for the loss of revenue that has resulted from shifting consumption patterns and, by some accounts, illegal downloading: these creators are not opposed to copyright and often voice the same justifications as their respective industries, but they are critical of the implementation of the current copyright system which sees artists receiving a small piece of the royalty pie. Streaming services, like YouTube, Netflix, LoveFilm and Spotify, represent one of the alternative forms of distribution (and, increasingly, production) available to creators in the digital age. Chapter 4 explored the position of such platforms as intermediaries in the debate over copyright and, while early excitement saw some creators supporting new technologies as the way forward, others have critiqued the platforms for producing negligible royalties and for redirecting most of these to the corporations that generally hold the rights to the material being distributed.

New technologies could be seen by creators as a more benevolent and fair mediator than the corporations to which they are contracted, but nobody has suggested that they could provide a reasonable income through royalties. The response to such technologies with respect to copyright has thus varied. Established artists have critiqued streaming platforms on the grounds that there is little money making its ways to artists and that, as a mediator, it is just as bad, if not worse, than the corporate behemoths who are on the receiving end of the small amount of royalties produced. Radiohead's Thom Yorke likened Spotify to a desperate last-ditch effort of a dying industry: 'I feel like as musicians we need to fight the Spotify thing. I feel that in some ways what's happening in the mainstream is the last gasp of the old industry. Once that does finally die, which it will, something else will happen' (Dredge, 2013b). David Byrne, best known as the Talking Heads frontman, offers a telling example of the limitations of streaming:

> For perspective, Daft Punk's song of the summer, 'Get Lucky', reached 104,760,000 Spotify streams by the end of August: the two Daft Punk guys stand to make somewhere around $13,000 each. Not bad, but remember this is just one song from a lengthy recording that took a lot of time and money to develop. That won't pay their bills if it's their principal source of income. And what happens to the bands who don't have massive international summer hits? (Byrne, 2013)

These critiques are grounded in the justification — often wheeled out by industry — that copyright is needed to reward artists even though what we see in the examples is that artists (even those who agree with that principle) are largely not rewarded through old or new industry structures. Critiques of the implementation of copyright do not necessarily challenge the dominant justifications used by the cultural industries and policymakers.

Independent and less-established artists tend to be more sanguine, with independent labels pointing to the services as an increasingly important source of revenue (Dredge, 2013b) and lesser-known artists viewing such platforms as beneficial in terms of promotion, even if their potential as a source of revenue is, for many, negligible. Essentially, creators who were already unlikely to make a living through copyright royalties (recall the widening gap between elites and everybody else discussed above) have practically removed copyright as a condition of evaluation. The recognition of copyright as unlikely to make or break an artistic career can be viewed as its own critique of the current system (or the triumph of a royalty system that has squeezed out the creators!). The promotional aspect of streaming platforms may of course lead fans to royalty-producing purchases or may lead them to contribute to revenue in other ways, and many creators have looked to streaming platforms as champions of less traditional or mainstream content. For example, Mitch Hurwitz, creator of *Arrested Development*, the sitcom whose fourth season comeback was produced by and broadcast on Netflix, has commended the platform for offering space to television that evolves and that doesn't necessarily fit the traditional mould or involve risk-free veterans (A. Lee, 2013).

Rather than strengthening copyright in the way championed by established artists, or tweaking new platforms until they reward artists in a way that has historically eluded the majority, some creators support revisiting those aspects of copyright that can reward creators or aid creativity. For many creators, the problem with copyright is not what is in the law but how it has been unevenly applied and how exceptions have been avoided by nervous lawyers or uncertain creators. With support from scholars and legal experts, artists have worked to ensure full use of the current copyright provision, especially when it comes to exceptions. Aufderheide and Jaszi (2011), for example, worked with documentary filmmakers in the US to reclaim fair use in documentary film. Their project was prompted by the shift in documentary filmmakers' concerns from fair use in their creations to the perceived threat of piracy, which led to a more conservative approach to copyrighted material: 'They typically regarded the draconian limits they imposed on their own use of copyrighted material as the price to be paid for copyright security as owners' (Aufderheide and Jaszi, 2011: 94). In order to avoid the use of copyrighted material (such as media playing in the background of filmed scenes), Aufderheide and Jaszi suggest that 'the people in charge of documenting reality were not just changing reality, but avoiding it altogether' (2011: 96). Discussions with filmmakers who described how they would like to be able to use material and how they would like their material to be used (a portrait that looked not unlike the current rules of fair use) led to the development of a code of practice — the Documentary Filmmakers' Statement of Best Practices in Fair Use — that has been applied in a range of filmmaking examples and has made it easier to insure films (where insurers were previously nervous of potential infringement claims). This is a particularly interesting example because it involved no legal change, but a production of discourse which allows for a less conservative interpretation and which led to changes in procedure. Furthermore, with a clearer understanding of fair use, filmmakers also became more open to fair use of their creations.

While people should be able to critique the copyright system without offering a solution, McLeod and Dicola's (2011) study of music sampling and the way in which copyright can stifle creativity is notable for its clear and detailed suggestions about how to improve the system to benefit both artists whose work is sampled and artists who seek to use samples, another example where the basic system and justifications remain supported but with tweaks to provide greater benefits to creators. After outlining issues of securing rights (or paying for them) and of royalty splits, they offer ideas for reform that could alleviate restraints on creative freedom while upholding the right of copyright holders to compensation. These include enhanced property rights (clarity might improve the sample clearance system and give rights holders more confidence); compulsory licences that include a price cap and prohibit rights holders from vetoing uses; an expansion of non-infringing uses (a minimal threshold; fair use covering creativity and commentary); and various innovations in voluntary licensing from Creative Commons and a one-stop sampling shop to an authentication database. Many of the suggestions resonate with those put forward by Toynbee in an earlier piece that likewise considered how 'copyright law doesn't mesh with the practice of popular music' (2004: 127), including sampling, but also forms of musical creativity including recordings and improvisation where there may not be a composition as such, but composition through performance. Both studies place the creator's perspective as key to redeeming copyright.

The adaptations or interpretations of copyright considered thus far have been concerned primarily with fair reward through royalties without impeding the creativity of subsequent creators. Ultimately, the drive to strike this balance supports the justification of copyright as offering incentive to create. But, as discussed earlier, direct financial reward is not the only incentive that has inspired creators and it is worth returning again to the role of moral rights, in order to emphasize that the division between non-economic and economic reward involves significant grey areas. Towse explains the economic role of moral rights: 'the moral right has an incentive effect for artistic production because it encourages artistic recognition of status and professionalism' (2006: 571), which itself can have subsequent effects on the market value of work. So strengthening moral rights is another suggestion that may empower and ultimately reward creators, although Towse notes the potential difficulty of identifying creators of some artistic works (such as multimedia) and, therefore, high transaction costs, an obstacle similar to that experienced by creators trying to negotiate the complex system of clearing rights for sampling.

Alternative perspectives on copyright and alternative approaches to funding creative work

For others, the solution to challenges presented by copyright in the digital age will not be found through strengthening or reinterpreting copyright law, but through moving away from copyright and relying on alternatives to fund creative work and, in some cases, reward creative workers. Below, we consider some of the alternatives represented and championed as better serving creators and creativity.

Piracy as promotion and incentive: the silver lining of infringement

One response from creators to the claims about the threat of copyright infringement has been to embrace the silver lining of unauthorized access and distribution. In Chapter 2 we discussed how the creators of television drama *Game of Thrones* have interpreted unauthorized access as an accolade and a promotional tool, echoing the long-term approach of HBO, which has treated illicit use as driving paid subscriptions. In the same arena, piracy has also proved a catalyst to the roll-out of new models of global distribution. Some users have taken to illegal downloading to pre-empt the long delays between the release of films or television series in different countries, and some creators and companies have responded by shortening or eliminating the lag time. US drama *Breaking Bad* gained a worldwide cult following, with many viewers using P2P platforms to obtain the show immediately after US broadcast. For the second half of the final series of the programme, UK viewers were able to access episodes within hours of broadcast via the streaming service Netflix. The delay between film release dates in different countries has been minimized and some blockbuster films have been released on the same date in multiple markets, in part as a strategy to combat piracy. Similarly, some films have recently been released through a combination of cinemas, DVD, online and television simultaneously. While the value of streaming services to creators is still being debated, this new model suggests that legal access, if adapted to the needs and desires of fans, can replace some unauthorized access. Although there remains a reliance on copyright in terms of funding creative work and providing creative reward, the view of piracy as promotion and incentive illustrates a shift away from anti-piracy campaigns and attempts to regulate or enforce and towards a different model of thinking about and responding to infringing use. Chapter 4 also documented ways in which infringement is monetized.

In other realms, piracy can be viewed as a promotion for other profitable activities: Gayer and Shy (2006) develop a model to explore how, under certain conditions, piracy can be profitable for musicians through higher demand for live performances. They also note studies in economics that show how piracy and samples can enhance demand for legal copies. While '360 deals' (described in Chapter 2) are an attempt to colonize revenues earned outside copyright, the study is an important reminder that much of the research exploring the financial threat of copyright infringement does not distinguish between artists and publishers even though, as we have explored, copyright serves these parties differently.

Crowdfunding and open source: minimizing the mediators and using the power of the crowd

Against the din of anti-piracy rhetoric, it can be easily forgotten that digitization has also offered many opportunities in terms of funding and making creative work. Some creators have explored alternative routes that excise many of the mediators in the traditional cultural industries and speak directly to fans as potential sources of funding and as co-creators.

Radiohead made headlines when they released their 2007 album *In Rainbows*, allowing individual fans to choose the price they were willing to pay for the download.

Of course, Radiohead had advantages over many creators: with a successful (major label-supported) career, they had the capital to fund the production of the album before selling it to fans and they had a pre-existing and substantial fan base to lower the risk. While other musicians have since utilized the pay-what-you-want model, the fact that it has not become a widespread method of distribution speaks to its drawbacks and, presumably, the concern that what people want to pay may not be as much as hoped. Still, the model points to possibilities in challenging the traditional market pricing system and a positive, user-driven approach to price discrimination.

For creators seeking funding for the production of creative work (rather than remuneration for completed work), crowdfunding has offered an alternative to reliance on traditional companies and contracts. Crowdfunding describes a model by which many small contributions are collected in order to support a particular project. While the model is not new, the internet has offered platforms for creators, the ability to reach a wide audience and ease of contribution. The largest of the platforms is currently Kickstarter, through which US- and UK-based creators can receive funding via Amazon Payments from anywhere in the world. Kickstarter describes itself and its success: 'Kickstarter is full of projects, big and small, that are brought to life through the direct support of people like you. Since our launch in 2009, 5.2 million people have pledged $873 million, funding 51,000 creative projects' (Kickstarter, 2014).

Crowdfunding is a modern version of arts patronage and, for many creators, is providing an alternative to working with traditional intermediaries (or being unable to secure a contract with a traditional intermediary). The presence of feature films, documentaries and short films funded through this model at the Sundance Film Festival speaks to its success. Likewise, the 2014 *Veronica Mars* film, based on the cult television series, was funded through Kickstarter and given a simultaneous release in theatres and through Video-on-Demand, an example of a release that was in essence a partnership between fans and creators.

In crowdfunding, the role of supporters is purely financial. Other models invite users to participate as co-creators. Perhaps most familiar is the open source development model, where the source code of computer software is shared and users are able to collaboratively modify and improve the software as a community (Berry, 2008). The open source concept has subsequently been applied to other collaborative processes that make source material available to contributors and to projects which result from the combination of contributions that are modifiable by users. In terms of creators and creativity, the open source model draws attention to the limitation of copyrighted proprietary software: the suggestion is that innovation is hampered by protecting software. While open source software may be used to make creative work (such as open source film-editing software), the process of contributing does not entail (or seek) financial reward. As an alternative model of creation, some critics see open source as only serving hobbyists.

The word crowdsourcing to describe outsourcing to the crowd gets applied in a variety of ways, including to projects adhering to an open source ethos, but a common use, and one that clearly distinguishes the model from open source relates to a model where people are invited to compete through the contribution of a specified idea, product or service, whether computer code, t-shirt design or music video. Brabham argues that crowdsourcing resolves the open source development model's reliance on free labour 'by providing a clear format for compensating contributors, a hybrid model that blends the transparent and democratizing elements of open source into a feasible model for doing profitable business, all facilitated through the web' (2008: 82). Far from being an uncontroversial solution, however, crowdsourcing introduces different problems and prompts different ethical questions. Brabham admits 'the intellectual labor the crowd performs is worth a lot more than winning solutions are paid' (2008: 83) and Kennedy is sympathetic to critics' claims that crowdsourced design competitions 'devalue design; they offer unfair compensation; they can result in problematic lawsuits; they employ minors; and they lead to a host of unethical practices, by clients, competition hosts and designers' (2013: 229). How and whether people can make a living though this route is only one question among many and it is difficult to see the disadvantages as a fair trade-off for giving a wider range of people the chance to be paid for creative work, and the innovation that such an approach may or may not bring.

Fairer distribution of funds

Attempts to address the inequalities produced by the copyright system include alternatives that seek to achieve a fairer distribution of funds to creators. One solution would involve a greater reliance on state subsidies. Towse writes that 'In most developed countries, copyright and subsidies to the arts, along with prizes and other such awards, co-exist and are usually complementary. The popular arts rely more on copyright as an incentive while subsidies are used as well to stimulate creativity in the "high" arts' (2006: 570). While the state subsidy system has potential advantages (it can take quality into account) and disadvantages (who determines quality or excellence?), its features provide an interesting contrast to the system of copyright which is easily taken for granted as the obvious and natural way to reward creative work. Indeed, the differences and potential advantages serve as one basis for public service media, which is funded in part by state subsidies.

Another alternative compensation model involves levies or taxes applied to content access or delivery devices, with revenue distributed to rights holders. Certain proposals focus on taxing a particular type of good or element of distribution: some countries, including Canada, Belgium and Finland, already tax some or all blank media with coverage expanding to catch up with technologies. However, many of the existing levies have been criticized for favouring the big media conglomerates and the approach to distribution does not ensure a greater percentage of revenue would reach creators (who may not be the rights holders). Flew et al. (2006) describe Fisher's levy-based model, which involves taxing all goods and services used to access media, with content owners paid a proportional share (as administered by the government). Such a system would present challenges: content owners could manipulate popularity figures and the tax rate could rise over time as traditional channels continue to be threatened.

Determining how to distribute revenue across different genres would be no mean feat and devices would be taxed even if not used to access copyrighted material. However, it is estimated that consumers spend more on recorded entertainment now than they would in levies (Fisher, 2004, cited in Flew et al., 2006). An effective levy-based system would require a simple form of DRM technology to mark content in order to trace use. There is a need for a prototype of this sort of system to provide evidence but Flew et al. (2006) suggest a greater percentage of revenue would go to creators and piracy would be eliminated.

Another version of a levy-based system would offer creators and content owners the choice to opt-in: 'Alternative compensation systems can be run on a voluntary basis, along the lines of existing collecting societies, whereby contributed content is centrally administered, stored, and made available to the public' (Flew et al., 2006: 9; see also Chapter 4). In the UK, the Electronic Frontier Foundation has offered their support for a voluntary collection system as an alternative to the proposed broadband tax which they argue 'would not only be unfair to fans, but reduce much-needed industry transparency by denying artists the chance to choose which society to join' (EFF, 2008).

As this chapter has demonstrated, creator experiences and views vary widely: copyright might be expected to figure less in the experiences of amateurs than professionals, and while some professionals benefit hugely in terms of copyright revenue, many more see little economic reward. The reason why it is so important to extricate the perspectives and positions of creators from the discourses of the cultural industries should by now be clear: creators do not always or necessarily support the justifications promoted by their respective industries and the views of creators, in terms of whether copyright should be strengthened, the extent to which copyright actually benefits creators, and what a viable alternative to copyright might look like, are wide-ranging. This makes the task of representing creators or acting in support of authors very difficult. Yet confronting this tangle of perspectives becomes particularly important when we consider how creator views and creative reward (real or imagined) are used to shape the beliefs of fans and patrons who want to support artists: ordinary user views of copyright is the focus of the next chapter.

6

CONSUMERS, CRIMINALS, PATRONS, PIRATES: HOW USERS CONNECT TO COPYRIGHT

LOCATING USERS

So far, this book has considered the positions and perspectives of a range of parties invested in debates about copyright, from cultural industry representatives and internet intermediaries to creative workers at all levels. But we have not yet looked at the positions and perspectives of the largest group with a relationship to copyrighted material: everyday users.

Firstly, it's important to clarify what we mean by 'users'. The term 'users' is employed here to represent those whose primary relationship to copyrighted material is as fans, purchasers, downloaders and sharers. They may also produce their own media content, but their role as media producer is secondary to that of user. Users may have worried about receiving a letter warning them to cease their infringing behaviour after downloading a television programme that is not available where they live or through their service. Users may have laughed at the anti-piracy campaigns aired before a DVD or film showing or they may have wondered about the legality of peer-to-peer (P2P) and streaming platforms. Or they may have never considered the role of copyright in their or anybody else's lives. Whatever the case, the fact remains that users are the most important party in the copyright debate: they are the focus of legal and policy reform, the target of industry appeals, the judges and supporters of creative workers. Indeed, users are present in one form or another throughout the book, often through characterizations that serve the needs of the groups articulating justifications. More often than not, users are characterized narrowly as consumers, perhaps not so surprising from commercial industries, but possibly worrying from policymakers, who we might expect to understand the population they represent primarily as citizens.

In this chapter, we explore the ways that users have been positioned in copyright discourse and how they have been studied by scholarly and industry researchers. We examine user practices as one strategy for understanding user perspectives before going straight to the source and looking at how users describe their own behaviour and views towards copyright. The chapter concludes by considering the role that users have played in the copyright debate (minimal) and where they might fit in a more democratic and deliberative process of consultation and policymaking.

FRAMING USERS

From the advent of copyright through to the present, users have been categorized and framed in legal, policy, popular, and industry discourses. Our understanding of the role of users with respect to copyright has been shaped by shifting and competing characterizations. We explore four key frames that position users as the public, as pirates, as partners, and as amateur producers, and consider how the choice of frame can alter the terms of the debate.

The public

You could say that users in the modern sense — those who use and consume the creative work protected by copyright — were present in the very earliest discussions of copyright as the beneficiaries of laws formulated to serve the public interest, one of the goals of copyright legislation, as noted in the brief history of copyright presented in Chapter 2. The role of the 'public interest' in early copyright debates and laws demonstrates the importance of users from the start.

Users, as we understand them in the modern sense, were initially visible as the 'public' in public interest: the end consumers who would benefit from the creation and circulation of copyrighted material such as literature and music scores. Users were present in early copyright debates through appeals to the 'public interest' directly, as the beneficiaries of laws to facilitate 'fair use' and 'fair dealing' and to encourage availability and accessibility of creative works. For example, the interest of the public was put forward as an argument against a temporary decision in 1768 to grant copyright in perpetuity: Joseph Yates argued against a common law copyright and claimed that the focus on the 'rights of the author as central protagonist' overlooked the interests of all others (Deazley, 2004: 177). Giving the author/proprietor such rights in perpetuity could lead to suppression of works or exorbitant prices, both of which would discourage propagation of learning for the general public. Users were also present in early debates indirectly, through the claim that a copyright system that rewards creative workers for their labour will encourage more creative production, ultimately benefiting the public as end-user. In other words, copyright must protect creative workers in order for the public to benefit from the production of creative work. As Davies explains, public policy must 'find a balance between two aspects of the public interest inherent to copyright: copyright as driving creative activity and thus promoting learning for the benefit of the public and exceptions to copyright that offer the widest availability of copyrighted material for the public' (2002: x).

Public interest arguments have continued to play a key role, as seen in the debates around open rights, more equitable pricing structures, new exceptions and extensions of copyright terms. In each of these cases, proposed changes are based in part on perceived benefits to the public, whether those benefits involve easier or more affordable access or providing an incentive to creators to produce more work to be enjoyed by the public.

Pirates

When users have infringed copyright, they are located in the copyright debate in an entirely different way: as pirates! The language of piracy has long had a place in the copyright debates, and became prominent especially in discussions of international copyright protection. In her chapter on nineteenth-century Anglo-US copyright relations, Seville considers 'the variations in the language of piracy as circumstances change through the century, and the debate progresses. What is revealed is an increasingly subtle and sensitive use of such language, as awareness of the complex issues underlying the international copyright question increases' (2010: 20). In this period, the label of pirate was applied to publishers who had not paid to reprint material, whether or not the law of a particular country required payment, depriving copyright holders of income and undermining publishers who had paid to reprint the same material. While some publishers and authors defended the activities of such pirates, by the end of the nineteenth-century, and with the passing of international copyright acts, any ambiguity around the morality of literary piracy was largely put to rest.

Whereas in the past infringement would necessarily have been undertaken on an organized scale and for commercial gain, today it is often carried out by ordinary users, enabled to produce and share illegal copies through technological advances (David, 2010). Users of P2P networks have inherited the pirate metaphor, which is as likely to be employed to describe individual copyright users as organized groups. From the British Phonographic Industry's 1980s *Home Taping is Killing Music* campaign, which replaced the skull of the Jolly Roger symbol with a cassette, to the 'Piracy is Theft' slogan used by the Federation Against Software Theft from the 1980s onwards and the *Piracy. It's a Crime* campaign used by the Motion Picture Association of America (MPAA) in the 2000s (see Chapter 3 for an analysis of campaign discourse), shifting technology and mass individualized reproduction have revived the discourse of piracy and have been central to industry representations of infringement. The use of the term 'pirate' to describe users engaged in media-sharing activities has been criticized for conflating very different types of infringement and for pushing the boundaries of the legal meaning of 'piracy'. Birmingham and David (2011), for example, note the difference between copyright infringement and criminal piracy, criticizing the application of the term to activities like P2P sharing. They also suggest 'this "success" in extending the term "piracy" beyond its legal meaning, may have been the content industry's worst mistake. The term "piracy" now confers a degree of rebel cool on practices that might otherwise be seen as simply penny pinching. From Jack Sparrow to The Pirate Bay, being labelled a pirate is not seen as a bad thing' (2011: 75). Indeed, some ordinary users responded to industry campaigns with parodies, highlighting the failure of the label to frighten many P2P platform users into legal behaviour (see Box 6.1).

Box 6.1
'You wouldn't steal a baby'

Media users and creators have produced parodies of anti-piracy campaigns which highlight the failure of the messages to result in the desired response. David (2013) considers how representations of file sharing as theft or piracy have failed or backfired, noting the parodies produced in response to anti-piracy campaigns and circulated on the internet: the hyperbole of the MPAA's *Piracy. It's a Crime* campaign, which compared piracy to stealing cars, handbags and televisions ('You wouldn't steal a car'), was met with faux-hysterical parodies. As well as user-created responses, parodies of the campaign were featured for the enjoyment of users in an episode of British comedy *The IT Crowd* and as a DVD extra for the American animated series *Futurama*. If viewers weren't already suspicious of the crime analogies employed by the campaign, *The IT Crowd* challenged the comparison by escalating the authoritative statements ('You wouldn't steal a handbag. You wouldn't steal a car. You wouldn't steal a baby. You wouldn't shoot a policeman', and so on) and setting them against absurd, dramatic imagery, including the downloader seizing a baby from its pram (see Figure 6.1) and using the hat of the intervening policeman as a toilet. The *Futurama* example similarly parodies the campaign through the robot pirate's disagreement with statements like 'You wouldn't steal a spaceship' and 'You wouldn't steal a human head'. The acronym of the campaign tagline – Downloading Often Is Terrible – is accentuated by the spacing between the characters (see Figure 6.2) and suggests the creators view piracy as undeserving of serious crime comparisons. (Though they would presumably prefer viewers to purchase the DVD on which the parody features.) Cvetkovski explores online parodies of anti-piracy campaigns, including examples in media, like the *IT Crowd* episode, and argues 'that anti-piracy parodies symbolize resistance to centralized and corporate control of popular culture' (2014: 248). Reflecting on the widespread participation in and circulation of such parodies, he suggests, 'Piracy spoofs invariably attract much attention on the internet because they reflect just how consumers resist having their attitudes shaped or influenced by corporate citizens' (2014: 254).

Figure 6.1

DOWNLOADING OFTEN IS TERRIBLE

Figure 6.2

Partners and legitimate consumers

The normalization of everyday infringement, encouraged by the increased ease and speed of copying introduced by digitization, has resulted in new conceptualizations of users in more recent campaigns, as outlined in Chapter 3's illustration of cultural industry perspectives and communication. Industry and government communication for and about users has started to eschew criminalization frames in favour of discourses of humiliation, where accessing copyright material illegally is shameful; education, in which users simply need to learn how and why to behave properly; and, most recently, responsibilization, suggesting creators and users alike are responsible for the success or failure of the cultural industries.

The 'consumer' language sets the terms of the debate because it suggests that the job of users is not to participate in discussions of policy, not to challenge the law and not to debate ideas about creative work and reward. To be a good consumer means to support the creative economy through legal and sanctioned activities and purchases. In trying to understand why consumers veer from this path, other parties have often described them as lacking the knowledge required to understand (and abide by) copyright. Anti-piracy campaigns and educational programmes designed for school use rely in part on the assumption that greater clarity and knowledge of copyright law will result in better behaviour. We return to the question of what users understand about copyright below.

Amateur creators

This book began with the premise that digitization has changed the role of and debates about copyright among a range of invested parties through the ability of consumers to make and distribute near exact copies of copyrighted work. The digital age has been heralded as bringing with it another new opportunity for users: the opportunity to generate and distribute their own creative contributions, often involving the use of manipulable platforms and sometimes involving re-working of copyrighted material. Indeed, interactive and collaborative activities are the cornerstone of what became known as 'Web 2.0'. Therefore, at the same time as users have been framed as pirates or as partners of industry, they have also been positioned in a different way as amateur creators themselves and encouraged to produce and share content online: to 'broadcast yourself', as the YouTube slogan put it. The emergence of Web 2.0 interactive technologies which encourage mass participation, cultural collaboration, and content creation has resulted in celebratory discourses of users as producers in their own right. By 2006, such was the pervasiveness of Web 2.0 technology that *TIME* famously named 'you' — the ordinary media users empowered to produce — person of the year 'for seizing the reins of the global media, for founding and framing the new digital democracy, for working for nothing and beating the pros at their own game' (Grossman, 2006).

To summarize, across legal, policy, and industry discourses, users have been characterized in various and sometimes conflicting ways: as the public, as pirates, as legitimate consumers, and as creators themselves. They have also been characterized as confused and in need of education. If this is how users have been framed discursively, what does research tell us about what people actually do in relation to copyrighted material and about how they understand and justify their own practices?

USER PRACTICES

Many researchers — academic, market, commissioned by governments — have been involved in investigations into user practices and behaviour around copyrighted material, including research on the extent of piracy versus legal consumption. Such studies range from large, quantitative surveys that seek a global picture of activity to smaller, qualitative projects that focus on the detail of particular activities and populations. This section explores a range of approaches in order to better understand what users do and what users think about copyright.

Legal consumption and piracy

There have been some major surveys conducted to understand internet user (and non-user) practices and attitudes on a global scale. The World Internet Survey includes 39 partner countries to study the social impact of the internet, though issues of illegal access or copyright are outside its broad scope (see World Internet Project, 2013, for the most recent report). On the other hand, The Research Bay project, which collected survey answers from 75,000 users visiting the temporarily renamed The Pirate Bay website, focused specifically on users visiting one of the most well-publicized sites of illegal sharing, telling us a lot about P2P users, but less about users more generally (www.thesurveybay.com/). Recent, large-scale surveys have sought to establish the role of unauthorized access in the activities across a more general population: for example, surveys of German, American and British users have suggested that many users access media through both authorized and unauthorized services and those who use illegal platforms spend the same amount or more money on legal media than their P2P-avoidant counterparts (Ofcom, 2012; Karaganis and Renkema, 2013).

Meanwhile industry groups continue to investigate user behaviour. For instance, PRS (Performing Rights Society) and Google published research in 2012 into business models for copyright-infringing sites. The report noted that although 'a large amount of quantitative and qualitative data has been collected in the past through consumer surveys into why people use these sites, there is insufficient data-driven analysis of the sites that are considered to facilitate copyright infringement' (2012: 3); of course, users still feature heavily, from how they access sites (directly or through links on social network or other sites), to how they should be differentiated into unintended, casual and regular users of infringing sites (PRS and Google, 2012). Research commissioned by industry groups tends to focus, unsurprisingly, on understanding the user for the purpose of improving enforcement or encouraging legal and profitable activities. Piracy is taken for granted as having swept the globe, with differences in national contexts irrelevant to parties intent on curbing illegal access wherever it takes place (see Box 6.2).

Box 6.2
Media piracy around the world

The 'problem' of piracy is repeatedly framed as a global one requiring international regulation and enforcement approaches. However, the situation of media users, and their relationship to pirated media, varies across the globe. In a report edited by Karaganis, *Media Piracy in Emerging Economies (2011)*, researchers explore the context of piracy in a range of countries, including South Africa, Russia, Brazil, Mexico, Bolivia and India.

While each country has its own particular context — with different successes and challenges — the studies taken together paint a more complex picture of the nature of piracy and the barriers to legal consumption than a one-size-fits-all model allows. Karaganis notes, 'High prices for media goods, low incomes, and cheap digital technologies are the main ingredients of global media piracy. If piracy is ubiquitous in most parts of the world, it is because these conditions are ubiquitous' (2011: i). No amount of education or enforcement can solve a problem that is caused by a lack of affordable access for most people and the framing of piracy as leading to a global loss hides the variation in impact on national economies. The report highlights the 'countervailing benefits of piracy to both industry and consumers in any model of total economic impact and, consequently, the importance of treating piracy as part of the economy rather than simply as a drain on it' (Karaganis, 2011: 13). In developing markets, the money that is not spent on legal media products (often a loss to US companies) will be spent on other services and products that support local and national economies: this 'consumer surplus from piracy might be more productive, socially valuable, and/or job creating than additional investment in the software and media sectors' (Karaganis, 2011: 16).

As well as examining the economic and industry contexts that frame media piracy, the report draws on surveys, focus groups and interviews with users. Strong user views reflected a clear understanding of the wider inequalities fuelling the battle over copyright: 'The consumer surplus generated by piracy is not just popular but also widely understood in economic-justice terms, mapped to perceptions of greedy US and multinational corporations and to the broader structural inequalities of globalization in which most developing-world consumers live. Enforcement efforts, in turn, are widely associated with US pressure on national governments and are met with indifference or hostility by large majorities of respondents' (Karaganis, 2011: 34). The user research conducted for the report demonstrates that users around the world have savvy and important views to contribute to the copyright debate.

Against the backdrop of attempts to capture, predict and control user behaviour, academics too have sought to understand users through various disciplinary lenses, including approaches from criminology, law, behavioural psychology, and media and communication. While scholars across these disciplines have shared an interest in better understanding users, specific research questions are driven by the objectives of the field: to position infringement within or against the context of criminal behaviour; to evaluate user practices in terms of the law; to understand the decision-making processes behind user choices; to consider infringing behaviour as one aspect of wider media use and media culture. The following section considers an area of activity that has been of particular interest to media and communication researchers and that highlights a key tension around users' creative engagement with copyrighted material.

Infringing creative practices

A range of scholars have studied a variety of related activities that have collapsed the boundary between users and creators, some of which activate issues involving copyright law's limitations in dealing with creative acts that are akin to fine art practices like collage (see McLeod, 2005, and below discussion of McLeod and Dicola, 2011), and others of which relate to issues addressed in Chapter 4 about contests over P2P distribution platforms (when does fan sharing become distribution?). Not all copyright infringement reflects the more typical representation of piracy as straightforward copying and sharing of copyrighted material. As noted above, one of the ways ordinary users are positioned within the copyright debates is as amateur producers or contributors to creative processes. A number of terms have been used and adopted by industry and scholars to capture such users and their activities: pro-ams (professional amateurs) (Manovich, 2009); produsers and produsage (Bruns, 2008); co-creators (Potts et al., 2008); user-generated content (van Dijck, 2009).

Amateur creative production, as indicated by the various phrases that have been introduced, takes many different forms. Scholars have explored how 'Co-creative media production is perhaps a disruptive agent of change that sits uncomfortably with our current understandings and theories of work and labour' (see overview in Banks and Deuze, 2009: 419) and we address some of the concerns around labour which affect both amateur and professional artists in the context of copyright in Chapter 5. However, for the present chapter, we focus specifically on those activities which highlight intersections of creative and infringing approaches to production.

Users participate in lots of activities which could reasonably be called 'creative' and which relate to copyright in different ways. Users contribute to open source software and Creative Commons content through websites like Wikipedia. They also contribute as co-creators of commercial media products like games, both illegally through 'modding' (making modifications not intended by the designer) and legally as invited contributors to game development, the latter of which prompts its own ethical questions: 'For waged labour, there is the threat of displacement by unpaid amateurs and the loss or redefinition of work. For amateurs, there is the question of whether pursuing their passions through creative production is something to be constructed as "enabled" by commercial entities or "exploited" by commercial entities' (Banks and Humphreys, 2008: 415).

Other activities relate directly to debates about copyright infringement. For example, a culture of subtitling and sharing has sprung up in response to the circulation of television programmes in markets where there is a long delay before broadcast or where the programmes are not broadcast at all. As Hu describes of fan cultures in China, activities range from sharing sources for copies and copies themselves (physical and torrents) to subtitling. Noting one subtitler's style, Hu writes, 'Her subtitling is an individual display of her mastery of language in articulation with her love for the drama' (2005: 177), a description which recognizes subtitling as a fan activity and creative act, not simply a technical skill. She draws attention to the statement included by the subtitler: 'This version is only for the purpose of friendly exchange. The copyright remains the property of Fuji TV station in Japan. Those who attempt to illegally market this product for commercial purposes must be responsible for possible outcomes' (2005: 178). While such activities are no doubt infringing copyright, the culture surrounding them seems far from the stereotypical image of piracy. Furthermore, research into infringing creative activities has suggested that the circulation of such material may in some cases offer benefits to the cultural industries. Erickson et al.'s study of parody music videos on YouTube, for instance, found that 'There is no evidence for economic damage to rights holders through substitution: The presence of parody content is correlated with, and predicts larger audiences for original music videos' (Erickson et al., 2013: 3). (Parody is often covered under a copyright exception if particular criteria are met, though in practice interpretation of permitted and non-permitted uses have varied within and between countries (see Erickson et al., 2013).)

Even in the face of conflicting evidence, cultural industries and intermediaries, including online platforms and companies such as Facebook and Google, tend to take a conservative view towards amateur creative production and copyright. Rather than modifying their practices around copyright to reflect the growth of user-driven creative activities, platforms have placed increasing restrictions on the creative practices of users. Burgess describes YouTube's changing copyright policy:

> Earlier phases of YouTube saw the rise and fall of a series of hugely popular UGC genres and fads that were rife with the reuse of professional media content — including home-made music videos and rapidly mashed up or wittily quoted clips from popular television shows. The innocent days where tween fans of teen idols could cut a rip of their favourite track to their favourite ripped images of the singer are, thanks to YouTube's copyright protection technologies, and automated takedowns, fading fast. (Burgess, 2013: 56)

Users can draw on and reflect on their involvement in creative processes online, and the obstacles they face, to form opinions about copyright issues. Amateur creative production reminds us that users have multiple identities, multiple purposes and multiple modes of interacting with copyrighted material and as a result cannot be boxed in, categorized and regulated in the way that policy and industry may want to do.

The international examples outlined above also highlight the importance of cultural context in understanding the role of copyright in the age of digitization, particularly in terms of user activities and perspectives. As copyright policy is increasingly proposed and approved on a global scale, differences between user activities and views in various cultural contexts offer the opportunity to broaden policy possibilities. While we can learn a lot about users through their legal and illegal activities, to really understand what users believe and communicate about copyright issues, we need to examine user comprehension, perspectives and discourses: the following section gathers together some of what we know about user views.

USER PERSPECTIVES AND DISCOURSES

Despite scholarly interventions challenging characterizations of users as deviants to be corrected or misinformed consumers lacking required knowledge, the cultural industries and the policymakers they influence continue to frame copyright infringement through powerful and entrenched ideas. These ideas have structured the development of copyright throughout history, making it difficult to re-imagine file sharing as pointing towards more open models of distribution or to see pirates as thoughtful contributors to a wider debate about the suitability of copyright law and regulation.

Even as space for alternative characterizations of users has been opened, the foundation of good versus bad behaviour persists in most government and cultural industry approaches: users tend to be implicated as either law-abiding or criminal, ethical or unethical, or as good or bad fans, with notions of piracy and the public interest continuing to constitute good or bad use. While any or all descriptions of users may be true of particular users in specific situations, they elide the complexities inherent to user attitudes and behaviour or make assumptions without empirically-grounded data. To get a clearer picture of how users understand copyright and their relationship to it, media users must be recognized, like the file sharers surveyed by Caraway, as 'knowledgeable social actors capable of furthering our understanding of the conditions under which their activities occur' (2012: 566). Commonsense or reductive characterizations of media users are challenged by research into the perspectives of users themselves, which offers detailed accounts of the varied behaviour and related justifications attached to file sharing (Kinnally et al., 2008; Cenite et al., 2009; Caraway, 2012; Edwards et al., 2013b).

What do users understand about copyright?

Some surveys of the general population have investigated the characterization of users as possessing limited knowledge of copyright and confused by distinctions between legal and illegal access and use of copyrighted material. Findings have offered support for the characterization: for example, in their 2012 online copyright infringement tracker benchmark study, the UK Office of Communications (Ofcom) found that 44 percent of internet users 'aged 12+ claimed to be either "not particularly confident" or "not at all" confident in terms of what is legal and what isn't online' (Ofcom, 2012). A German survey of digital content usage, also published in 2012, found that, while awareness of the illegality of P2P and sharing has grown over time, younger users and users of illegal platforms are more likely to believe that illegal platforms and options are legal (GfK, 2012). Karaganis and Renkema's *Common Culture* report, based on a survey of American and German users, also highlights the inability of users to accurately differentiate legal from illegal platforms, noting that surveying the issue of unauthorized streaming 'is difficult because of the lack of clear differentiators between many legal and unauthorized services' (2013: 26). Such findings have similarly been borne out through qualitative research which has given a platform to the voices of users themselves, an approach explored in greater detail below.

It seems that users are confused because copyright is confusing. One reason is that the language of law and policy requires specialist knowledge and terms. Another is that users are rarely exposed to the history, detail and purpose of copyright, which tend to be taken for granted in user-directed campaigns that link consumer behaviour to criminal activity or to financially-threatened cultural industries (see Chapter 3) and which tend to be absent in other arenas of public discussion. As Frith and Marshall note, 'Copyright is not normally taken to be a topic of political or public interest. It is rarely written about in newspapers or featured in policy debate', which explains in part how 'the rationale of copyright laws and why they matter tends to be determined by the interest of the corporate lobbyists' (2004: 4).

There are exceptions to this tendency, however, when copyright becomes the focus of news stories or educational curricula, offering rare opportunities for users to encounter, and possibly reflect on, key issues. In this way, users may learn about copyright through particular controversies, lawsuits, and policy reviews, as well as formal educational initiatives.

Copyright and the Beatles: learning through controversy

In order for an advertiser to use a pre-existing song in a commercial, the song must be licensed from the copyright holder. Nowadays, many commercials use pre-existing songs by well-known and unknown artists, but in the 1980s such uses were less common and some resulted in heated public debates. As Klein (2009) describes, a 1987 Nike commercial featuring The Beatles' 'Revolution' introduced the public to aspects of US copyright law when the living members of the band objected to the use of the song. Many Beatles fans were surprised to discover that the Beatles themselves did not control the licensing of the track. Like most music released by major record labels, the recording was owned by the label that financed the recording (in this case, Capitol-EMI). And the rights to the composition — which are originally assigned to the songwriter/s — had been purchased by Michael Jackson, who had been previously advised by his friend Paul McCartney to invest in music publishing. The use of 'Revolution' by Nike was legal, but didn't sit well with fans who felt that the band should have a right to reject such uses on moral grounds (and, as noted in Chapter 2, other countries do acknowledge varying degrees of moral rights). This case underlines a contradiction between a public sense of moral rights, expressed through the debate over the commercial, and the actual system of music copyright, where an author may have no control over licensing.

Almost two decades later, the Beatles found themselves again at the centre of a debate about uses of copyrighted material, although this time in favour of an unsanctioned use. McLeod and Dicola (2011) look at the history of sampling in popular music, lawsuits that resulted from cases of sampling and how these have shaped copyright law. According to McLeod and Dicola, the current system of copyright is inefficient and stifles creativity: they demonstrate how some classic hip-hop albums would not be made today because of the constraints of copyright. One example they analyse is Dangermouse's 2004 *The Grey Album*, a mash-up of Jay-Z's *Black Album* and the Beatles' *White Album*, made without licensing either album. *The Grey Album* was both popular and critically acclaimed despite EMI issuing cease-and-desist orders around the world. They argue that 'EMI are reacting to the fact that digital technologies help level the playing field between individual artists and the culture industry machine' (McLeod and Dicola, 2011: 177) and that the industry reaction is disingenuous, and overprotective of a system that has served them well in the past. This case illustrates the way that the public views mash-ups as creative acts in and of themselves, like montage or sound collage, an approach which, ironically, already had a precedent in popular music with the Beatles' own use of sound and recording samples.

They fought the law: learning through lawsuits

Details of copyright have also emerged for users through the press coverage and publicity surrounding high-profile lawsuits against owners of websites that encourage P2P sharing of media. Previous chapters have documented a range of lawsuits related to such platforms and the infringing activities involved, though two, bookending the 2000s, have proved most significant in terms of publicity and results. Filed in December 1999 and decided in February 2001, *A&M Records, Inc. v. Napster, Inc.* was the earliest legal case to deal with copyright law and P2P downloading. As detailed in Chapter 4, it brought together Recording Industry Association of America (RIAA) plaintiffs who argued against the fair use claims asserted by Napster representatives, with the RIAA ultimately prevailing. For many users who had accessed media through P2P platforms, this case removed any ambiguity about how their activities would be viewed through a court of law, even if the arguments in favour of file sharing seemed persuasive. It's worth noting that a consortium of 18 copyright law professors responded to the outcome, explaining that they were 'concerned that the District Court's approach to these issues would, if followed by other courts, significantly impede the deployment of useful technology that could greatly enhance the value of the Internet for copyright owners as well as consumers' (Litman et al., 2000). In other words, the copyright law professors noted that copyright law is not meant to protect business models at the risk of preventing new models from developing. Their intervention also demonstrated that it was not simply ordinary users who supported Napster, but experts as well.

In 2009 The Pirate Bay Trial in Sweden revived some of the same debates and, like the Napster case, the platform can be understood as standing in for the ordinary, file-sharing user. The defendants in this case were found guilty of being accessories to crimes against copyright law. Critiques regarding the role of copyright law in innovation followed, alongside some approving responses from artists: Paul McCartney, for example, responded to the verdict: 'If you get on a bus you've got to pay. And I think it's fair, you should pay your ticket … Anyone who does something good, particularly if you get really lucky and do a great artistic thing and have a mega hit, I think you should get rewarded for that' (quoted in McKenzie and Cochrane, 2009). Again, the view of the law is revealed through the lawsuit outcome, though users were able to poke holes into the assumptions and arguments underpinning the prosecution's case, questioning the applicability of theft analogies for non-physical property; raising an eyebrow at claims about the suffering of creators; and insisting that not all P2P activities are the same. Knowledge that platforms can be used to access out-of-print material, material outside the user's market and to replace media purchased in an analogue form can form the basis for challenging a legal approach that does not differentiate. Even for users who have generally supported the outcomes of legal action, the punishment of platform owners and ordinary users may seem over-the-top: The Pirate Bay defendants were initially given prison sentences and ordered to pay fines of $1million each and, following its successful lawsuit against Napster, the RIAA did not curry favour with the public when it prosecuted grandparents and children.

Copyright revisited: learning through policy reviews

Reviews of and changes to copyright law also attract press coverage and can highlight for users antiquated or inconsistent aspects of copyright, which are often the aspects that result in recommendations for change. Users who pay close attention to such coverage may notice that actual changes to copyright law, following government-commissioned reviews, are sometimes at odds with the recommendations or that the least controversial recommendations, from a user's perspective, take longer to implement than the more contentious recommendations.

As we describe in the following chapter, there have been a number of government-commissioned consultations and reviews of copyright in the United Kingdom over the last decade, with the most recent reported in *Digital Opportunity* (Hargreaves, 2011). The report acknowledged the modern British copyright system as complicated and complex, and recognized that those without institutional support or training, such as users and independent creators, can be easily left confused by the detail of copyright law.

The recommendations, which included updates to copyright law intended to increase consumer confidence, were generally supported by the relevant government committees and the government's formal, published response. In June 2014, three years after the report was published, the recommendation to make format shifting of CDs and e-books legal was implemented (to much bewilderment: few users realized the everyday activity was *not* legal) (Arthur, 2014).

On the other hand, within a few months of the report's publication, another change to copyright seemed to contradict the report, suggesting that the modifications to copyright law are the result of competing interests. The review had concluded, supporting the findings of the 2006 UK review, that there was no evidence to support an extension to the rights of owners of sound recordings and that proposals should be based on economic evidence, yet an extension was approved soon after.

Copyright in the classroom: learning through formal educational initiatives

As copyright's role in the lives of everyday users has grown more significant through digitization, so too has its presence in educational curricula. Because educational programmes are often produced and provided by bodies located within or linked to the cultural industries, their orientation towards copyright and evident objectives are pretty obvious. Yar (2008) examines educational campaigns about intellectual property (IP) produced by the Copyright Society of America, the Software & Information Industry Association (SIIA), the Business Software Alliance (BSA), the MPAA and the Government of Western Australia's Department of Education and Training, in order to identify the common themes.

He organizes the identified themes under four key myths, which will not be new to readers of this book. The first is the myth of property as a natural right, by which Yar means the tendency of programmes to treat the notion of individual property rights in the context of copyright as normal and uncontested. The second, the myth of equivalence between tangibles and intangibles, highlights the way the educational programmes treat IP as the same as material property, avoiding the obvious differences (for example, that a 'stolen' intangible good can still be used by other parties). The myth of individual creativity is the third: the programmes thus rely on the Romantic notion of the individual creator, ignoring the centrality of borrowing (of generic and narrative conventions, for instance) to much creative and copyrighted work. The fourth, the myth of harm, emphasizes the material damage caused by infringement to individual creators and damage caused to cultural production by removing incentives, despite evidence to the contrary on both counts.

What the schoolchildren who encounter these classroom programmes don't get, however, is any sense of alternative perspectives. As Yar puts it, 'From a critical perspective, one must note the absence of any acknowledgement that the concept of intellectual property is itself contested and contestable, or any consideration of alternative views about how access to cultural goods might be organized' (2008: 619). The contested nature of IP represents a missed opportunity to encourage participation in the debate over copyright, though probing questions no doubt emerge organically in lessons.

These examples suggest that learning about copyright — through particular controversies, lawsuits, policy reviews, and formal educational initiatives — does not simply fill a gap in knowledge, which will necessarily lead to law-abiding behaviour. Instead, users enter into unresolved debates about why copyright law is what it is, whom it serves and how it fits, or doesn't fit, with social norms. The examples also demonstrate the limited information about copyright that most users have available to them: in Chapter 7 we consider how users have managed to mobilize against particular policies despite their disadvantageous position and in Chapter 8 we return to the possibility of education as an intervention and consider what an effective approach might entail.

In sum, it is probably fair to say, as industry and government representatives have, that many users have minimal understanding or misunderstanding of the formal system of copyright and its attendant issues. And yet, even users who are hesitant to make claims about the content of copyright law and who are confused about what constitutes a legal use of copyrighted material, are willing and able to challenge industry claims regarding piracy and to debate issues relevant to the cultural industries and copyright.

What do users have to say about copyright?

Explorations of media users, especially those that have been commissioned by the cultural industries or that have fed policy consultations, have been largely quantitative in nature. As Freedman notes, 'The policymaking process continues to privilege quantitative data and large-scale statistical evidence' (2008: 101). While the surveys mentioned above offer some useful statistics for understanding what users do, multiple choice questions and short answers are less successful in identifying *why* users do what they do. A preference for large-scale surveys thus ignores the rich data and complex picture that can be achieved through qualitative approaches such as open-ended surveys, focus groups or interviews. A qualitative approach can encourage engagement with users as citizens with valuable voices, and their own (legitimate) perspectives and justifications on copyright, in a way that quantitative data simply cannot. The belief that users offer worthy views and valuable contributions to the larger policy discussion was a basis for the focus groups conducted by Edwards et al. (2013b) (see Box 6.3).

Box 6.3
Communicating copyright: users in their own voices

By giving user voices a platform, we are able to examine and challenge the assumptions that sustain characterizations of users present in the discourse of other groups, such as rights holders or policymakers. Edwards et al. (2013b) conducted focus groups in the UK which illustrated media users as complex, contradictory and conflicted, but also, at times, understandably cynical and acutely rational.

Users presented a complex combination of behaviour and views with respect to copyrighted material, often describing patterns of use that included both legal and illegal access: a student described, 'A film comes out in the movies. And if it looks really good, I'll go watch it. And then, I dunno, a couple of weeks go by, and you can get a relatively good quality [copy] online and download it illegally. And, I'll do that so I can watch it at home. And then another few months go by and I can buy the DVD for a quid.'

Users displayed some awareness of industry structures, which informed their views of copyright: some users were suspicious that many creatives do not receive a substantial share of copyright revenue (such as newer artists reliant on the promotion of large media companies) and this concern was paired with the widespread belief that some creatives receive too

(Continued)

(Continued)

much reward. As a retiree noted, 'I think it's fair to protect the income stream of the property owner to a point. I mean, there comes a point where you might even say, do you know what, I think the world has paid you amply for your intellectual property, and you should now say, thank you very much, world, and hand it over.'

Users of P2P networks expressed specific and rational justifications for behaviour, from the belief that such behaviour was temporary (relating to income, employment and age) to the recognition of new social norms that sanction the breaking of copyright law in this way: a member of a mother's group explained, 'I understand why people who ... who spend the time to create these things need paying for them, but if I buy an actual book or a CD, you don't think twice about lending it to a friend for a couple of weeks. ... I think once I've purchased it, I now think it's mine to do with what I wish.'

Ordinary users may deploy their awareness of the role of power in the cultural industries to contest claims that piracy is damaging to artists, by rightly pointing out that many of the normal practices of recording companies — for example, the percentage of music sales that goes to the artist — can also be viewed as damaging to artists. At the same time, users may accept the basic tenets of copyright as being rooted in common sense: for instance, expressing a belief in or sympathy for the underlying principles of copyright as providing an incentive to produce creative work and as a reward for creative labour. Finally and unsurprisingly, users form perspectives on copyright in terms of the relevance of copyright to their own lives, and it is through this process that the gap between the law and everyday behaviour is revealed.

Marshall and Frith describe the predictable consequence of a law that is out of alignment with everyday behaviour: 'There currently seems to be a radical disjuncture between the law and the social practices it supposedly governs. ... If copyright law is counter-intuitive, if it contradicts widely-held beliefs about the avaricious nature of the recording industry, then it is unlikely to be followed' (2004: 213). More recently, Hargreaves acknowledged in the *Digital Opportunity* report, 'The copyright regime cannot be considered fit for the digital age when millions of citizens are in daily breach of copyright, simply for shifting a piece of music or video from one device to another. People are confused about what is allowed and what is not, with the risk that the law falls into disrepute' (2011: 5).

If we locate piracy within our ordinary, everyday cultural lives, as Marshall did in his consideration of music 'infringers' (2004), we must accept social practices as following rules, patterns and rationales that deserve exploration, not simply regulation. What goes unacknowledged by many industry and policy voices is that user behaviour towards copyrighted material is guided by a logic, just not the same logic embedded in the law. For instance, users have views on when creators have been adequately rewarded for their creative endeavours and what material should be freely available to end users, with such opinions driving the actions of internet activists (see Box 6.4).

Box 6.4
The case of internet activist Aaron Swartz

The line between ordinary user and activist is a fluid one, and many users have been galvanized into activism by strong convictions and the desire for change that emerged through their own online experiences. The internet has also made it easier than ever for like-minded users to come together as a movement, with extraordinary results. As Sell notes of the defeat of the Stop Online Piracy Act (SOPA) and PROTECT IP Act (PIPA) in 2012, 'While US private rights holders powerfully have shaped the global intellectual property system (projecting their preferences globally), this time a transnational network of Internet users altered domestic intellectual property outcomes in the United States' (2013: 68). One of the activists opposed to the bills, and a key proponent of the campaign to defeat them, was computer programmer Aaron Swartz, whose suicide in 2013 was a tragic example of the unintended consequences of criminalizing infringement regardless of context.

In 2010 and 2011 Swartz, a longtime advocate of open access, had downloaded a large number of academic journal articles from the digital library JSTOR and was charged by federal authorities, who claimed that Swartz intended to distribute the documents to unauthorized users via P2P platforms (Swartz himself was authorized to access the articles through a university affiliation). Following an increase in the number of charges and with the threat of severe penalties, including 35 years in prison, 26-year-old Swartz took his own life. Many felt that the prosecution was attempting to make an example of Swartz and that the charges were inappropriate and excessive for actions that were rooted in a belief in open access rather than personal gain. Swartz's death served as a catalyst for a proposed bill (known as 'Aaron's Law') that limits the scope of the Computer Fraud and Abuse Act and its application to everyday activities. The case is relevant to our exploration of the copyright debate as comprising competing justifications and uneven platforms to voice positions: ordinary users, including the activists that speak on their behalf, have limited opportunities to communicate their perspectives and influence policymaking, forcing them to rely on alternative methods. That these alternative methods are met with criminal prosecution illustrates how those in power are effectively shutting down any possibility of productive deliberation.

Indeed, in the early days of file sharing, Vaidhyanathan (2001) celebrated P2P networks and the MP3 movement as a 'rational revolt' and an example of citizens challenging the control of the music industry that prompted conversations about the relevance of copyright. While some of Vaidhyanathan's predictions are less convincing today (for example, he suggested that people would continue to buy media because official releases are higher quality or more convenient), his characterization of such activities as a 'rational revolt' gives users a metaphorical seat at the table. But who could be assigned the seat to speak for all users? Various political and activists groups, including The Pirate Party, Electronic Frontier Foundation, Open Rights Group, Creative Commons, are often assumed to have this responsibility, 'representing' the voices of users and acting as visible and audible sources of user discourses. Lindgren (2013) analyses the pro-piracy discourses of blogs in Sweden in order to capture the views and voices of pirates and pro-piracy actors; while pro-piracy bloggers can hardly represent all users, they can be seen as representing the interests of file sharers and they illustrate how 'moral entrepreneurship may be exercised not only by traditional actors such as politicians, educators, news institutions, or representatives of churches and the legal system, but also by online grassroots organizations, mobilized subcultures or digitally literate individuals' (2013: 3).

The following chapter will explore the perspectives and roles of some of the organized groups in greater detail. For now, it is worth noting that activism has had some success in resisting certain policies such as SOPA and PIPA, but this is different from users (activist or not) having a constructive influence on the policymaking process. As we discuss in the following chapter, there are serious limitations attached to what Rosanvallon (2008) describes as a 'democracy of rejection' rather than 'democracy of proposition', where ordinary citizens only have the choice to say no to what those in power propose, rather than the ability to propose alternatives.

WHERE'S THE CONSULTATION?

This chapter has drawn attention to the gulf between users, as imagined in the communications and campaigns of the cultural industries and the policies of government, and the complex reality of the end-user experience of copyright in the digital age, where ideas of pirates and the public meet and clash with everyday activities. As the section on user research demonstrated, the importance of identifying what users understand or don't understand about copyright has entered the agenda of researchers from a broad range of perspectives and with various objectives. However, while some voices have expressed that the disjuncture between user experiences and copyright law requires legislative reforms, there continues to be an emphasis on influencing user behaviour through enforcement, industry campaigns and narrow educational aims. Organizations like the Electronic Frontier Foundation have offered alternatives to traditional educational campaigns — their *Teaching Copyright* curriculum provides the balance that Yar (2008) identified as missing in mainstream campaigns — but they lack the access and funding that powerful cultural industries have to insert them into classrooms or beyond.

Consumer and educational campaigns about copyright have concentrated on communicating the laws and the morality of abiding by them, with the expectation that users will then follow them. Clearer communication of the history of copyright and the claims that lead to policy change or policy challenges would better position users as partners in deliberation who, with industry and policymakers, can map a way forward. Educators have often turned to media literacy to equip people to critically analyse media production, distribution and reception: in Chapter 8 we consider the possibilities and limitations of a literacy approach to media policy.

This chapter has highlighted the voice of consumers as offering a contribution to the debate, but one that would be enhanced through the encouragement of a more informed public and a more deliberative policymaking process, where the interests and values of all groups are represented and reflected upon equally, marking a return of the public interest to the heart of copyright legislation. Whether the policymaking process is able or willing to include user voices remains to be seen. In the next chapter, we turn our attention to the policymakers whose role is to balance the various interests and perspectives that contribute to the copyright debate.

7

COPYRIGHT POLICY: HOW POLICY REPRESENTS (OR FAILS TO REPRESENT) DIFFERENT GROUPS

INTRODUCTION

There is nothing natural or inevitable about copyright or the specific form it takes. While copyright law has converged around the world in recent years, historically countries have taken different decisions about what protection, if any, to give to cultural works. To understand copyright today and how it might change in future, we need to examine the processes by which decisions about copyright are made. In this chapter, we focus on the copyright policymaking process and assess the extent to which it reflects the interests and values of the different groups considered in this book.

Ideally, the process that decides copyright policy would be a democratic one. We advocate a specifically 'deliberative' understanding of democratic decision-making in this book. In this view, all groups affected by the policy should be able to participate in determining what it is. Decisions should follow open public discussion — where all options and perspectives are considered and where participants seek to convince others through arguments, rather than through other sources of influence and power — and the aim should be to formulate a policy that reflects the common good or at least a fair compromise among the interests and values of different groups (Habermas, 1997; Mansbridge et al., 2010). However, as we describe in this chapter, the copyright policymaking process falls short of these ideals. The larger corporations in the cultural industries tend to dominate the process, using their economic resources and position in order to have more influence over policy decisions. Meanwhile, the imbalance of power in the policymaking process at a national level is evident too at an international level, where countries in favour of stronger copyright policy, such as the United States and members of the European Union, have been able to internationalize and export their own policies to other countries through various international agreements.

Although the policymaking process is unequal and skewed in favour of certain economic groups, it cannot be reduced to economic forces. Policymakers have some independence and are always able to make different political choices (Hay, 2002; Marsh, 2002; Hesmondhalgh, 2005). Discourse is significant in how policymakers interpret policy problems and solutions and alternative discourses that express different interests and values can emerge and become influential in policy. The relative autonomy of policymakers is extended further by the fact that corporations from different sectors (for example, rights holders in the cultural industries and technology companies) may have conflicting interests and so offer different discursive visions which policymakers can choose from. Although typically distant from the policymaking process, media users may at times also become politically engaged and challenge prevailing discourses. We describe some recent examples in this chapter where the public has mobilized against particular copyright policies. The normative challenge, we conclude, is to find a way to ensure that such public involvement is a more central and regular part of the copyright policymaking process.

POWER AND THE POLICYMAKING PROCESS

It is sometimes said that politics gets in the way of good policymaking. In this view, policymaking is best left to 'the experts', who should base their decisions about policies on an objective analysis of the 'facts' and 'evidence' rather than on political considerations. Certainly, evidence does and should play an important role in the policymaking process and good policymaking requires relevant expertise. However, policymaking also involves making choices among competing interests and values and often gives rise to disagreements among groups that cannot simply be solved by examining the 'facts' more closely. Put differently, the policymaking process cannot but be political (Freedman, 2008).

Policymaking is best understood, then, as a political process, which involves deciding among competing values and the interests of different groups. But how might we think about that process more specifically? In liberal representative democracies, elected representatives play the central political role in the policymaking process. The people elect political representatives in order to represent their interests and to act on their behalf. Formally speaking, the government makes decisions about the policy their country will adopt, passing new laws where it can command an effective majority of representatives and entering into international agreements with other countries. The national level remains central to policymaking, but political representatives also operate at a local level and, significantly, at a supranational and regional level in the case of the European Union. As we explore in more detail in the next section of this chapter, bilateral and multilateral trade agreements among countries, and participation within international organizations such as the World Trade Organization (WTO) and United Nations, are also a crucial aspect of copyright policy (see Box 7.1).

Box 7.1

Copyright and international and supranational institutions

National policymakers, governments, and regulatory authorities are central to copyright policymaking and the implementation of copyright regulation. The national level is often where the public has the clearest connection to copyright policymaking. However, there are also

(Continued)

(Continued)

important international and supranational institutions and forums through which national policymakers operate.

The European Union (http://europa.eu/index_en.htm) is an economic and political union of 28 European countries and is a unique example of regional or supranational governance above the level of national governments. Policies are formulated by the European Commission, the European Council of Ministers (which represents national governments) and by the European Parliament (the members of which are elected by all European citizens), while the Commission may conduct consultations in order to elicit broader input into policy. The European Union has worked to standardize copyright policy among its member states and it usually represents its members in trade negotiations in the World Trade Organization (WTO) and the World Intellectual Property Organization (WIPO).

The World Trade Organization (WTO) (www.wto.org/) is an international or supranational organization for negotiating trade arrangements, which emerged out of smaller free-trade negotiations among countries. It was established in 1995 and 159 countries around the world are members. The WTO administers the Agreement on Trade-Related Aspects of Intellectual Property Rights (TRIPS), discussed further below.

The World Intellectual Property Organization (www.wipo.int/portal/en/index.html) is an agency of the United Nations that focuses specifically on copyright and other aspects of intellectual property. It was established in 1967 and 187 countries are now member states. WIPO administers a number of international treaties, including the Berne Convention for the Protection of Literary and Artistic Works.

Although central to the policymaking process, elected representatives do not make policy in isolation, and so to understand the policymaking process more fully we need to look beyond the role of representatives alone. Policymaking involves a range of other people working in and around government, from policy advisors and government officials to the regulatory bodies that implement policy. Meanwhile, various groups outside government (private corporations, trade unions, researchers and academics, think tanks, consumer and activist groups, and so on) also seek to influence policymakers and shape policy decisions outside election times. We must therefore examine the wider networks of groups that shape (or try to shape) policy within particular policy areas.

A critical question for policy analysts is the relative power of groups within these policy networks and the extent to which power is shared evenly among them. One prevalent way of thinking about this is 'pluralist', a perspective most often associated with the political scientist Dahl (1961) (for more comprehensive accounts of different theories of the policymaking process see M. Hill, 2013; and John, 2013). Responding to earlier writers such as C. Wright Mills (1956), who argued that a 'power elite' dominated politics and society, Dahl (1961) maintained that the political system in the United States was pluralist in so far as all groups in society have the ability to influence different issues and outcomes. While the pluralist perspective does not assume that all groups are equal in all respects, it does maintain that power is distributed broadly across society and the policymaking process is therefore open and competitive. No group dominates the policy process and any group can influence decisions if they are sufficiently organized and motivated.

We can evaluate the merits of pluralism as either a normative theory (an account of what the policymaking process should be like) or a descriptive one (an account of what the policymaking process is like) (M. Hill, 2013: 28). As a normative theory, the pluralist perspective is attractive. Pluralism recognizes different interests and values in society and the need for all groups to have an opportunity to influence policy decisions. But, arguably, pluralism is not ambitious enough as a normative theory. While all groups may be able to influence decisions through a pluralist politics, their perspectives are viewed as fixed and incompatible with one another and so there is a little sense in which a more general agreement about the common good might be generated through the policy process (Knops, 2007). Later, we consider an alternative, deliberative view of democratic policymaking, which at least keeps open the possibility of reaching an agreement on the common good, however difficult to arrive at and defeasible such an agreement may be.

But what about pluralism as a descriptive account of the policymaking process? On the face of it, the policymaking process appears pluralist. Various groups do take part in the process and seek to influence policy decisions. Governments and regulatory authorities encourage this participation by holding policy consultations that ask for public input. In the United Kingdom, for example, a number of government reviews related to copyright policy have been held in recent years, including, most notably, *The Gowers Review of Intellectual Property* in 2006 and *Digital Opportunity: A Review of Intellectual Property and Growth* led by Hargreaves in 2011. Both reviews generated a significant number of responses from industry, trade associations, consumer and campaign groups, and individuals: the Gowers panel received over 500 submissions and the Hargreaves panel nearly 300. The European Commission reported that a recent consultation on copyright rules in the European Union had 'generated broad interest with more than 9,500 replies to the consultation document and a total of more than 11,000 messages, including questions and comments, sent to the Commission's dedicated email address' (European Commission, 2014: 3). Responses were received from a range of 'stakeholders' and a large number were categorized as being from 'end users/consumers' (European Commission, 2014: 5). However, the fact that groups take part in consultations like this does not mean that power is equally or even widely shared among them. For writers from a more critical perspective, the pluralist view of policymaking fails to account for the way in which certain social groups — and, in particular, large private corporations — have more power and a privileged position in the policymaking process (Marsh, 2002; Hesmondhalgh, 2005; Freedman, 2008; Freedman, 2010). If the pluralist perspective may not be ambitious enough as a normative account of what the policymaking process should be like, critics argue that it is too optimistic as a descriptive account of what the process is like in practice. Indeed, pluralist writers such as Dahl recognized the limitation of pluralist theory to some extent and so revised their positions in subsequent writings (M. Hill, 2013: 36).

There are various ways that private companies use their economic resources to influence policymaking. Firstly, they can employ lobbyists, consultancy companies, and policy and legal experts to work on their behalf in order to help shape policy and influence the decisions of policymakers. As noted in Chapter 3, the links between corporations and policymakers can be supported by a 'revolving door', where government officials move into industry lobbying positions (Sell, 2013: 73–4). Secondly, corporations can invest in research to generate evidence to support their position. Policymakers often rely on the expertise and research data of corporations and may not have access to impartial evidence. As Hargreaves recently commented following his review of copyright policy, 'Much of the data needed to develop empirical evidence on copyright and designs is privately held. It enters the public domain chiefly in the form of "evidence" supporting the arguments of lobbyists ("lobbynomics") rather than as independently verified research conclusions' (Hargreaves, 2011: 18). Finally, corporations may fund parties and political campaigns, supporting political representatives who are likely to promote their interests. As Sell describes in the case of the United States, 'Due to the high costs of running political campaigns in the United States, candidates must rely on big donors to help them win. The deep pockets of intellectual property-based sectors such as software, pharmaceuticals, movies, and music have earned them a favored place at the political table' (Sell, 2013: 72). For corporations, spending money to influence policy can be viewed as a financial investment, which, like any other, is made with the expectation of economic returns. As Crouch notes, 'they [corporations] can wield enormous funds for their lobbying, not just because they are resource rich to start with, but because the success of lobbying will bring increased profits to the business: the lobbying costs constitute investment' (Crouch, 2004: 17–18).

Corporate influence on the policy process is not limited to lobbying and political funding. As emphasized by more critical theories of government and politics, economic forces can also have a more 'structural' effect on policymaking within capitalist societies (Marsh, 2002: 22–6). Though initially an advocate of the pluralist perspective, Lindblom (1977, 1982) developed a critique of early pluralist theory along these lines, arguing that corporations have greater sway over policy than other groups because of the economic position they hold in society. In capitalist societies at least, economic success and employment are reliant to a large extent upon the activities of private firms. Given that electoral success often rests on economic success ('it's the economy, stupid', as an election campaign manager for former US president Bill Clinton famously put it), governments depend on these corporations and are understandably keen to attract and sustain their investment. As a result, for Lindblom, governments will tend to privilege economic interests in their decision making. Lindblom concludes that the economic system is therefore a 'prison' for policymakers in a way that pluralists fail to recognize: 'For a broad category of political/economic affairs, it imprisons policymaking, and imprisons our attempts to improve our institutions' (Lindblom, 1982: 329).

The influence of private business on policy may be evident in particular policy decisions taken, but its effects may also be less observable and harder to detect. In a well-known critique of pluralism, Bachrach and Baratz (1962) argued that the pluralist perspective fails to recognize how power may be exercised by controlling the agenda. To grasp power in the policymaking process fully, we need to consider how certain issues come to be included or excluded from the policy agenda in the first place. For example, online copyright infringement or 'piracy' is framed as a pressing 'problem' that requires the attention of policymakers (in line with the interests of corporate rights holders), while the inequitable nature of contracts and the distribution of revenue within cultural industry structures is not. Policy analysts need to be alert, as Freedman puts it, not just to 'policy noise but policy *silence*, not policy visibility but policy *opacity*, not decision making but *non-decision making*' (Freedman, 2010: 347). Media corporations may also seek to influence the policy agenda through media coverage and public campaigns (see Chapters 3 and 6). Calculations about media coverage can then be another structural factor that shapes policy decisions. Freedman explains that 'a major influence on government decisions to pursue or bury specific policy proposals is the likely reaction of powerful media moguls, hardly a glowing endorsement of a fully competitive and decentralized bargaining system' (2008: 89).

In recent years, the influence of private business on policymaking appears, if anything, to have grown. As discussed in Chapter 3, the cultural industries are diverse and include numerous small companies, but there is also a well-known tendency for ownership to become more concentrated and for corporations to become bigger and more global in scope (Baker, 2007). At the same time, organizations that have traditionally counterbalanced corporate power, such as Trade Unions, or public institutions such as public service broadcasters, have faced relative decline in many countries (M. Hill, 2013: 36). The power of corporations in the policymaking process has risen as a consequence. Crouch (2004, 2011, 2013) goes so far as to say that some corporations have become 'insiders' in the policy process today, rather than just 'lobbyists'. He writes that 'In principle the "lobby" is a place outside the decision-making chamber, where those not involved in the formal governmental process can make their case to those who are. In important respects corporations are today "inside the chamber"' (Crouch, 2013: 221). Freedman (2008) reaches a similar conclusion in his study of the media policymaking process in the UK and US. He finds that decision-making power rests with a small, like-minded elite, which includes representatives of media corporations as well as policymakers. While various groups seek to influence media policy, the media policymaking process is therefore far from a fully pluralist and democratic one. As he concludes, 'When debates and disagreements do take place in the process of policy formation, both the terms of these conflicts and their eventual resolution in specific policy instruments are drawn up, not by members of a dispersed policy "network" but by a small decision-making elite' (Freedman, 2008: 88).

There are a number of reasons, therefore, to expect large corporations to have more sway than other groups in the policymaking process. However, their control over policy is not total. As Hesmondhalgh puts it, 'policy is not utterly at the mercy of the wealthy and powerful. Political institutions and processes have some autonomy' (2005: 97). It is important to avoid a crude economically-deterministic perspective that reduces politics to economics (Hay, 2002; Marsh, 2002). Firstly, corporations across different sectors are not homogeneous and have competing interests (Marsh, 2002: 33). As noted in previous chapters, different businesses related to copyright have opposing interests and so adopt different discourses and positions in relation to copyright. Policymakers may therefore be presented with different options, even within the constraints of the 'market prison' (Lindblom, 1982). Secondly, while the playing field is less equal than the pluralist perspective may suggest, less powerful groups that represent other interests and values can at times influence policymaking, especially when they are able to engage the public. We consider examples below where the public has been mobilized to challenge particular copyright policies. The need to win public support in order to be elected and re-elected (and the threat, if not, of being removed from power) remains a central consideration for political representatives in democratic political systems that ensures accountability. More positively, elections can also authorize and empower political representatives to bring about more substantial change. Thirdly, and relatedly, discourse remains significant to how policymakers interpret policy problems and solutions and justify policy publicly (Fairclough, 2013; Edwards et al., 2014). Conflicts among competing discourses are an important part of the policy process. Policymakers may always potentially be persuaded by different and — let us hope — good arguments.

Looking ahead to the next section, we can clarify the point here by considering how to interpret the recent internationalization or globalization of copyright policy. As we describe, copyright policy has converged across countries in recent years through a number of international organizations and agreements. We might read these developments as evidence of the increasing power of global economic forces and the declining ability of national governments to make different and independent policy decisions. However, policy convergence does not necessarily mean that governments have no political independence or power. As we describe in the next section, the internationalization of copyright policy was something actively promoted and pursued by Western governments and can be interpreted as a political project as much as an economic one. Other options were always possible and contests over copyright policy and discourse remain evident. While economic factors are important in explaining policy, politics cannot be reduced to economics. As Hay notes, 'fatalism and resignation are the antithesis of politics' (2007: 67). Whatever our view of what copyright law and policy should be, it is important to keep in mind that it is something that is made through — and so can be transformed through — politics. The policymaking process is not an equal one, but neither are its outcomes entirely predetermined.

COPYRIGHT ON THE RISE

Copyright law was originally a national issue, decided by individual governments. Historically, countries adopted different positions on what rights, if any, to afford to the owners of cultural works. However, there has been an increased standardization and globalization of copyright over time around certain minimum requirements. Encouraged by corporate rights holders in the cultural industries, the United States and other Western governments have taken measures not only to strengthen their own domestic copyright policy, but also to promote and export 'Western' copyright law to other countries.

The international regulation of copyright began in the nineteenth century when the movement of cultural products across borders appeared to necessitate some agreement among countries. The Berne Convention for the Protection of Literary and Artistic Works was established in 1886 and was initially agreed among ten countries: Belgium, France, Germany, Haiti, Italy, Liberia, Spain, Switzerland, Tunisia, and the United Kingdom (Burger, 1988). The key principle of the convention was non-discrimination: those who signed the convention were required to treat rights holders from other countries who signed the agreement in the same way as rights holders within their own countries and provide them with the same rights. At the same time, national governments had some scope to decide their own copyright policy in line with their interests and values. As Sell describes, 'States had considerable autonomy to craft laws that reflected their levels of economic development and comparative advantages in either innovation or imitation' (2003: 12). An international office was established to administer the Berne Convention (the United International Bureaux for the Protection of Intellectual Property or BIRPI), which later became the World Intellectual Property Organization (WIPO) in 1967. Berne was amended over time, with members agreeing, among other things, a minimum copyright term of the life of the author plus fifty years in 1908. Meanwhile, more countries signed the convention and most are now signatories, indicating how global copyright has become.

Significantly, the United States was reluctant to recognize international copyright initially. It was not among the original signatories of the Berne Convention and did not sign the agreement until 1988. However, from the 1980s onwards, policy in the United States changed markedly and it became the most energetic promoter of copyright internationally. What explains the shift? As described by Sell (2003; see also Drahos and Braithwaite, 2002), the change in policy must be seen against a backdrop of broader changes at the time associated with economic globalization, new technology, and the growth of a neoliberal discourse emphasizing free markets and deregulation. Within this structural context, a group of corporate rights holders were able to successfully lobby the United States and other Western governments for changes in international copyright policy. Corporations connected intellectual property (IP) with global trade and persuaded Western governments of the need to protect IP rights within a new competitive global economy and in the face of technological change (Sell, 2003: 44). A discourse that emphasized the economic importance of the cultural industries (and so of copyright) in providing Western countries with a comparative advantage in trade in an increasingly competitive global economy was important (see Chapter 3). Copyright was pushed up national policy agendas as a result, while, internationally, Western governments worked alongside corporate rights holders in order to ensure recognition and better protection of copyright in other countries.

The 1994 WTO's Agreement on Trade-Related Aspects of Intellectual Property Rights (TRIPS) was a significant agreement in extending copyright internationally. TRIPS required members of the WTO to enforce copyright and to create penalties for copyright infringement. Meanwhile, governments were able to impose trade sanctions on other countries as a means of pressuring them to observe the rules. The TRIPS agreement was not as flexible as Berne, leaving less room for national decision-making, and marked a move towards greater standardization in international copyright policy (Sell, 2003). Major corporate rights holders played a critical role in developing TRIPS, as well as lobbying for it. Forming a group called the Intellectual Property Committee (IPC), corporations were 'insiders' in the TRIPS policymaking process. As May describes, 'given the general perception of the specialized nature of intellectual property law, the IPC capitalized on the assumption that extensive technical knowledge was needed to "support" the negotiating teams. Thus, the IPC essentially drafted the TRIPs agreement, while the actual negotiations fine-tuned the text and made some concessions to developing countries' negotiators' (2007: 28–9). The close involvement of corporate actors in drafting policy is not unique to TRIPS and is typical of policy in this area more generally.

It is not difficult to understand why the United States and other developed countries might support TRIPS and similar international agreements. As Boyle explains, 'the United States has taken an eager interest in the international copyright framework — hardly surprising given that the country has steadfastly moved from being a net importer to a net exporter of copyrighted works, a shift that has made it increasingly important to secure protection for American authors abroad' (2008: 1802). The position of less-developed countries in relation to copyright is more complicated. The copyright regimes of many of these countries are influenced in complex ways by colonial legacies inherent in legal systems as well as country-specific norms. For some, compliance with international agreements has meant exceeding the benchmarks set and generally favouring rights holder protection over user access (Armstrong et al., 2010). Of course, compliance with TRIPS in practice does not always look as harmonized as envisaged: enforcement is often weak and local contexts have shaped interpretation of the law and resulted in some resistance (see Box 7.2). Still, it is far from clear that such international trade agreements are in the interests of developing countries, which import more copyrighted work than they export. Indeed, developing countries and their advocates have sought to connect IP issues discursively with human rights and development rather than markets and trade (Hamelink, 1994). A trade discourse tends to favour dominant market players, while human rights and development discourses speak primarily to developing nations (Boateng, 2011). Moreover, the colonial legacy of exploiting indigenous cultural work such as music or performance, without acknowledging its origins and/or compensating its creators, exacerbates the asymmetric distribution of power between developed and less developed nations within the global copyright regime. However, the general point about the disjuncture between TRIPS and the interests of developing countries stands. For Hesmondhalgh (2008), as we noted in Chapter 2, agreements such as TRIPS can be interpreted as a form of 'cultural imperialism', which are imposed by Western countries on developing ones.

Box 7.2
Tanzania and Kenya: music, history and copyright

Although critics have been rightly concerned about the way in which TRIPS clearly benefits certain countries while offering little benefit to other WTO members, studies suggest that the vision of harmonization embedded in the agreement is a long way off, with national contexts shaping different rights regimes. Perullo and Eisenberg (2014) have explored the different interpretations of supposedly 'harmonized' copyright law in East Africa: although Tanzania and Kenya are bound by the same TRIPS requirements, in reality the adoption of the requirements have taken different paths.

Specifically, their analysis illustrates how the implementation of musical rights policies have been shaped in Tanzania and Kenya 'by historical differences between the two countries with respect to: (1) language and educational policy; (2) the culture of bureaucracy; (3) the organization of musical unions and collective management organizations; and (4) state orientations toward music as national culture' (Perullo and Eisenberg, 2014: 149). For example, the commercialization of music is more formally embedded in Kenya, where a music industry modelled on those in the US and Europe has been in operation since the 1960s. The existence in Kenya of a commercial music industry that could be threatened by the spectre of piracy encouraged a more serious approach to infringement by legal professionals and music industry insiders. In Tanzania, however, language barriers divided those who understood copyright law from those who understood the local music economy: although copyright law is printed and discussed largely in English, most Tanzanians rely primarily on Swahili. Moreover, the notion of music as property that copyright relies on collided with a history and context of socialist policies in Tanzania that challenge the concept of private ownership.

Perullo and Eisenberg demonstrate how 'efforts to harmonize copyright legislation through TRIPS, as well as various regional organizations, has not been strong enough to counter local interests in and conceptions of rights, property, and music. Instead, the specific environments that absorb these laws reinterpret their meaning based on the specific lived experiences of those who can exert the most control over them' (2014: 149).

But why would developing countries sign agreements such as TRIPS? Even if developing countries may have tried to oppose TRIPS, the greater economic power of the United States as well as the members of the European Union and Japan — spurred by the lobbying of rights holders — meant that they were able to impose TRIPS in the face of resistance (Drahos, 2002; Sell, 2003; May, 2007). The United States Trade Representative (USTR) played a decisive role. Using a provision of the 1998 Omnibus Trade and Competitiveness Act called 'Special Provision 301', the USTR threatened to blacklist and impose sanctions against countries that were opposed to copyright principles. Meanwhile, the United States also worked to establish bilateral trade agreements with developing countries where, in exchange for recognizing copyright principles, countries were promised access to agricultural markets without discrimination (May, 2007). The imbalance of power between developed and developing countries is especially stark in bilateral agreements, where developing countries are isolated and not able to form coalitions with similar countries (Yu, 2012, 2013).

From the 2000s onwards, the United States, the European Union, and other countries have supplemented the requirements set out in TRIPS through further bilateral trade agreements. The agreements that have resulted appear to reflect the interests of developing countries even less. As Yu concludes, 'Because the intellectual property provisions in these so-called "TRIPS-plus agreements" often mandate protections in excess of the levels required by the TRIPS Agreement and other international IP agreements, they threaten to ignore the local needs, national interests, technological capabilities, institutional capacities and public health conditions of many less developed countries' (2013: 2). There have also been efforts to establish further multilateral agreements, such as the Anti-Counterfeiting Trade Agreement (ACTA) and the Trans-Pacific Partnership (TPP). ACTA was negotiated from 2007 to 2010 among a number of countries with the aim of achieving stronger international copyright protection. However, as we describe further below, the agreement was criticized in many respects, including for the opaque and exclusive nature of the decision-making process as well as for some of the measures it proposed to take in order to tackle copyright infringement (Levine, 2012). Following public pressure, some governments decided to withdraw from the agreement, including, notably, the European Union.

In addition to internationalizing key copyright principles, corporate rights holders have also sought to strengthen rights in other ways. As noted in Chapter 2, copyright law is commonly traced back to the British Statute of Anne in 1709. Under the Statute of Anne, copyright lasted for 14 years and was renewable for another 14 years. But since then governments have lengthened copyright substantially. We have already noted the minimum standards set by the Berne Convention. In 1993, the European Union decided to extend the duration of copyright by 20 years beyond what was required by Berne, so that the term of copyright was now the life of the author plus 70 years for its members. Following that, in order to harmonize its law with the European Union, the United States extended its duration by 20 years in the Copyright Term Extension Act of 1998. At the same time, it extended copyright terms for corporate works beyond that of the European Union to 95 years from the year of publication or 120 years from its creation (depending on which expires first). The extension was applied retroactively in order to apply to existing cultural products, as well as to new works. The fact that extensions apply to work *already* produced belies any instrumental claim that extending copyright is about providing an incentive for new cultural products. Corporations have subsequently continued to lobby for extensions to copyright terms, despite the seeming poverty of arguments in favour of them (see Box 7.3).

Box 7.3

Evidence-based policy? Duration of copyright in sound recordings and performers' rights

In 2011, the European Union agreed to extend the copyright duration for sound recordings and performers' rights from 50 to 70 years. This extension clearly benefits existing rights holders economically, but many commentators argue that long copyright terms are detrimental in other respects by restricting access to cultural works and limiting the public domain (Lessig, 2004a; Toynbee, 2004). Government-commissioned reviews have also questioned the economic rationale for extending the copyright term. For example, Gowers (2006) concluded that there was no economic rationale and public benefit for extending the term beyond 50 years. He writes:

> The Review finds the arguments in favour of term extension unconvincing. The evidence suggests that extending the term of protection for sound recordings or performers' rights prospectively would not increase the incentives to invest, would not increase the number of works created or made available, and would negatively impact upon consumers and industry. Furthermore, by increasing the period of protection, future creators would have to wait an additional length of time to build upon past works to create new products and those wishing to revive protected but forgotten material would be unable to do so for a longer period of time. (Gowers, 2006: 56)

Similarly, in 2011, Hargreaves wrote in his review that: 'Economic evidence is clear that the likely deadweight loss to the economy exceeds any additional incentivizing effect which might result from the extension of copyright term beyond its present levels. This is doubly clear for retrospective extension to copyright term, given the impossibility of incentivizing the creation of already existing works, or work from artists already dead' (Hargreaves, 2011: 19). Despite this, the European Union agreed in 2011 that the copyright term for sound recordings and performers' rights would be extended to 70 years and this was implemented by the UK government in 2013. This example indicates how the decisions of policymakers do not necessarily follow the considered judgements and recommendations of policy reviews and consultations.

In addition to lobbying for increases in the duration of copyright, corporations have also campaigned for greater protection and enforcement of copyright online. Through WIPO, governments agreed important treaties in the 1990s in order to ensure that copyright applied to the internet and measures were put in place to protect it (Yu, 2013). Also, as described in Chapters 4 and 6, various legal actions have been taken by rights holders against individuals or intermediaries accused of involvement in online copyright infringement. More recently, by emphasizing the threat that 'piracy' poses to the cultural industries, corporate rights holders have sought to persuade policymakers to take additional actions to tackle illegal file sharing and downloading. In particular, they have lobbied for policies which would require internet service providers (ISPs) to help to tackle the problem of copyright infringement, turning internet intermediaries from being 'mere conduits' to regulators which monitor and police the behaviour of their users (see Chapter 4).

Corporations lobbied governments across countries for new 'graduated-response' copyright policies, which would require ISPs to take 'technical measures' against users who ignored initial warnings about copyright infringement. In France, the HADOPI law (Haute Autorité pour la diffusion des œuvres et la protection des droits sur internet, or 'law promoting the distribution and protection of creative works on the internet') was passed in 2009 and included provisions for ISPs to warn and potentially suspend the internet accounts of recidivist copyright infringers. Meanwhile, the Digital Economy Act passed in the UK in 2010 included similar measures (Digital Economy Act 2010, section 10) (Corrigan, 2011). Further policies to enforce copyright and tackle online copyright infringement have been introduced and considered in other countries. However, these policies have also proven controversial and have faced resistance. In 2012, two bills that sought to tackle copyright infringement were rejected in the United States (the Stop Online Piracy and the PROTECT IP Acts), while ACTA, as already noted, was also rejected by the European Union — we discuss these cases further in the next section. Meanwhile, controversial provisions to disconnect internet users were removed from the HADOPI law in 2013 (although users may be still fined) (Andy, 2013). As we noted in Chapter 4, ISPs in the UK as well as campaign groups were critical of the Digital Economy Act; as of 2014, the Act has still not been implemented in the UK.

The privileged position of particular interests and discourses in copyright policy-making has meant that alternative discourses tend to be left at the margins. So, as noted above, free trade considerations have tended to trump the importance of access to knowledge or human rights in international discussions of copyright. In national contexts, meanwhile, even small changes to copyright that may benefit groups other than rights holders have been slow to emerge. As noted previously, overly strict digital copyright can undermine amateur creativity. Mash-ups, parodies of copyrighted material, and home videos have all been subject to infringement claims. As Hesmondhalgh puts it, 'copyright, intended to foster creativity, has become an almost insane restriction on it in many cases' (2013: 163). Compared with the system of 'fair use' in the United States, which provides some flexibility to use copyrighted material, the limited nature of exceptions in the UK has been especially marked. The recent Hargreaves Review (Hargreaves, 2011) recognized the problem, arguing for more flexibility around copyright to benefit users and other organizations wishing to use copyright material. While the proposals faced significant opposition, the government eventually implemented the changes in 2014, three years after the report was published, including exceptions to allow caricature, parody, or pastiche. This change in policy has been put down by some to lobbying by technology corporations and most notably Google. When initiating the Hargreaves Review, the UK prime minister said that 'The founders of Google … feel our copyright system is not as friendly to this sort of innovation as it is in the United States. Over there, they have what are called "fair use" provisions, which some people believe gives companies more breathing space to create new products and services' (Cameron, quoted in Hargreaves, 2011: 44). Reflecting on the Hargreaves Review, a committee of members of parliament in the UK that reviews media policy reported that it had 'heard numerous complaints from across the creative spectrum about the perceived power and influence of Google in the government's inner, policy-making sanctum' (Culture, Media and Sport Select Committee, 2013: paragraph 52). They wrote, 'We are deeply concerned that there is an underlying agenda driven at least partly by technology companies (Google foremost among them) which, if pur-sued uncritically, could cause irreversible damage to the creative sector on which the United Kingdom's future prosperity will significantly depend' (Culture, Media and Sport Select Committee, 2013: paragraph 55). This example indicates how private corporations do not all share the same interests and how technology companies and internet intermediaries have become an increasingly significant voice within copyright policymaking, a point to which we return in the next section.

DEMOCRATIZING COPYRIGHT POLICY?

While corporate rights holders and governments have successfully strengthened copyright in recent years, these policy developments have not gone uncontested. Organizations and campaign groups representing the other groups discussed in this book (intermediaries, creative workers and users) have questioned the direction of copyright policy. Meanwhile, as already noted in Chapter 6, users themselves have also resisted copyright regulation, not just through their everyday media practice (by continuing to commit online copyright infringement in significant numbers), but more recently through joining public protests against particular copyright policies. Recent protests against the Stop Online Piracy Act (SOPA) and the PROTECT IP Act (PIPA) in the United States and the international Anti-Counterfeiting Trade Agreement (ACTA) are important examples.

Given the implications copyright may have for people's media practices, we might expect the public to be more engaged with the copyright policymaking process. Yet, generally speaking, public engagement is low. Drahos and Braithwaite (2002) draw on Olson's theory of collective action to explain why corporate rights holders are more likely to organize politically to defend and further their interests than mem-bers of the public. They argue that 'diffuse public interests tend to be unrepresented because the costs to individuals of organizing large groups are not matched by the small gains for each individual', meaning that 'producer interests' (for example, cor-porations) are likely to be 'more organized than consumer interests' (for example, media users) (Drahos and Braithwaite, 2002: 193). The costs and benefits generated by being involved in politics are important considerations, but there is a danger that we reduce collective action to calculations of individual self-interest and reward. Shared values and a sense of justice can also motivate people politically and publics may be mobilized through the circulation of alternative discourses within the public sphere that raise public awareness and challenge dominant discourses.

Against this backdrop, the recent public protests against copyright policies have been significant. As already mentioned, SOPA and PIPA were new pieces of legislation considered in the United States in 2011–2012 in order to strengthen copyright protection and tackle infringement on sites hosted outside the United States. Controversially, the bills proposed using the Internet's Domain Name System to prevent access to websites suspected of copyright infringement and to stop advertising and financial companies from supporting them. Corporate rights holders (such as Comcast, News Corporation, Time Warner and Viacom) and industry associations (such as the Motion Picture Association of America (MPAA) and the Recording Industry of America (RIAA)) supported SOPA and PIPA (Sell, 2013: 71). However, the bills were opposed by a range of other groups, including technology corporations and intermediaries (such as Facebook, Google, and Yahoo!) and campaign organizations (such as the Electronic Frontier Foundation and the American Civil Liberties Union) (Sell, 2013: 72). Significantly, by representing SOPA and PIPA as a form of internet censorship that threatened free speech online, those who opposed the bill were able to generate significant public support for their campaign. On Wednesday, 18 January 2012, a number of websites staged a protest against the bills through blackouts, with Wikipedia displaying a message to say, 'the US Congress is considering legislation that could fatally damage the free and open Internet' (E. Lee, 2013: 17) (see Figure 7.1). Other tactics were employed as part of the campaign, including digital civil disobedience or 'hacktivism': denial of service attacks, which involve overloading servers with requests, were used against the websites of organizations that supported the bills. Members of the public responded to the campaign in large numbers, signing petitions and contacting their elected representatives (for example, a petition organized by Google reportedly collected between 4.5 and 7 million signatures) (Sell, 2013: 77). The result, according to Lee, was 'the largest online protest in history' (2013: 17).

Figure 7.1

In the face of opposition, SOPA and PIPA were abandoned or have at least been deferred for the time being.

Not long after the campaign against SOPA and PIPA, a new copyright agreement being negotiated internationally (the Anti-Counterfeiting Trade Agreement or ACTA) sparked similar public protests, but this time in Europe. ACTA was an international agreement to ensure greater copyright protection. Australia, Canada, Korea, Japan, Morocco, New Zealand, Singapore, and the United States all signed the agreement in 2011. The EU initially supported the agreement on behalf of its member states, but subsequently withdrew from it following public opposition (Levine, 2012). ACTA proved controversial not just because of the provisions that sought to tackle copyright infringement, but because of a lack of transparency and consultation. Indeed, the opaque nature of the decision-making process seemingly led to confusion among the public about the provisions the agreement contained, some of which had been modified by the time the agreement was finalized (Levine, 2012; Yu, 2014). Aside from leaks, early drafts of the agreements were limited to governments and particular private corporations. Kader Arif, the European Parliament's rapporteur for ACTA, resigned after the agreement was initially signed in January 2012, stating, 'I condemn the whole process which led to the signature of this agreement: no consultation of the civil society, lack of transparency since the beginning of negotiations, repeated delays of the signature of the text without any explanation given, rejection of Parliament's recommendations as given in several resolutions of our assembly'. At the same time, public protests had begun to surface and were brought together on 7 June 2012, with demonstrations reportedly taking place in over 100 cities across Europe (Matthews and Žikovská, 2013). Since the Treaty of Lisbon (an important agreement which adapted the constitutional procedures of the European Union), international trade agreements like ACTA must be supported by the members of the European Parliament in order to be passed. A petition with 2.8 million signatures was sent to the European Parliament, calling on it 'to stand for a free and open internet' (Baraliuc et al., 2013: 93). Following this, the European Parliament rejected ACTA in a vote in July 2012. Thirty-nine Members of the European Parliament voted in favour of ACTA, while 478 voted against it (165 MEPs abstained).

What explains the success of these protests and the failure on these occasions of rights holders to secure their favoured policy outcomes? Firstly, as already noted, the opponents to the bills included corporations as well as members of the public. Prominent internet intermediaries such as Amazon, eBay, Facebook, Google, and Yahoo! were among those who opposed SOPA and PIPA. While these firms may emphasize the value of free speech and freedom of information in defending their position discursively, they are also pursuing their own economic interests in opposing the bills (like corporate rights holders were in supporting them) and were willing to employ the resources available to them (like corporate rights holders were) to achieve the desired policy objectives. As Sell observes, 'Google has established a strong presence in Washington, DC, and spent $5.9 million dollars on lobbying in 2011, more than any other computer or Internet company by a large margin' (2013: 79). As we mentioned earlier and was discussed in Chapter 4, it is mistaken to treat corporations as if they are homogeneous and all send the same messages to policymakers (Marsh, 2002). A conflict of interests between rights holders on the one side (which were in favour of SOPA and PIPA) and of technology companies and intermediaries on the other (which were opposed) was arguably significant in explaining the policy outcome.

However, while the involvement of technology corporations and intermediaries was significant, it does not explain the success of the campaigns against SOPA, PIPA and ACTA alone. As other commentators have documented, consumer and citizen groups and the high levels of participation by members of the public also played a major role in influencing the decisions of political representatives (E. Lee, 2013; Sell, 2013). It would be mistaken, therefore, to reduce SOPA and ACTA to a contest between corporate interests. The internet was arguably a significant factor in helping to facilitate the public protest. By making it easier to reach and find those with similar interests and views and to organize distributed networks and campaigns, social media and the web help to address the collective action problem discussed above (the benefits to individuals involved in organizing do not match the costs of participation) (Bimber, 2012). But, in addition, a discourse which raised public awareness about the policies and represented them as threat to fundamental values and rights — in particular, people's freedom of speech online — was important in establishing and mobilizing the public to participate (Sell, 2013).

The protests against SOPA, PIPA and ACTA are noteworthy in showing how the public can have the power to influence copyright policymaking. However, the protests are also limited in a crucial respect. Opposing and preventing an undesirable policy from being implemented is different from being involved in the formulation of an alternative policy. The power to resist political decisions remains a negative one, what Rosanvallon has termed a 'democracy of rejection' rather than a 'democracy of proposition' (2008: 15). What is missing, in Couldry's terms, is not just 'opportunities for citizens to express their dissatisfaction with government', but rather 'the means by which these voices can be valued within a wider process of policy development' (Couldry, 2010: 143). But then how might it be possible for the public to have more influence over the formation of copyright policy in the first place?

As mentioned above, in standard theories of liberal representative democracy, elected representatives provide the crucial link between the public and the policymaking process. However, political parties have tended not to put forward alternative copyright discourses and policies that the public may support. A notable, and somewhat remarkable, exception to this is the Pirate Party, which emerged in Sweden in 2006 and has subsequently been established in many other countries (Burkart, 2014). The Pirate Party campaigns for copyright reform, such as the reduction of copyright terms, as well as for individual rights such as freedom of speech and respect for privacy online. The party has been able to garner electoral support: for example, it performed particularly well in the Swedish elections for the European Parliament in 2009, where it received an impressive 7.1 percent of the vote (Erlingsson and Persson, 2011). The party also played a central role in the campaign against ACTA discussed above. It is not clear whether pirate parties can repeat such successes in future, but their accomplishments to date show support for alternative copyright discourses and policies when they are put forward to the public (Burkart, 2014).

Voting for elected representatives is not the only way the public can seek to influence policymaking. As already noted, governments also host policy consultations and reviews where they ask for public input into the process of policy formation outside election times. Even if members of the public may not be involved in the consultation process directly, organizations and groups that seek to represent their interests (as well as the interests of other groups such as creative workers) may participate. These groups can provide an additional link between the public and the policymaking process and may adopt alternative discourses that challenge dominant positions and perspectives (see Box 7.4).

Box 7.4
Copyright discourse and critique

Edwards et al. (2014) explore the role of discourse in the policymaking process by examining responses to government consultations in the UK. They examine how rights holders use discourse strategically in order to pursue their own interests, but also how alternative and oppositional discourses from other groups may emerge. Drawing upon Boltanski and Chiapello's (2005 [1999]) sociology of capitalism and Boltanski and Thévenot's (2006 [1991]) sociology of justification, they emphasize that in making policy arguments actors often must appeal to general justificatory principles — about what is good, right and just — which involve a broader claim to public legitimacy beyond their particular interests. Such justificatory claims provide some scope for opposition and critique, as other groups contest the interpretation of these principles and the evidence used to support them.

In their submissions to government reviews, rights holders defend the existing copyright regime robustly. To do so, the submissions draw primarily upon an instrumental view of copyright, where the copyright regime is represented as being essential in order to support and facilitate cultural production. Indeed, creativity tends to be conflated with the copyright regime, such that the only incentive for creativity is financial. Alongside general market-based discourses, the submissions also appeal more specifically to national economic interests. The 'creative industries' are represented as crucial in allowing the UK to find a niche and succeed in a global economy. Statistics are liberally scattered throughout submission documents, to emphasize the knowledge and expertise of the industry. For example, in its submission to the 2011 *Hargreaves Review of Intellectual Property and Growth* (Hargreaves, 2011), the BPI states that 'The recorded music industry as a whole employs over 100,000 people and has a combined turnover of around £4 billion' (BPI, 2011: 16). The economic value that the cultural industries represent provides a strong foundation for arguing that copyright is indispensable: it is presented as the 'bedrock' (UK Music, 2011: n.p.), 'cornerstone' (FAST, 2011: 5), or 'currency' (BPI, 2011: 14) of healthy creative industries. Yet, while the submissions tend to rely mostly on an instrumental view of copyright, rights holders also draw at times on a more intrinsic

(Continued)

(Continued)

conception that justifies copyright as a valuable end in itself and a reward that creators rightfully deserve. For example, UK Music states 'Enforcement of copyrights is also about equality and justice. Individual creators, performers, rights holders should have access to justice when their rights are infringed' (UK Music, 2011: n.p.). Copyright is represented as legitimate, then, because it is aligned with moral concerns relating to justice, to which creative workers and corporate rights holders are both entitled because their moral claims over cultural products are apparently one and the same.

However, Edwards et al. (2014) point to how these discourses are open to challenge by other groups which — while they do not necessarily disagree with the principles espoused — question their interpretation and the evidence used to support them. For example, some groups, such as the Creative Commons and Open Rights Group (ORG), question the claim that creativity is synonymous with the current copyright regime by locating creativity outside as well as inside industry structures. Rights holders are seen as exaggerating the instrumental benefits of the existing copyright system and as ignoring how copyright may obstruct as well as promote creativity. The claim by rights holders that the current copyright regime best serves the UK's national economic interests is also disputed by some submissions. For example, despite stating that it supports UK Music's submission to the Hargreaves Review, the Association of Independent Music (AIM) argues on behalf of the independent music sector that 'Independent music companies are now the only UK-owned, UK-run music industry sector: all the major multinationals are now foreign-owned' and hence do not function 'as part of indigenous UK business' (AIM, 2011: 1). AIM's observations, therefore, seek to undermine the music industry's claim about the need to protect British interests (creativity, revenue and employment). Finally, other submissions challenge the presentation of the cultural industries as having singular interests. For example, the Featured Artists Coalition/Music Managers Forum (FAC/MMF) contest rights holders' simplistic, unitary presentation of a recording 'industry' with singular 'interests' in their marketing and government communication, instead highlighting the reality that power is concentrated in the hands of multinational corporations. They argue for fairer contract negotiations between artists, performers and rights holders, for a limited transfer of copyright, and a return to transparent and collective licensing processes (FAC/MMF, 2011). By pointing to the power imbalances that exist within the copyright system and calling for fairness on behalf of creative workers, FAC/MMF render questionable the moral terrain underlying the cultural industries' intrinsic justifications of copyright and pleas for 'justice and equality'.

In those countries that adopt them, consultations are a valuable means of participation that supplement elections. However, they are also limited in terms of how far they democratize policymaking. Firstly, although some of the groups that participate in consultations seek to represent media users as we've noted, members of the public themselves are typically absent from the process. A more democratic policymaking process would be more inclusive, involving all groups affected by the policy. Secondly, given the structure of consultations, the different groups involved need not always respond to the views of others and justify their positions. Consultations are usually limited to single, discrete contributions, leaving little to no room for others to contest or develop each other's arguments (Edwards et al., 2014). Thirdly, the judgements reached through consultations are not necessarily mirrored in political decisions. The aim of a deliberative policymaking process should be to agree on a policy that reflects the common good or, if such a 'rationally-motivated consensus (*Einverständnis*)' is not possible, at least achieve 'a negotiated agreement (*Vereinbarung*) that balances conflicting interests' (Habermas, 1997: 166). But policy consultations do not always translate neatly into political outcomes and may be short-circuited by other processes, such as the direct lobbying of politicians (Freedman, 2008: 80–105). Outcomes may then reflect the particular interests of the lobbyists and the corporations they represent, rather than the common good or a compromise among the interests of all groups.

There are barriers preventing wider public participation in copyright policymaking. Given a lack of public understanding about copyright, media literacy and education programmes which address people's understanding of media policy and the policymaking process are important (see Chapter 8). At the same time, media users are not necessarily apathetic about copyright policy, as demonstrated by public participation in recent protests. Indeed, low levels of political engagement can be viewed as much as a 'supply-side' problem, as a 'demand-side' one, stemming from the relative lack of meaningful and attractive opportunities offered by the political system (Hay, 2007). As already noted, we advocate a more inclusive and 'deliberative' system of democratic policymaking. What might realizing this more deliberative vision entail? A more deliberative approach to policymaking would require a twin focus, emphasizing the importance of both public discourse in the public sphere and more focused deliberation with policymakers around particular policies (Habermas, 1997; Hendriks, 2006; Coleman and Blumler, 2009; Moss and Coleman, 2013). Firstly, a more deliberative system is reliant upon the '"wild" complex' (Habermas, 1997: 307) of public discourses that circulate in the public sphere. Ways must be found to connect these informal discourses with policy decisions by opening up the channels through which public concerns can inform the policy agenda and public views feed into the policymaking process. Secondly, a more deliberative system would seek to radicalize existing consultation procedures in order to promote more inclusive debate around particular policy proposals. To do so, selected groups of media users might be recruited alongside representatives of other groups (rights holders, intermediaries and creative workers) in order to ensure that all perspectives are represented and debated fully. In both cases, for this more deliberative system to work, public authorities would need to demonstrate a willingness to listen to all groups and to reflect this in policy decisions taken.

The copyright policymaking process, skewed as it is in favour of the economically most powerful, may seem far removed from this deliberative vision. Yet, as we've argued, it is possible for the public to become mobilized and influence the policymaking process. When democratic protests emerge, it's important that they aim not just to influence this or that policy, but also to reform the policymaking process itself, making the most of the channels of public participation that exist already and campaigning for more inclusive and deliberative ones both within and above the level of national governments. Meanwhile, if public authorities are to resolve the digital copyright debate in a sustainable and fair way, they will need to encourage and support this broader participation. For while much about the copyright debate remains contested, it's clear that the only legitimate resolution to it is one grounded in widespread public participation and deliberation.

THE FUTURE OF COPYRIGHT: HOW WE CAN LEARN FROM THE DEBATE

SLIGHT RETURN

At the start of this book, we argued that in order to understand copyright in the digital age, we must understand how copyright is communicated. To explore copyright as a structured disagreement where various discourses meet and clash, we concentrated on the perspectives of different groups — cultural industries, policymakers, creative workers, internet intermediaries, and media users — while recognizing the diversity within and overlap between them. We examined justifications in favour of strengthening copyright as well as challenges to the current copyright regime, attempts to produce international standards around copyright and cases that refuse such standardization.

In Chapter 2, we examined how copyright has been stretched to breaking point by the strong pulls of history and technology. The historical roots of copyright continue to reassert themselves in modern debates: early legal cases determined our understanding of copyright concepts which remain central to disagreements and legal decisions. Property, the public domain and the scope of protection (in terms of what is covered and for how long) are among the ideas that underpin modern discussions, as they did historical ones, providing foundational principles but also preventing radical reimagining of systems of reward and access for creative work. Even prior to digitization, copyright was a contentious subject: assumptions about authorship and ownership, for example, were regularly challenged by instances that did not fit cleanly with copyright law. But digitization increased the challenges of a one-size-fits-all copyright law exponentially. Digitization has resulted in opportunities and challenges for which existing copyright law and regulation were unprepared. The same technologies that enabled new business models to develop within the cultural industries were also available to other players, and piracy, once primarily the preserve of professionals, became a hobby for many ordinary users. Attempts to extend laws internationally and technologically have seen winners and losers as the balance of power has been alternately tipped and restored.

In Chapters 3 and 4 we discussed the positions of the cultural industries and intermediaries in the debate about copyright. The cultural industries have used a range of arguments to shore up their rights and suggest that a stronger copyright regime, in favour of enforcement rather than flexibility, is the way to protect long-term economic growth and creativity. In their efforts to communicate their position, they have constructed infringement as criminal, socially irresponsible and shameful. However, such arguments are not uncontested, and resistance on the part of users and anti-copyright activists has emerged both in continued illegal downloading as well as in the discursive arena. Cultural industry claims are challenged both on the basis of evidence that the cultural industries are growing, not declining, and through alternative framings of user creativity — infringing or not — as a fundamental and healthy part of cultural economies in the digital age.

Given their role in hosting, distributing and locating copyrighted work, internet intermediaries are viewed by rights holders as an important site of regulatory control that can be used to enforce and protect copyright. Chapter 4 illustrated how some intermediaries have resisted being co-opted by the cultural industries in their efforts to clamp down on infringement (for example, because they fear it will alienate their customers or reduce the quality of service they provide). Internet service providers (ISPs) such as the UK's TalkTalk or file-sharing sites such as Sweden's The Pirate Bay have taken a clear stance in opposition to current copyright regulation and have defended their position in court, although they have been largely unsuccessful. Other internet intermediaries have collaborated with rights holders, helping to regulate copyright, limit infringement and generate revenue in new ways. In some cases, intermediaries are rights holders themselves with an economic interest in enforcing copyright, making their role more complex. Complicating the picture even further, there are other intermediaries — like sites such as Wikipedia — which have pursued alternative discourses of copyright and contribute to a digital commons where knowledge and creative work may be more freely shared among creators and users.

Creators and users (and the sometimes blurred line between them) were the focus of Chapters 5 and 6. Perhaps most striking about both groups is the huge variation in terms of experiences and views, with the latter obviously linked to the former. We would expect amateur creators to have a different set of expectations and needs with respect to copyright than professional creators would. And within the professional category (that is, people who try to make a living through creative work), inequality between creative workers across the cultural industries is reflected in part in the uneven distribution of revenue derived through copyright. Assumptions about Romantic authors, authorship as a solitary activity, and the link between financial incentive and innovation encourage creators to take copyright conditions for granted even as the reality offers serious contradictions: that creators can (and often have to) assign their copyright to others means that the greatest beneficiaries of copyright revenue are often not themselves creators. While representing the views of creators is made impossible by the plurality of views, one thing is for sure: despite implicit and explicit statements otherwise, not all creators agree with the justifications communicated by the industries and policymakers that claim to support them.

Users similarly challenge the neat categories into which they have been positioned in the copyright debate. While characterizations of users as the public, as pirates, as partners, and as amateur producers all hold truths, a more nuanced understanding of user perspectives can be found through examining user practices and by listening to user voices as they describe their own behaviour and views towards copyright. Through this approach we discover that, even with a minimal understanding or misunderstanding of the system of copyright, users can challenge industry claims about piracy and can debate issues relevant to copyright. However, incorporating their views into formal consultation and the policymaking process remains a challenge.

As discussed in Chapter 7, the copyright policymaking process is far from an equal and fully democratic one. Corporate rights holders in the cultural industries have tended to dominate the process, using their economic resources and position in order to have more sway over policymakers and policy decisions. At the same time, countries in favour of stronger copyright policy, such as the United States and members of the European Union, have been able to internationalize and export their own policies to other countries across the globe through international agreements. However, the direction of copyright policy has also been resisted by the other groups considered in this book. Intermediaries, creative workers, and at times media users have contested and challenged copyright policies and the discourses used to justify them publicly. Chapter 7 concluded by arguing that public engagement, especially through deliberative-democratic procedures, needs to become a more central and regular part of the copyright policymaking process.

Teasing out the positions of different actors in the copyright debate, we can identify some key justificatory themes that both drive the debate and unite or separate the different positions within it. The first is the economic value provided by copyright. For many actors in the debate, copyright is understood as a way of enabling the producers of information goods (authors, performers, technicians and others) to make money from their work and power the creative economy. For the cultural industries, it is a means of structuring supply and demand, and maintaining control over the price of cultural work, thereby helping producers to manage the risk and return associated with their creative efforts. However, positions within the economic theme are diverse. While the cultural industries and some authors vociferously defend copyright as an important cornerstone for their business models, some artists believe that a more flexible copyright regime, where creative work can be more easily shared, could generate more income, rather than less, for artists. For users, copyright adds to the cost of their consumption, while infringement can save them money. 'Fair use' regimes are gradually recognizing that some everyday user practices, such as format shifting and parody, are both rational and reasonable. However, high volume file sharing, even when users are dispersed and anonymous and sharing is facilitated by technological connections rather than 'knowing' agents, remains beyond the pale for rights holders and the law because of the significant economic losses they suggest it represents.

The second theme relates to culture. Perhaps predictably, the cultural industries argue that they protect culture, in that the rights they enforce provide a mechanism through which creators are incentivized to produce their work. In contrast, organizations and individuals in favour of a flexible copyright regime often base their arguments on the value and importance of the free circulation of cultural work. They point out that sharing, copying and mixing different cultural forms has always been part of creative practice, and that too strong a focus on enforcement will stifle innovation, limiting the potential that the digital age offers for expanding creativity beyond the boundaries of cultural industry structures. Introducing flexibility into copyright law requires a re-balancing of policy towards the public interest, fair use and a digital commons that ensures much wider access to cultural work. Policymakers, then, also take culture into account when considering how to regulate the use of copyrighted work.

The third theme that connects all actors is power. The way that copyright is constructed in law, and talked about in debates, reflects the relative power of those engaged in economic and cultural struggles over creative work. Put bluntly, the cultural industries want to preserve the structural power they enjoy in determining the market for cultural texts. Others want to change those structures, or abandon them altogether, redistributing the power to make and distribute cultural texts away from institutions and towards creators and users. And policymakers act as the arbiters of power through the decisions they make about how to balance different interests in copyright law. Often, power is wielded implicitly rather than explicitly: through copyright discourse that paints infringers as criminals, or artists as Romantic geniuses deserving of rewards, and through the work of lobbying national and international policymakers by industry and opposition groups alike. There is an imbalance of power between users and other actors in the copyright debate because some groups and organizations can more readily access policymakers and thereby influence copyright law. Moreover, their behind-the-scenes work is often difficult to identify and challenge.

To some extent, users reclaim power through their actions and rationalities when they consume copyrighted work. Indeed, as we have described, the persistence of copyright infringement in the face of industry and government attempts to eradicate it has posed a significant challenge to copyright regulation (David, 2010). However, the power users may have to circumvent copyright is limited in crucial respects. Firstly, whereas technological change has helped to facilitate copyright infringement, it could just as easily bring greater control over copyrighted material in future. As we noted in Chapter 4, the move to the 'cloud' and more closed, controllable devices (Zittrain, 2009a) and the use of increased traffic management by ISPs may offer additional ways to regulate copyright and the behaviour of users. But secondly and more importantly, even if media users have the technical means to infringe copyright, a position where large numbers of people are in breach of a law that they may neither understand nor fully support is not a sustainable or legitimate solution. What media users lack is the power to participate and shape the formation of the policy in the first place, to be 'the authors of the laws to which they are subject as addressees' (Habermas, 1997: 408). There is a difference, in Rosanvallon's terms, between the 'democracy of rejection' and the 'democracy of proposition' (2008: 15).

In Chapter 7, we argued that policymaking should take a more deliberative form, where all affected groups are included in the debate and where the aim is to arrive at a rational agreement or at least to balance the interests of different groups (Habermas, 1997). The gap between the way the current copyright debate is conducted, as it has been described in this book, and deliberative ideals is significant. Indeed, ideal deliberation may never be fully achievable in practice, but if public authorities are serious about resolving the copyright debate in a legitimate way, then efforts need to be made to at least achieve a 'more deliberative democracy' (Coleman and Blumler, 2009: 38).

As we describe below, attempts to encourage greater public participation in copyright policymaking will need to proceed on two fronts. The first aim must be to promote media policy literacy, helping to improve public understanding and participation. We have recognized in previous chapters the expectation within the cultural industries that education will solve the problem of copyright infringement, with public campaigns and industry-supported curricula being two weapons in their arsenal. Could the education approach be adapted to encourage participation rather than obedience? Educators and governments have in recent decades often turned to notions of media literacy in an attempt to enable users to better understand the media that occupy a central role in their everyday lives, but media policy has rarely featured in conceptions of media literacy. We review debates about media literacy and copyright, highlighting the principles that must support educational programmes if they are to avoid teaching users about copyright simply in order to make them more obedient citizens rather than active citizens who contribute to policymaking. But however extensive it is, media literacy education will only go so far. Media literacy programmes must be met halfway by a genuine commitment to deliberative democratic procedures as the way in which the most legitimate resolution to the copyright debate might be found.

CHANGING THE DEBATE

As Lunt and Livingstone explain, 'The expectation that ordinary people can and will become informed decision makers, competent in maximizing their opportunities and minimizing their risks, is widely promoted in terms of "literacy"' (2012: 117). Indeed, literacies have cropped up across a range of sectors, both media-related and not, and sometimes in ways that test the metaphor (Buckingham, 2007; Livingstone, 2008; Lunt and Livingstone, 2012). Buckingham highlights the growth of 'literacies' both within media education and beyond: 'This proliferation of literacies may be fashionable, but it raises some significant questions … "Literacy" comes to be used merely as a vague synonym for "competence", or even "skill"' (2007: 43). And yet researchers, educators and governments continue to return to the term in hope that, in the right hands, it may fill perceived gaps. Media policy literacy (under various titles) has recently thrown its hat in the ring as a potential emancipator. Before we consider the possibilities and limitations of such a concept, we consider the role of policy in more general media literacy programmes and agendas.

Media literacy has set up residence in school curricula around the world, though the purpose of programmes has varied over time and space:

> Media education has been taught in schools in many countries for decades, sometimes as part of a protectionist agenda (teaching children to critique and be wary, all the better to defend themselves against mass culture), sometimes as part of a creative agenda (teaching children to appreciate the cultural forms and genres, all the better to extend their aesthetic and critical understanding), and more recently as part of an empowerment agenda (teaching children to use the technical tools of self-expression, all the better to participate in modern society). (Lunt and Livingstone, 2012: 118)

While competing definitions continue to circulate, within media educator and media researcher circles, media literacy almost certainly contains a serious critical dimension. 'Literacy is inevitably related to the question of who owns and controls information, and the means by which it is generated and distributed' and the approach of modern media educators connects literacy to 'broader questions of social power' (Buckingham, 2007: 47). Through media education, young people are enabled to cast a critical eye across issues of representation, language, production and audiences (the four essential components of media literacy described by Buckingham (2003). Media policy remains a supporting player, lurking behind production or emerging rarely as information to inform debates rather than as the focus of debates. Even if policy were to take a more central role, the existence of media literacy almost entirely within school classrooms suggests further limitations, given the limited rights of school-children as citizens. (Buckingham (2003) notes some sites of media education beyond the classroom, such as community media workshops, churches, independent activist groups, but also recognizes that theirs are not necessarily progressive social goals.)

The movement of media literacy out of the classroom and into the regulatory realm comes with different advantages and disadvantages. When part of the policy agenda, media literacy has been defined and employed in various ways by different organizations and countries, though usually including notions of access and evaluation and sometimes creation: the European Parliament and Council tends to a protectionist approach; Ofcom in the UK shifted their focus from a protectionist to an empowerment approach following input from academic review; and UNESCO likewise relies on an empowerment frame (Lunt and Livingstone, 2012). But while the empowerment discourse may be welcome, outcomes are uncertain and true beneficiaries unclear. Worryingly, media literacy is endorsed as a way to place greater responsibility on individuals to regulate their own activities, 'legitimating the reduction of top-down regulatory intervention in a converging and globalizing media market (e.g. by relaxing the restrictions on product placement) while simultaneously sustaining a promise (little evaluated in outcome) of "empowerment" to the public' (Lunt and Livingstone, 2012: 128). The potential of media literacy as part of the policy agenda to reach a wider public, rather than just schoolchildren, must be weighed against its potential use as an excuse to deregulate. And, notably, media literacy *as* policy still does not address policy *in* media literacy, either absent or, as in the formal educational programmes described in Chapter 6, taken-for-granted and indisputable.

Given the growing interest among media policy researchers in encouraging public engagement, it follows that a notion of 'media policy literacy' has recently emerged, in notion, if not always name. For example, Hasebrink (2012) suggests that stronger user involvement in media governance could be encouraged through media literacy by including avenues to participation (as representatives in controlling bodies, for example) among the elements addressed. Lentz (2014a) argues for the creation of media policy educational experiences akin to those available in other policy fields, such as environmental and human rights, and stresses the importance of media policy literacy as a cultivator of citizenship, which should be instilled from school through to adult education. She focuses on how media policy literacy may be advanced for higher education students by opportunities for 'situated learning' (or learning within a community of practice) through university and non-profit organization programmes (Lentz, 2014b). Participants have a lot to gain through the selective programmes, but it's more difficult to imagine how they could be made widely available to members of the public. The convergence of researchers around the idea of media policy literacy suggests that once again the literacy metaphor and model is offering a path through a difficult thicket between media and ordinary users. And yet, to garner serious interest in development and take-up, the criticisms levelled at literacies past must be considered carefully.

The policymaking process could be enhanced through the incorporation of media policy literacy, but the approach would need to avoid some pitfalls that have marked previous literacies. In terms of content, to achieve the goal of enabling users to participate meaningfully in the policymaking process, a media policy literacy would need to teach not simply what media policy is, but how the policymaking process functions, who has a say, and who benefits. Teaching people about copyright so that they can adjust their behaviour to be on the right side of the law is very different from teaching people about copyright so that they can contribute to deliberative processes underpinning policy decisions. In terms of setting, media policy literacy cannot be limited to formal media education programmes delivered through schools: ongoing engagement with the policymaking process through various sites and over time is needed to produce active citizens who are able to challenge taken-for-granted aspects of media policy and policymaking.

Furthermore, media policy literacy, no matter how extensive it is, can only go so far. It needs to be one element within a wider structure of support for public participation in policymaking. Media policy literacy, in this way, must be an ethos shared by all parties involved in relevant debates and activities, not just formal educators. For the copyright debate to achieve its potential as a dynamic and democratic discussion, a greater range of justificatory discourses, including those of ordinary users, must be able to vie for legitimacy. To achieve this, public authorities would need to demonstrate a genuine commitment to achieving a more open and deliberative system of policymaking.

What would a more deliberative approach entail? In Chapter 7, we argued that it would require a twin focus (Habermas 1997; Hendriks 2006; Coleman and Blumler, 2009; Moss and Coleman 2013). A more deliberative system would seek to open up the channels through which the public discourses and concerns that circulate among groups in the public sphere can influence the policy agenda and feed into the policymaking process. At the same time, it would also seek to promote more inclusive public discussion around particular policy proposals, bringing together groups, including users, to debate copyright policy. In both cases, the aim would be to voice and consider the perspectives of all groups so that they may influence policy decisions. To stand a chance of achieving a copyright policy that reflects the common good, or at least strikes a fair compromise between different interests and values, requires us first to represent and understand all perspectives: this book, we hope, is one small contribution towards that goal.

REFERENCES

AIM (Association of Independent Music) (2011) *Association of Independent Music Submission to the Hargreaves Review of Intellectual Property and Growth*. Available at: http://webarchive.nationalarchives.gov.uk/20140603093549/http://www.ipo.gov.uk/ipreview-c4e-sub-aim.pdf

Alexa (2014) 'The top 500 sites on the web'. Available at: http://www.alexa.com/topsites

Andersen, B. and Frenz, M. (2010) 'Don't blame the P2P file-sharers: the impact of free music downloads on the purchase of music CDs in Canada', *Journal of Evolutionary Economics*, 20(5): 715–40.

Andy (2013) 'France set to dump 3 strikes anti-piracy law but automated fines will live on', *TorrentFreak*, 14 May. Available at: http://torrentfreak.com/france-set-to-dump-3-strikes-anti-piracy-law-but-automated-fines-will-live-on-130514/

APC (Association for Progressive Communications) (2014) *APC Internet Rights Charter*. Available at: http://www.apc.org/en/node/5677/

Armstrong, C., De Beer, J., Kawooya, D., Prabhala, A. and Schonwetter, T. (eds) (2010) *Access to Knowledge in Africa: The Role of Copyright*. Cape Town: UCT Press.

Arthur, C. (2014) 'UK copyright tweak in June will finally allow ripping of CDs', *The Guardian*, 31 March. Available at: http://www.theguardian.com/technology/2014/mar/31/uk-copyright-tweak-legally-rip-cds-ipod

Aufderheide, P. and Jaszi, P. (2011) *Reclaiming Fair Use: How to Put the Balance Back in Copyright*. Chicago, IL: University of Chicago Press.

Bachrach, P. and Baratz, M.S. (1962) 'Two faces of power'. *American Political Science Review*, 56(04): 947–52.

Baker, C.E. (2007) *Media Concentration and Democracy: Why Ownership Matters*. Cambridge: Cambridge University Press.

Bakhshi, H., Freeman, A. and Higgs, P. (2013) *A Dynamic Mapping of the UK's Creative Industries*. London: NESTA.

Banks, J. and Deuze, M. (2009) 'Co-creative labour', *International Journal of Cultural Studies*, 12(5): 419–31.

Banks, J. and Humphreys, S. (2008) 'The labour of user co-creators', *Convergence*, 14(4): 401–18.

Baraliuc, I., Depreeuw, S. and Gutwirth, S. (2013) 'Copyright enforcement in the digital age: a post-ACTA view on the balancing of fundamental rights', *International Journal of Law and Information Technology*, 21(1): 92–104.

Barron, A. (2002) 'Copyright law and the claims of art', *Intellectual Property Quarterly*, 4: 368–401.

BBC (2005) 'Movie body hits peer-to-peer nets', *BBC News*, 11 February. Available at: http://news.bbc.co.uk/1/hi/technology/4256449.stm

BBC (2011) 'BT ordered to block links to Newzbin 2 website', *BBC News*, 28 July. Available at: http://www.bbc.co.uk/news/technology-14322957

BBC (2013a) 'US Internet 'six strikes' anti-piracy campaign begins', *BBC News*, 26 February. Available at: http://www.bbc.co.uk/news/technology-21591696

BBC (2013b) 'Apple reveals iOS 7 design revamp and iTunes Radio', *BBC News*, 10 June. Available at: http://www.bbc.co.uk/news/technology-22846725

BBC (2014) 'Netflix users rise past 44 million', *BBC News*, 22 January. Available at: http://www.bbc.co.uk/news/business-25854296

Beam, C. (2009) 'Bootleg nation: how strict are Chinese copyright laws?', *Slate*, 22 October. Available at: http://www.slate.com/articles/news_and_politics/explainer/2009/10/bootleg_nation.html

Becker, H.S. (1982) *Art Worlds*. Berkeley, CA: University of California Press.

Bell, D. and Jayne, M. (2004) *City of Quarters: Urban Villages in the Contemporary City*. Aldershot: Ashgate.

Benjamin, W. (1968) 'The work of art in the age of mechanical reproduction', in H. Arendt (ed.), *Illuminations*. London: Fontana, pp. 219–26.

Berry, D.M. (2008) *Copy, Rip, Burn: The Politics of Copyleft and Open Source*, London: Pluto Press.

Bettig, R. (1996) *Copyrighting Culture: The Political Economy of Intellectual Property*. Boulder, CO: Westview Press.

Bimber, B. (2012) 'Digital media and citizenship', in H. Semetko and M. Scammell (eds), *The SAGE Handbook of Political Communication*. London: SAGE, pp. 115–27.

Birmingham, J. and David, M. (2011) 'Live-streaming: will football fans continue to be more law abiding than music fans?', *Sport in Society*, 14(1): 69–80.

Boateng, B. (2011) 'Whose democracy? Rights-based discourse and global Intellectual Property rights activism', in R. Mansell and M. Raboy (eds), *The Handbook of Global Media and Communication Policy*. Malden, MA: Wiley Blackwell, pp. 261–75.

Boltanski, L. and Chiapello, È. (2005[1999]) *The New Spirit of Capitalism*. Trans. G. Elliott. London: Verso.

Boltanski, L. and Thévenot L. (2006[1991]) *On Justification: Economies of Worth*. Trans. C. Porter. Princeton, NJ: Princeton University Press.

Bourdieu, P. (1984) *Distinction: A Social Critique of the Judgement of Taste*. London: Routledge & Kegan Paul.

Bourdieu, P. (1993) *The Field of Cultural Production: Essays on Art and Literature*. Cambridge: Polity Press.

Boyle, J. (1996) *Shamans, Software and Spleens: Law and the Construction of the Information Society*. Cambridge, MA: Harvard University Press.

Boyle, J. (2008) 'Harmonizing copyright's internationalization with domestic constitutional constraints', *Harvard Law Review*, 121(7): 1798-819. Available at: http://harvardlawreview.org/2008/05/harmonizing-copyrights-internationalization-with-domestic-constitutional-constraints/

BPI (British Recorded Music Industry) (2011) *Independent Review of Intellectual Property and Growth: Response of the BPI (British Recorded Music Industry)*. Available at: http://webarchive.nationalarchives.gov.uk/20140603093549/http://www.ipo.gov.uk/ipreview-c4e-sub-bpi.pdf

BPI (2012) 'Digital revenues overtake physical in UK recorded music market'. Available at: https://www.bpi.co.uk/searchresult/digital-revenues-overtake-physical-in-uk-recorded-music-market.aspx

BPI (2013) *Digital Music Nation*. London: BPI (British Recorded Music Industry). Available at: https://www.bpi.co.uk/assets/files/BPI_Digital_Music_Nation_2013.PDF

BPI (2014) 'Our campaigns: Music Matters'. Available at: http://www.bpi.co.uk/music-matters.aspx

Brabham, D.C. (2008) 'Crowdsourcing as a model for problem solving: an introduction and cases', *Convergence*, 14(1): 75–90.

Brainz (n.d.) 'The 14 most ridiculous lawsuits filed by the RIAA and the MPAA'. Available at: http://brainz.org/14-most-ridiculous-lawsuits-filed-riaa-and-mpaa/

Brewster, T. (2012) 'Newzbin dies a miserable death', *Techweek Europe*, 29 November. Available at: http://www.techweekeurope.co.uk/news/piracy-newzbin-ends-100584

Bridy, A. (2010) 'Graduated response and the turn to private ordering in online copyright enforcement', *Oregon Law Review*, 89: 81–132.

Bruns, A. (2008) *Blogs, Wikipedia, Second Life, and Beyond: From Production to Produsage.* New York: Peter Lang.

Buckingham, D. (2003) *Media Education: Literacy, Learning and Contemporary Culture*. Cambridge: Polity Press.

Buckingham, D. (2007) 'Digital media literacies: rethinking media education in the age of the Internet', *Research in Comparative and International Education*, 2(1): 43–55.

Bull, D. (2010) *Home Taping is Killing Music*. Available at: https://www.youtube.com/watch?v=R3jkUhG68wY

Burger, P. (1988) 'The Berne Convention: its history and its key role in the future', *Journal of Law and Technology*, 3(1): 1–69.

Burgess, J. (2013) 'YouTube and the formalisation of amateur media', in D. Hunter, R. Lobato, M. Richardson and J. Thomas (eds), *Amateur Media: Social, Cultural and Legal Perspectives*. Oxford: Routledge, pp. 53–8.

Burkart, P. (2014) *Pirate Politics: The New Information Policy Conflicts*. Cambridge, MA: MIT Press.

Burkart, P. and McCourt, T. (2006) *Digital Music Wars: Ownership and Control of the Celestial Jukebox*. Lanham, MA: Rowman and Littlefield.

Byrne, D. (2013) 'The internet will suck all creative content out of the world', *The Guardian*, 11 October. Available at: http://www.theguardian.com/music/2013/oct/11/david-byrne-internet-content-world

Cammaerts, B., Mansell, R. and Meng, B. (2013) *Copyright and Creation: A Case for Promoting Inclusive Online Sharing*. London: London School of Economics and Political Science. Available at: http://www.lse.ac.uk/media@lse/documents/MPP/LSE-MPP-Policy-Brief-9-Copyright-and-Creation.pdf

Cammaerts, B. and Meng, B. (2011) *Creative Destruction and Copyright Protection: Regulatory Responses to File-sharing*. London: London School of Economics and Political Science. Available at: http://www.lse.ac.uk/media@lse/documents/MPP/LSEMPPBrief1.pdf

Caraway, B.R. (2012) 'Survey of file-sharing culture', *International Journal of Communication*, 6: 564–84.

Cave, D. (2000) 'Come on, Eileen: Napster CEO Eileen Richardson is walking on sunshine. But with lawsuits piling up, is she really dancing on a grave?', *Salon*, 8 May. Available at: http://www.salon.com/2000/05/08/napster_richardson/

Caves, R. (2000) *Creative Industries: Contracts between Art and Commerce*. Cambridge, MA: Harvard University Press.

CCI (Center for Copyright Information) (2014) 'What do teachers need to know?' Available at: http://www.copyrightinformation.org/resources-faq/what-do-teachers-need-to-know/

Cenite, M., Wang, M.W., Peiwen, C. and Chan, G.S. (2009) 'More than just free content: motivations of peer-to-peer file sharers', *Journal of Communication Inquiry*, 33(3): 206–21.

Cloonan, M. (2007) *Popular Music and the State in the UK: Culture, Trade or Industry?* Aldershot: Ashgate.

Coleman, S. and Blumler, J. (2009) *The Internet and Democratic Citizenship: Theory, Practice, and Policy*. Cambridge: Cambridge University Press.

Corrigan, R. (2011) 'Information policy making: developing the rules of the road for the information society (or the anatomy of a Digital Economy Act)', in M. Ramage and D. Chapman (eds), *Perspectives on Information*. London: Routledge, pp. 134–53.

Couldry, N. (2010) *Why Voice Matters: Culture and Politics after Neoliberalism*. London: SAGE.

Creative Commons (2014) 'About'. Available at: http://creativecommons.org/about

Crouch, C. (2004) *Post-democracy*. Cambridge: Polity Press.

Crouch, C. (2011) *The Strange Non-death of Neo-liberalism*. Polity Press.

Crouch, C. (2013) 'From markets versus states to corporations versus civil society?', in A. Schäfer and W. Streeck (eds), *Politics in the Age of Austerity*. Cambridge: Polity Press, pp. 219–38.

Culture, Media and Sport Select Committee (2013) *Supporting the Creative Economy: Third Report*. Available at: http://www.publications.parliament.uk/pa/cm201314/cmselect/cmcumeds/674/67402.htm

Cvetkovski, T. (2014) 'The farcical side to the war on media piracy: a popular case of Divine Comedy?', *Media, Culture & Society*, 36(2): 246–57.

Dahl, R.A. (1961) *Who Governs?: Democracy and Power in an American City*. New Haven, CT: Yale University Press.

Darch, C. (2014) 'The political economy of traditional knowledge, trademarks and copyright in South Africa', in M. David and D. Halbert (eds), *The SAGE Handbook of Intellectual Property*. London: SAGE, pp. 263–78.

David, M. (2010) *Peer to Peer and the Music Industry: The Criminalization of Sharing*. Thousand Oaks, CA: SAGE.

David, M. (2013) 'File-sharing and beyond: cultural, legal, technical and economic perspectives on the future of copyright online', in W.H. Dutton (ed.), *The Oxford Handbook of Internet Studies*. Oxford: Oxford University Press, pp. 464–85.

Davies, G. (2002) *Copyright and the Public Interest* (2nd edition). London: Sweet & Maxwell.

DCMS (Department for Culture, Media and Sport) (1998) *Creative Industries Mapping Documents 1998*. London: Department for Culture, Media and Sport.

DCMS (2013) *Classifying and Measuring the Creative Industries*. London: Department for Culture, Media and Sport.

Deazley, R. (2004) *On the Origin of the Right to Copy: Charting the Movement of Copyright Law in Eighteenth-Century Britain (1695–1775)*. Oxford: Hart Publishing.

Deazley, R. (2006) *Rethinking Copyright: History, Theory, Language*. Cheltenham, UK: Edward Elgar.

DiCola, P. (2013) 'Money from music: survey evidence on musicians' revenue and lessons about copyright incentives', *Arizona Law Review*, 55: 301–70.

Dixon, S. (2013) 'Discursive intervention in international intellectual property policymaking: how developing countries and civil society employ text to challenge and change the status quo', *Communication, Culture and Critique*, 6(4): 598–615.

Dobusch, L. and Schüßler, E. (2014) 'Copyright reform and business model innovation: regulatory propaganda at German music industry conferences', *Technological Forecasting and Social Change*, 83: 24–39.

Doctorow, C. (2012) 'Why the death of DRM would be good news for readers, writers and publishers', *The Guardian*, 3 May. Available at: http://www.theguardian.com/technology/2012/may/03/death-of-drm-good-news

Doyle, G. (2013) *Understanding Media Economics* (2nd edition). London: SAGE.

Drahos, P. (1996) *A Philosophy of Intellectual Property*. London: Dartmouth Publishing.

Drahos, P. (2002) 'Negotiating intellectual property rights: between coercion and dialogue', *International Intellectual Property Law & Policy*, 7: 1–18.

Drahos, P. and Braithwaite, J. (2002) *Information Feudalism: Who Owns the Knowledge Economy?* London: Earthscan.

Dredge, S. (2013a) 'Hotfile to pay Hollywood studios $80m damages in filesharing settlement', *The Guardian*, 4 December. Available at: http://www.theguardian.com/technology/2013/dec/04/hotfile-hollywood-filesharing-damages-mpaa

Dredge, S. (2013b) 'Thom Yorke calls Spotify "the last desperate fart of a dying corpse"', *The Guardian*, 7 October. Available at: http://www.theguardian.com/technology/2013/oct/07/spotify-thom-yorke-dying-corpse

Dredge, S. (2014) 'Forget suing filesharers: in 2014, anti-piracy efforts follow the money', *The Guardian*, 2 April. Available at: http://www.theguardian.com/technology/2014/apr/02/infringing-websites-list-anti-piracy

Dryzek, J. (2000) *Deliberative Democracy and Beyond: Liberals, Critics, Contestations.* Oxford: Oxford University Press.

Duff, A. (2008) 'The normative crisis of the information society', *Cyberpsychology: Journal of Psychosocial Research on Cyberspace*, 2(1). Available at: http://cyberpsychology.eu/view.php?cisloclanku=2008051201

Edlund, M. (2002) 'Lyin' eyes: the recording artists coalition's bogus crusade to save the little guy', *Slate*, 11 February. Available at: http://www.slate.com/articles/arts/culturebox/2002/02/lyin_eyes.html

Edwards, L. (2009) *The Role and Responsibility of Internet Intermediaries in the Field of Copyright and Related Rights.* World Intellectual Property Organization. Available at: http://www.wipo.int/export/sites/www/copyright/en/doc/role_and_responsibility_of_the_internet_intermediaries_final.pdf

Edwards, L., Klein, B., Lee, D., Moss, G. and Philip, F. (2013a) 'Framing the consumer: copyright regulation and the public', *Convergence*, 19(1): 9–24.

Edwards, L., Klein, B., Lee, D., Moss, G. and Philip, F. (2013b) 'Isn't it just a way to protect Walt Disney's rights?: media user perspectives on copyright', *New Media & Society* [online first]. doi: 10.1177/1461444813511402

Edwards, L., Klein, B., Lee, D., Moss, G. and Philip, F. (2014) 'Discourse, justification, and critique: towards a legitimate digital copyright regime?', *International Journal of Cultural Policy* [online first]. doi: 10.1080/10286632.2013.874421

EFF (Electronic Frontier Foundation) (2008) 'RIAA v. the people: five years later'. Available at: https://www.eff.org/wp/riaa-v-people-five-years-later

EFF (2013) 'Lawrence Lessig strikes back against bogus copyright takedown'. Available at: https://www.eff.org/press/releases/lawrence-lessig-strikes-back-against-bogus-copyright-takedown

EFF (2014) 'Teaching copyright'. Available at http://www.teachingcopyright.org

Erickson, K., Mendis, D. and Kretschmer, M. (2013) *Copyright and the Economic Effects of Parody: An Empirical Study of Music Videos on the YouTube Platform and an Assessment of the Regulatory Options.* London: Intellectual Property Office.

Erlingsson, G.Ó. and Persson, M. (2011) 'The Swedish Pirate Party and the 2009 European Parliament election: protest or issue voting?', *Politics*, 31(3): 121–8.

Estavillo, M. (2012) 'Special report: Focus on intermediaries' role rises as internet matures', *Intellectual Property Watch*, 21 March. Available at: http://www.ip-watch .org/2012/03/21/special-report-focus-on-intermediaries-role-rises-as-internet-matures/

European Commission (2014) *Report on the Responses to the Public Consultation on the Review of the EU Copyright Rules*. Available at: http://ec.europa.eu/internal_market/ consultations/2013/copyright-rules/docs/contributions/consultation-report_en.pdf

FAC/MMF (Featured Artists Coalition and Music Managers Forum) (2011) *The FAC and MMF Submission to the Hargreaves Review*. Available at: http://webarchive. nationalarchives.gov.uk/20140603093549/http://www.ipo.gov.uk/ipreview-c4e-sub-featured.pdf

Fairchild, C. (2008) *Pop Idols and Pirates: Mechanisms of Consumption and the Global Circulation of Popular Music*. Aldershot: Ashgate.

Fairclough, N. (2003) *Analysing Discourse: Textual Analysis for Social Research*. London: Routledge.

Fairclough, N. (2004) 'Critical discourse analysis and change in management dis-course and ideology: a transdisciplinary approach to strategic critique'. University of Lancaster. Available at: http://www.ling.lancs.ac.uk/staff/norman/paper5.doc.

Fairclough, N. (2013) 'Critical discourse analysis and critical policy studies', *Critical Policy Studies*, 7(2): 177–97.

FAST (Federation Against Software Theft (2011) *Response to the Call for Evidence: FAST*. Available at: http://webarchive.nationalarchives.gov.uk/20140603093549/ http://www.ipo.gov.uk/ipreview-c4e-sub-fast.pdf

Flew, T. (2002) 'Beyond ad hocery: defining creative industries'. *Cultural Sites, Cultural Theory, Cultural Policy: The Second International Conference on Cultural Policy Research*, Wellington, New Zealand, 23–26 January.

Flew, T., Leisten, S.H. and Hearn, G.N. (2006) 'Alternative systems for intellectual property in the digital age', in J. Servaes and P. Thomas (eds), *Intellectual Property Rights Communication in Asia: Conflicting Traditions*. New Delhi: SAGE, pp. 226–40.

Flood, A. (2012) 'Pay-what-you-want ebooks "bundle" makes $1.1 m in two weeks', *The Guardian*, 23 October. Available at: http://www.theguardian.com/books/2012/ oct/23/pay-what-you-want-ebooks

Franda, M. (2002) *China and India Online: Information Technology Politics and Diplomacy in the World's Two Largest Nations*. Lanham, MD: Rowman and Littlefield.

Freedman, D. (2008) *The Politics of Media Policy*. Cambridge: Polity Press.

Freedman, D. (2010) 'Making media policy silences: the hidden face of communi-cations decision making', *The International Journal of Press/Politics*, 15(3): 344–61.

Freedman, D. (2012a) 'Outsourcing internet regulation', in J. Curran, N. Fenton and D. Freedman (eds), *Misunderstanding the Internet.* London: Routledge, pp. 95–120.

Freedman, D. (2012b) 'Web 2.0', in J. Curran, N. Fenton and D. Freedman (eds), *Misunderstanding the Internet*. London: Routledge, pp. 69–94.

Frith, S. (2000) 'Power and policy in the British music industry', in H. Tumber (ed.), *Media Power, Professionals and Policies*. London: Routledge, pp. 70–83.

Frith, S. (2004) 'Music and the media', in S. Frith and L. Marshall (eds), *Music and Copyright* (2nd edition). New York: Routledge, pp. 171–88.

Frith, S. and Marshall, L. (2004) 'Making sense of copyright,' in S. Frith and L. Marshall (eds), *Music and Copyright* (2nd edition). New York: Routledge, pp. 1–18.

Galloway, S. and Dunlop, S. (2007) 'A critique of the definitions of the cultural and creative industries in public policy', *International Journal of Cultural Policy*, 13(1): 17–31.

Gans, H. (1999) *Popular Culture and High Culture: An Analysis and Evaluation of Taste*. New York: Basic Books.

Garnham, N. (1990) *Capitalism and Communication: Global Culture and the Economics of Information*. London: SAGE.

Garnham, N. (2005) 'From cultural to creative industries', *International Journal of Cultural Policy*, 11(1): 15–29.

Gayer, A. and Shy, O. (2006) 'Publishers, artists, and copyright enforcement', *Information Economics and Policy*, 18: 374–84.

GfK (2012) *Survey on Digital Content Usage (DCN Survey) 2011*. Available at: http://www.musikindustrie.de/fileadmin/piclib/presse/Dokumente_zum_Download/DCN-Studie_2012_engl_Presseversion_Final.pdf

Giblin, R. (2014) 'Evaluating graduated response', *Columbia Journal of Law & the Arts*, 37(2): 147–210.

Gillespie, T. (2006) 'Designed to "effectively frustrate": copyright, technology and the agency of users', *New Media & Society*, 8(4): 651–69.

Gillespie, T. (2010) 'The politics of "platforms"', *New, Media & Society*, 12(3): 347–64.

Google (2012) 'An update to our search algorithms'. Available at: http://insidesearch.blogspot.co.uk/2012/08/an-update-to-our-search-algorithms.html

Google (2014a) 'Google Transparency Report'. Available at: https://www.google.com/transparencyreport/removals/copyright/

Google (2014b) 'FAQ'. Available at: https://www.google.com/transparencyreport/removals/copyright/faq/

Google (2014c) 'How content ID works'. Available at: https://support.google.com/youtube/answer/2797370?hl=en-GB

Gower, P. (2009) 'National stalls law to block internet pirates', *The New Zealand Herald*, 24 February. Available at: http://www.nzherald.co.nz/nz/news/article.cfm?c_id=1&objectid=10558313

Gowers, A. (2006) *Gowers Review of Intellectual Property*. London: HM Treasury.

Greenfield, S. and Osborn, G. (2004) 'Copyright law and power in the music industry', in S. Frith and L. Marshall (eds), *Music and Copyright* (2nd edition). New York: Routledge, pp. 89–102.

Grossman, L. (2006) 'You — yes, you — are TIME's person of the year', *Time*, 25 December. Available at: http://content.time.com/time/magazine/article/0,9171,157 0810,00. html

Habermas, J. (1997) *Between Facts and Norms: Contributions to a Discourse Theory of Law and Democracy*. London: Polity Press.

Halliday, J. (2012) 'BT and TalkTalk lose challenge against Digital Economy Act', *The Guardian*, 6 March. Available at: http://www.theguardian.com/technology/2012/mar/06/internet-provider-lose-challenge-digital-economy-act

Hamelink, C. (1994) *The Politics of World Communication*. London: SAGE.

Hargreaves, I. (2011) *Digital Opportunity: A Review of Intellectual Property and Growth*. London: HM Treasury.

Harris, M. (n.d.) 'Top 5 DRM removal programs', *About.com*. Available at: http://mp3.about.com/od/essentialsoftware/tp/best_drm_removal_software.htm

Hasebrink, U. (2012) 'The role of the audience within media governance: the neglected dimension of media literacy', *Media Studies*, 3(6): 58–73.

Hay, C. (2002) *Political Analysis: A Critical Introduction*. Basingstoke: Palgrave Macmillan.

Hay, C. (2007) *Why We Hate Politics*. London: Polity Press.

Heitner, D. (2013) 'Is the NFL committing copyright infringement by using photos without consent?', *Forbes*, 23 October. Available at: http://www.forbes.com/sites/darrenheitner/2013/10/23/is-the-nfl-committing-copyright-infringement-by-using-photos-without-consent/

Hendriks, C.M. (2006) 'Integrated deliberation: reconciling civil society's dual role in deliberative democracy', *Political Studies*, 54(3): 486–508.

Herman, B.D. (2008) 'Breaking and entering my own computer: the contest of copyright metaphors', *Communication Law and Policy*, 13(2): 231–74.

Herman, B.D. (2013) *The Fight over Digital Rights: The Politics of Copyright and Technology*. Cambridge: Cambridge University Press.

Hesmondhalgh, D. (2005) 'Media and cultural policy as public policy', *International Journal of Cultural Policy*, 11(1): 95–109.

Hesmondhalgh, D. (2008) 'Neoliberalism, imperialism and the media', in D. Hesmondhalgh and J. Toynbee (eds), *The Media and Social Theory*. Abingdon: Routledge, pp. 95–111.

Hesmondhalgh, D. (2013) *The Cultural Industries* (3rd edition.). London: SAGE.

Hesmondhalgh, D. and Baker, S. (2011) *Creative Labour: Media Work in Three Cultural Industries*. Abingdon: Routledge.

Hesmondhalgh, D. and Pratt, A. (2005) 'Cultural industries and cultural policy', *International Journal of Cultural Policy*, 11(1): 1–13.

Hill, A. (2013) 'Internet users unaware of illegal downloading', *The Guardian*, 22 April. Available at: http://www.theguardian.com/technology/2013/apr/22/internet-users-unaware-illegal-downloading

Hill, M. (2013) *The Public Policy Process* (6th edition). Harlow: Pearson.

Hintz, A. and Milan, S. (2011) 'User rights for the internet age', in R. Mansell and M. Raboy (eds), *The Handbook of Global Media and Communication Policy*. Malden, MA: Wiley Blackwell, pp. 231–41.

Hogan, M. (2012) 'Shades of grey: anti-piracy legislation and independent labels', *Pitchfork*, 27 January. Available at: http://pitchfork.com/features/articles/8763-shades-of-gray-anti-piracy-legislation-and-independent-labels/

Hu, K. (2005) 'The power of circulation: digital technologies and the online Chinese fans of Japanese TV drama', *Inter-Asia Cultural Studies*, 6(2): 171–86.

IFPI (International Federation of the Phonographic Industry) (2014) 'Music subscription revenues help drive growth in most major markets'. Available at: http://www.ifpi.org/news/music-subscription-revenues-help-drive-growth-in-most-major-markets

Industry Trust (2013) '"Moments worth paying for" grows up'. Available at: http://www.industrytrust.co.uk/industry-trust-annual-review-2013-2/moments-worth-paying-for-grows-up/

Industry Trust (2014) 'You make the movies'. Available at: http://www.industrytrust.co.uk/campaigns/you-make-the-movies/

Jaszi, P. and Woodmansee, M. (1996) 'The ethical reaches of authorship', *South Atlantic Quarterly*, 95: 947–77.

John, P. (2012) *Analyzing Public Policy*. Abingdon: Routledge.

Jowitt, T. (2011) 'BT given two weeks to block Newzbin2', *Techweek Europe*, 26 October. Available at: http://www.techweekeurope.co.uk/news/bt-given-two-weeks-to-block-newzbin2-43776

Karaganis, J. (ed.) (2011) *Media Piracy in Emerging Economies*. Social Science Research Council. Available at: http://piracy.americanassembly.org

Karaganis, J. and Renkema, L. (2013) *Copy Culture in the US and Germany*. New York: The American Assembly. Available at: http://piracy.americanassembly.org

Keall, C. (2013) 'First music pirate nailed under new copyright law', *National Business Review*, 30 January. Available at: http://www.nbr.co.nz/opinion/first-music-pirate-nailed-under-new-copyright-law

Kennedy, H. (2013) 'Against amateur economies: spec work competitions and the anti-spec movement', *Cultural Studies Review*, 19(1): 228–48.

Kickstarter (2014) 'Seven things to know about Kickstarter'. Available at: https://www.kickstarter.com/hello

Kinnally, W., Lacayo, A., McClung, S. and Sapolsky, B. (2008) 'Getting up on the download: college students' motivations for acquiring music via the web', *New Media & Society*, 10(6): 893–913.

Klang, M. and Murray, A. (2005) *Human Rights in the Digital Age*. London: GlassHouse Press.

Klein, B. (2009) *As Heard on TV: Popular Music in Advertising*. Aldershot: Ashgate.

Knops, A. (2007) 'Debate: agonism as deliberation – on Mouffe's theory of democracy', *Journal of Political Philosophy*, 15(1): 115–26.

Kohl, U. (2012) 'The rise and rise of online intermediaries in the governance of the Internet and beyond – connectivity intermediaries', *International Review of Law, Computers & Technology*, 26(2–3): 185–210.

Kohl, U. (2013) 'Google: the rise and rise of online intermediaries in the governance of the Internet and beyond (Part 2)', *International Journal of Law and Information Technology*, 21(2): 187–234.

Kravets, D. (2007) 'Napster trial ends seven years later, defining online sharing along the way', *Wired*, 31 August. Available at: http://www.wired.com/2007/08/napster-trial-e/

Kretschmer, M. and Kawohl, F. (2004) 'The history and philosophy of copyright', in S. Frith and L. Marshall (eds), *Music and Copyright* (2nd edition). New York: Routledge, pp. 21–53.

Kretschmer, M. and Pratt, A.C. (2009) 'Legal form and cultural symbol', *Information, Communication & Society*, 12(2): 165–77.

Kretschmer, M., Bently, L. and Deazley, R. (2010) 'The history of copyright history: notes from an emerging discipline', in R. Deazley, M. Kretschmer and L. Bently (eds), *Privilege and Property: Essays on the History of Copyright*. Cambridge: OpenBook Publishers, pp. 1–20.

Laing, D. (2004) 'Copyright, politics, and the international music industry', in S. Frith and L. Marshall (eds), *Music and Copyright* (2nd edition). New York: Routledge, pp. 70–85.

Lee, A. (2013) 'NYTVF: "Arrested Development's" Mitch Hurwitz wants a Bluth movie and Season 5 at Netflix', *Hollywood Reporter*, 22 October. Available at: http://www.hollywoodreporter.com/news/nytvf-arrested-developments-mitch-hurwitz-650002

Lee, D. (2012) 'Spotify: Metallica ends Napster feud with new deal', *BBC News*, 6 December. Available at: http://www.bbc.co.uk/news/technology-20634944

Lee, E. (2013) *The Fight for the Future: How People Defeated Hollywood and Saved the Internet – For Now*. LULU Press.

Lentz, B. (2011) 'Regulation as linguistic engineering', in R. Mansell and M. Raboy (eds), *The Handbook of Global Media and Communication Policy*. Hoboken, NJ: Wiley, pp. 432–48.

Lentz, B. (2014a) 'The media policy Tower of Babble: a case for policy literacy pedagogy', *Critical Studies in Media Communication*, 31(2): 134–40.

Lentz, B. (2014b) 'Building the pipeline of media and technology policy advocates: the role of "situated learning"', *Journal of Information Policy*, 4: 176–204.

Lessig, L. (2004a) *Free Culture*. New York: The Penguin Press.

Lessig, L. (2004b) 'Copyrighting the President', *Wired*, August. Available at: http://archive.wired.com/wired/archive/12.08/view.html?pg=5

Lessig, L. (2006) *Code 2.0*. New York: Basic Books.

Levine, D.S. (2012) 'Bring in the nerds: secrecy, national security and the creation of international intellectual property law', *Cardozo Arts & Entertainment Law Journal*, 30(2): 105–51.

Lindblom, C.E. (1977) *Politics and Markets: The World's Political-Economic Systems*. New York: Basic Books.

Lindblom, C.E. (1982) 'The market as prison', *The Journal of Politics*, 44(2): 323–36.

Lindgren, S. (2013) 'Pirate panics: comparing news and blog discourse on illegal file sharing in Sweden', *Information, Communication & Society* [online first]. doi: 10.1080/1369118X.2012.757632

Litman, J. (2000) 'The demonization of piracy'. *The 10th Conference on Computers, Freedom and Privacy*, Toronto, Canada, 6 April. Available at: http://www.wayne.edu/litman/papers/demon.pdf

Litman, J. et al. (2000) *Brief Amicus Curiae of Copyright Law Professors in Support of Reversal, Consortium of 18 Copyright Law Professors, Napster Inc. v. A&M Records et al.* Available at: http://www-personal.umich.edu/~jdlitman/briefs/Amicus.pdf

Livingstone, S. (2008) 'Engaging with media – a matter of literacy?', *Communication, Culture & Critique*, 1(1): 51–62.

Lunt, P. and Livingstone, S. (2012) *Media Regulation: Governance and the Interests of Citizens and Consumers*. London: SAGE.

MacKenzie, R. (2010) 'Chile breaks new ground in regulating IP liability', *WIPO Magazine*, 3 June. Available at: http://www.wipo.int/wipo_magazine/en/2010/03/article_0009.html

Madden, M. (2004) *Artists, Musicians and the Internet*. Washington, DC: Pew Internet and American Life Project. Available at: http://www.pewinternet.org/2004/12/05/artists-musicians-and-the-internet/

Manovich, L. (2009) 'The practice of everyday (media) life: from mass consumption to mass cultural production?', *Critical Inquiry*, 35(2): 319–31.

Mansbridge, J., Bohman, J., Chambers, S., Estlund, D., Føllesdal, A., Fung, A., Lafont, C., Manin, B. and Luis Martí, J. (2010) 'The place of self-interest and the role of power in deliberative democracy', *Journal of Political Philosophy*, 18(1): 64–100.

Marsden, C.T. (2010) *Net Neutrality: Towards a Co-Regulatory Solution*. London: Bloomsbury Academic.

Marsh, D. (2002) 'Pluralism and the study of British politics: it is always the happy hour for men with money, knowledge and power', in C. Hay (ed.), *British Politics Today*. Cambridge: Polity Press, pp. 14–38.

Marshall, L. (2004) 'Infringers', in S. Frith and L. Marshall (eds), *Music and Copyright* (2nd edition). New York: Routledge, pp. 209–14.

Marshall, L. (2005) *Bootlegging: Romanticism and Copyright in the Music Industry*. London: SAGE.

Marshall, L. (2013) 'The 360 deal and the "new" music industry', *European Journal of Cultural Studies*, 16(1): 77–99.

Marshall, L. and Frith, S. (2004) 'Afterword: where now for copyright?', in S. Frith and L. Marshall (eds), *Music and Copyright* (2nd edition). New York: Routledge, pp. 189–208.

Mato, D. (2009) 'All industries are cultural: a critique of the idea of "cultural industries" and new possibilities for research', *Cultural Studies*, 23(1): 70–87.

Matthews, D. and Žikovská, P. (2013) 'The rise and fall of the anti-counterfeiting trade agreement (ACTA): lessons for the European Union', *IIC – International Review of Intellectual Property and Competition Law*, 44(6): 626–55.

May, C. (2003) 'Digital rights management and the breakdown of social norms', *First Monday*, 8: 11–13. Available at: http://firstmonday.org/htbin/cgiwrap/bin/ojs/index.php/fm/rt/printerFriendly/1097/1017

May, C. (2007) *The World Intellectual Property Organization: Resurgence and the Development Agenda*. London: Routledge.

McChesney, R. (2013) *Digital Disconnect*. New York: New Press.

McKenzie, G. and Cochrane, G. (2009) 'Paul McCartney: Pirate Bay verdict "fair"', *BBC Newsbeat*, 20 April. Available at: http://news.bbc.co.uk/newsbeat/hi/music/newsid_8007000/8007950.stm

McLeod, K. (2001) *Owning Culture: Authorship, Ownership, & Intellectual Property Law*. New York: Peter Lang.

McLeod, K. (2005) 'Confessions of an intellectual (property): Danger Mouse, Mickey Mouse, Sonny Bono, and my long and winding path as a copyright activist-academic', *Popular Music & Society*, 28(1): 79–93.

McLeod, K. and Dicola, P. (2011) *Creative License: The Law and Culture of Digital Sampling*. Durham, NC: Duke University Press.

Miège, B. (1987) 'The logics at work in the new cultural industries', *Media, Culture and Society*, 9(3): 273–89.

Miège, B. and Garnham, N. (1979) 'The cultural commodity', *Media, Culture and Society*, 1(1): 297–311.

Millaleo, S. and Cadenas, H. (2014) 'Intellectual property in Chile: problems and conflicts in a developing society', in M. David and D. Halbert (eds), *The SAGE Handbook of Intellectual Property*. London: SAGE, pp. 130–47.

Moss, G. (2011) 'Media CAT vs Adams: the cat that did not get the cream', *Journal of Intellectual Property Law and Practice*, 6(11): 813–20.

Moss, G. and Coleman, S. (2013) 'Deliberative manoeuvres in the digital darkness: e-democracy policy in the UK', *The British Journal of Politics & International Relations* [online first]. doi: 10.1111/1467-856X.12004

MPDA (Motion Picture Distributors Association (India)) (2013a) 'Indian screen community calls for protection of online content to ensure vibrant digital marketplace'. Available at: http://mpaa-india.org/press/Final%20Press%20Release_%20 Digital%20conference.pdf

MPDA (2013b) 'Motion Picture Distributors Association (India) joins screen community in celebration of World IP Day'. Available at: http://mpaa-india.org/press/ Final%20MPDA%20-World%20IP%20ay%202013.pdf

Murdock, G. (2004) 'Building the digital commons: public broadcasting in the age of the internet'. *The 2004 Spry Memorial Lecture*, Vancouver/Montreal, Canada, 18 and 22 November. Available at: http://www.fondsgrahamspryfund.ca/previous-conferences/conference-2004/

Murdock, G. (2014) 'Another people: communication policy and the Europe of citizens', in K. Donders, C. Pauwels and J. Loisen (eds), *The Palgrave Handbook of European Media Policy*. Basingstoke: Palgrave Macmillan, pp. 143–71.

Murray, A. (2010) *Information Technology Law: The Law and Society*. Oxford: Oxford University Press.

Negus, K. (1999) *Music Genres and Corporate Cultures*. London: Routledge.

Negus, K. (2006) 'Rethinking creative production away from the cultural industries', in J. Curran and D. Morley (eds), *Media and Cultural Theory*. Abingdon: Routledge, pp. 197–208.

NME (2008) 'Radiohead reveal how successful "In Rainbows" download really was', *New Musical Express*, 15 October. Available at: http://www.nme.com/news/radiohead/40444

NPR (2013) 'Pirates steal "Game of Thrones": why HBO doesn't mind', *All Things Considered*, 7 April. Available at: http://www.npr.org/2013/04/07/176338400/ pirates-steal-game-of-thrones-why-hbo-doesnt-mind

Oakley, K. (2006) 'Include us out: economic development and social policy in the creative industries', *Cultural Trends*, 15(4): 255–73.

O'Connor, J. (2000) 'The definition of the cultural industries', *The European Journal of Arts Education*, 2(3): 15–27.

O'Connor, J. (2010) *The Cultural and Creative Industries: A Literature Review* (2nd edition). Creativity, Culture and Education Series. Newcastle upon Tyne: Creativity, Culture and Education.

OECD (Organization for Economic Co-Operation and Development) (2010) *The Role of Internet Intermediaries in Advancing Policy Objectives*. OECD Publishing. Available at: http://www.oecd-ilibrary.org/science-and-technology/the-role-of-internet-inter-mediaries-in-advancing-public-policy-objectives_9789264115644-en

Ofcom (Office of Communications) (2012) *OCI Tracker Benchmark Study Q3 2012: Introduction and Key Findings*. London: Ofcom. Available at: http://stakeholders.ofcom.org.uk/market-data-research/other/telecoms-research/copyright-infringement-tracker/

ORG (Open Rights Group) (2011) *Hargreaves Review of IP and Growth: Open Rights Group (ORG) submission*. Available at: http://webarchive.nationalarchives.gov.uk/20140603093549/http://www.ipo.gov.uk/ipreview-c4e-sub-org.pdf

ORG (2014) 'Copyright reform'. Available at: https://www.openrightsgroup.org/issues/copyright-reform

Pang, L. (2008) '"China who makes and fakes": a semiotics of the counterfeit', *Theory, Culture & Society*, 25(6): 117–40.

Park, J. (2013) 'Open curriculum alternatives to MPAA's new anti-piracy campaign for kids', *Creative Commons*, 25 September. Available at: https://creativecommons.org/weblog/entry/39781

Patry, W. (2009) *Moral Panics and the Copyright Wars*. Oxford: Oxford University Press.

Perullo, A. and Eisenberg, A.J. (2014) 'Musical property rights regimes in Tanzania and Kenya after TRIPS', in M. David and D. Halbert (eds), *The SAGE Handbook of Intellectual Property*. London: SAGE, pp. 148–64.

Pessach, G. (2013) 'Deconstructing disintermediation: a skeptical copyright perspective', *Cardozo Arts & Entertainment Law Journal*, 31(3): 833–73.

Potts, J. and Cunningham, S. (2008) 'Four models of the creative industries', *International Journal of Cultural Policy*, 14(3): 233–47.

Potts, J., Hartley, J., Banks, J., Burgess, J., Cobcroft, R., Cunningham, S. and Montgomery, L. (2008) 'Consumer co-creation and situated creativity', *Industry & Innovation*, 15(5): 459–74.

Prakash, P. (2012) 'Analysis of the Copyright (Amendment) Bill 2012', *The Centre for Internet & Society*, 23 May. Available at http://cis-india.org/a2k/blog/analysis-copyright-amendment-bill-2012

Pratt, A. (2005) 'Cultural industries and public policy', *International Journal of Cultural Policy*, 11(1): 31–44.

Pratt, A. (2008) 'Cultural commodity chains, cultural clusters, or cultural production chains?', *Growth and Change*, 39(1): 95–103.

Price, D. (2013) *Sizing the Piracy Universe*. London: NetNames. Available at: https://copyrightalliance.org/sites/default/files/2013-netnames-piracy.pdf

Primo, N. and Lloyd, L. (2011) 'South Africa', in J. Karaganis (ed.), *Media Piracy in Emerging Economies*. New York: Social Science Research Council, pp. 99–147. Available at: http://piracy.americanassembly.org/wp-content/uploads/2011/06/MPEE-PDF-1.0.4.pdf

PRS for Music and Google (2012) *The Six Business Models of Copyright Infringement*. Available at: http://www.prsformusic.com/aboutus/policyandresearch/researchand economics/Documents/TheSixBusinessModelsofCopyrightInfringement.pdf

Rens, A., Prabhala, A. and Kawooya, D. (2006) *Intellectual Property, Education and Access to Knowledge in Southern Africa*. Tralac Working Paper No. 12. Stellenbosch: US Printers. Available at: http://www.tralac.org/wp-content/blogs.dir/12/files/2011/uploads/20061002_Rens_IntellectualProperty.pdf

Richter, F. (2014) 'The LP is back!', *Statista*, 5 January. Available at: http://www.statista.com/chart/1465/vinyl-lp-sales-in-the-us/

Rohrer, F. (2009) 'Getting inside a downloader's head', *BBC News Magazine*, 18 June. Available at: http://news.bbc.co.uk/1/hi/magazine/8106805.stm

Rosanvallon, P. (2008) *Counter-Democracy: Politics in an Age of Distrust*. Cambridge: Cambridge University Press.

Rose, M. (1993) *Authors and Owners: The Invention of Copyright*. Cambridge, MA: Harvard University Press.

Schultz, M. (2006) 'Copynorms: copyright and social norms', in P. Yu (ed.), *Intellectual Property and Information Wealth: Issues and Practices in the Digital Age*, vol. 1. Westport, CT: Praeger, pp. 201–36.

Sell, S.K. (2003) *Private Power, Public Law: The Globalization of Intellectual Property Rights*. Cambridge: Cambridge University Press.

Sell, S.K. (2013) 'Revenge of the "nerds": collective action against Intellectual Property maximalism in the global information age', *International Studies Review*, 15(1): 67–85.

Seville, C. (2010) 'Nineteenth-century Anglo–US copyright relations: the language of piracy versus the moral high ground', in L. Bently, J. Davis and J.C. Ginsburg (eds), *Copyright and Piracy: An Interdisciplinary Critique*. Cambridge: Cambridge University Press, pp. 19–43.

Solsman, J. (2013) 'Hulu in 2013: sales up nearly half to $1B with 5M paid users', *Cnet.com*, 18 December. Available at: http://www.cnet.com/uk/news/hulu-in-2013-sales-up-nearly-half-to-1b-with-5m-paid-users/

Sorrel, C. (2011) 'How to strip DRM from Kindle E-Books and others', *Wired*, 17 January. Available at: http://www.wired.com/gadgetlab/2011/01/how-to-strip-drm-from-kindle-e-books-and-others/

Stahl, M. (2010) 'Cultural labor's "democratic deficits": employment, autonomy and alienation in US film animation', *Journal for Cultural Research*, 14(3): 271–93.

Stahl, M. (2011) 'From seven years to 360 degrees: primitive accumulation, recording contracts, and the means of making a (musical) living', *tripleC*, 9(2): 668–88.

Stahl, M. and Meier, L.M. (2012) 'The firm foundation of organizational flexibility: the 360 contract in the digitalizing music industry', *Canadian Journal of Communication*, 37(3): 441–58.

Sutter, G. (2005) 'Internet service providers and liability', in M. Klang and A. Murray (eds), *Human Rights in the Digital Age*. Abingdon: Routledge, pp. 71–84.

Tao, Q. (2012) 'Legal framework of online intermediaries' liability in China', *info*, 14(6): 59–72.

Techdirt.com (2013) 'Surprise: MPAA told it can't use terms "piracy", "theft" or "stealing" during Hotfile trial', *techdirt.com*, 2 December. Available at: http://www.techdirt.com/articles/20131130/15263725410/surprise-mpaa-told-it-cant-use-terms-piracy-theft-stealing-during-hotfile-trial.shtml

The Economist (2012) 'Intellectual property in China: still murky', *The Economist*, 21 April. Available at: http://www.economist.com/node/21553040

Thielman, S. (2013) 'Bewkes: Game of Thrones piracy "better than an emmy": exec talks streaming, stealing and the Time Inc. spin-off, *Adweek*, 7 August. Available at: http://www.adweek.com/news/television/bewkes-game-thrones-piracy-better-emmy-151738

Thomas, P. (2014) 'Copyright and copyleft in India: between global agendas and local interests', in M. David and D. Halbert (eds), *The SAGE Handbook of Intellectual Property*. London: SAGE, pp. 335–69.

Throsby, D. (2008) 'Modelling the cultural industries', *International Journal of Cultural Policy*, 14(3): 217–32.

Topel, F. (2013) 'Interview: Metallica on "Metallica through the never" & beyond', *Crave Online*, 16 September. Available at: http://www.craveonline.com/film/interviews/571521-tiff-2013-metallica-on-metallica-through-the-never

Towse, R. (2006) 'Copyright and artists: a view from cultural economics', *Journal of Economic Surveys*, 20(4): 567–85.

Towse, R. (2011) 'Creative industries', in R. Towse (ed.), *Handbook of Cultural Economics*. Cheltenham: Edward Elgar, pp. 125–31.

Toynbee, J. (2004) 'Musicians', in S. Frith and L. Marshall (eds), *Music and Copyright* (2nd edition). New York: Routledge, pp. 123–38.

Toynbee, J. (2013) 'How special? Cultural work, copyright, politics', in M. Banks, R. Gill and S. Taylor (eds), *Theorizing Cultural Work: Labour, Continuity and Change in the Cultural and Creative Industries*. London: Routledge, pp. 86–100.

Tschmuck, P. (2009) 'Copyright, contracts and music production', *Information, Communication & Society*, 12(2): 251–66.

Uhelszki, J. (2000) 'Metallica sue Napster for copyright infringement: Metallica cite Napster and three universities in copyright suit', *Rolling Stone*, 13 April. Available at: http://www.rollingstone.com/music/news/metallica-sue-napster-for-copyright-infringement-20000413

UK Music (2011) *UK Music Response to the Call for Evidence of the Independent Review of Intellectual Property and Growth*. Available at: http://webarchive.nationalarchives.gov.uk/20140603093549/http://www.ipo.gov.uk/ipreview-c4e-sub-ukmusic.pdf

Vaidhyanathan, S. (2001) *Copyrights and Copywrongs: The Rise of Intellectual Property and How It Threatens Creativity*. New York: NYU Press.

Van der Sar, E. (2013) 'Six strikes fails to halt U.S. Pirate Bay growth', *TorrentFreak*, 13 September. Available at: http://torrentfreak.com/six-strikes-fails-to-halt-u-s-pirate-bay-growth-130903/

van Dijck, J. (2009) 'Users like you? Theorizing agency in user-generated content', *Media, Culture & Society*, 31(1): 41–58.

Visser, C. (2006) 'Technological protection measures: South Africa goes *overboard. Overbroad*', *Southern African Journal of Information and Communication*, 7: 54–63.

Wang, L. (2008) 'Searching for liability: online copyright infringement in China'. Available at: http://www.chinalawandpractice.com/Article/1886194/Channel/9937/Searching-for-Liability-Online-Copyright-Infringement-in-China.html

Wang, S. and Zhu, J. (2003) 'Mapping film piracy in China', *Theory, Culture & Society*, 20(4): 97–125.

Wikipedia (2014) 'Wikipedia: about'. Available at: http://en.wikipedia.org/wiki/Wikipedia:About

WIPO (World Intellectual Property Organization) (2011) *From Screen to Script*. World Intellectual Property Organization. Available at: http://www.wipo.int/export/sites/www/freepublications/en/copyright/950/wipo_pub_950.pdf

WIPO (2014a) 'What is intellectual property?' Available at: http://www.wipo.int/about-ip/en/

WIPO (2014b) 'Limitations and exceptions'. Available at: http://www.wipo.int/copyright/en/limitations/

Woodmansee, M. (1984) 'The genius and the copyright: economic and legal conditions of the emergence of the "author"', *Eighteenth-Century Studies*, 17(4): 425–48.

World Internet Project (2013) *World Internet Project Report 2013*. Available at: http://www.worldinternetproject.net/

Yar, M. (2005) 'The global "epidemic" of movie "piracy": crime-wave or social construction?', *Media, Culture & Society*, 27(5): 677–96.

Yar, M. (2007) 'Teenage kicks or virtual villainy? Internet piracy, moral entrepreneurship, and the social construction of a crime problem', in Y. Jewkes (ed.), *Crime Online*. London: Routledge, pp. 95–108.

Yar, M. (2008) 'The rhetorics and myths of "anti-piracy" campaigns: criminalisation, moral pedagogy and capitalist property relations in the classroom', *New Media & Society*, 10(4): 605–23.

Yarow, J. (2014) 'Amazon says it has at least 20 million prime members', *Business Insider*, 6 January. Available at: http://www.businessinsider.com/amazon-prime-members-2014-1

Yu, P.K. (2012) 'Trade agreement cats and the digital technology mouse'. SSRN Scholarly Paper, Rochester, NY: Social Science Research Network. Available at: http://papers.ssrn.com/abstract=2220278

Yu, P.K. (2013) 'The non-multilateral approach to international intellectual property normsetting'. SSRN Scholarly Paper, Rochester, NY: Social Science Research Network. Available at: http://papers.ssrn.com/abstract=2325766

Zeller Jr, T. (2004) 'Pew file-sharing survey gives a voice to artists', *New York Times,* 6 December. Available at: http://www.nytimes.com/2004/12/06/arts/06down.html

Zittrain, J. (2009a) *The Future of the Internet: And How to Stop It* (New edition). London: Penguin.

Zittrain, J. (2009b) 'Lost in the cloud', *New York Times*, 19 July. Available at: http://www.nytimes.com/2009/07/20/opinion/20zittrain.html

Zittrain, J. (2012) 'Don't let software patents stop us standing on the shoulders of giants', *The Guardian,* 18 April. Available at: http://www.guardian.co.uk/commentis-free/2012/apr/18/software-patents-shoulders-of-giants

Zittrain, J. (2013) 'Digital books are under the control of distributors rather than readers', *Wired UK*, 8 July. Available at: http://www.wired.co.uk/magazine/archive/2013/07/ideas-bank/how-amazon-kindled-the-bookburners-flames

INDEX